ⱽ VALIANT.

Dan Mintz Chairman   **Fred Pierce** Publisher   **Walter Black** VP Operations
Travis Escarfullery Director of Design & Production   **Peter Stern** Director of International Publishing & Merchandising
Lysa Hawkins & **David Wohl** Senior Editors   **Rob Levin** Executive Editor   **Jeff Walker** Production & Design Manager
John Petrie Senior Manager - Sales & Merchandising   **Danielle Ward** Sales Manager   **Gregg Katzman** Marketing & Publicity Manager

Russ Brown President, Consumer Products, Promotions & Ad Sales

SHADOWMAN

WRITER
CULLEN BUNN

ARTIST
JON DAVIS-HUNT

COLORIST
JORDIE BELLAIRE

LETTERER
CLAYTON COWLES

COVERS BY
JON DAVIS-HUNT

EDITORIAL ASSISTANT
AUDREY MEEKER

ASSOCIATE EDITOR
DAVID MENCHEL

SENIOR EDITORS
HEATHER ANTOS
LYSA HAWKINS

GALLERY
JORDIE BELLAIRE
CULLEN BUNN
JON DAVIS-HUNT
DAVE JOHNSON
ROBBI RODRIGUEZ
MICHAEL WALSH
CASPAR WIJNGAARD
ANNIE WU

COLLECTION COVER ART
TONY MOORE
JENNY FRISON
(Kowabunga Comics Edition)

COLLECTION FRONT ART:
FRANCESCO FRANCAVILLA
JOHNNY DESJARDINS

COLLECTION BACK COVER ART
JEFF DEKAL

COLLECTION EDITOR
IVAN COHEN

COLLECTION DESIGNER
STEVE BLACKWELL

Shadowman® Book One. Published by Valiant Entertainment LLC. Office of Publication: 239 West 29th Street, New York, NY 10001. Compilation copyright © 2021 Valiant Entertainment LLC. All rights reserved. Contains materials originally published in single magazine form as Shadowman #1-4. Copyright © 2021 Valiant Entertainment LLC. All rights reserved. All characters, their distinctive likeness and related indicia featured in this publication are trademarks of Valiant Entertainment LLC. The stories, characters, and incidents featured in this publication are entirely fictional. Valiant Entertainment does not read or accept unsolicited submissions of ideas, stories, or artwork. Printed in Korea. First Printing. ISBN: 9781682153741. ISBN (Kowabunga Comics edition): 9781682153789.

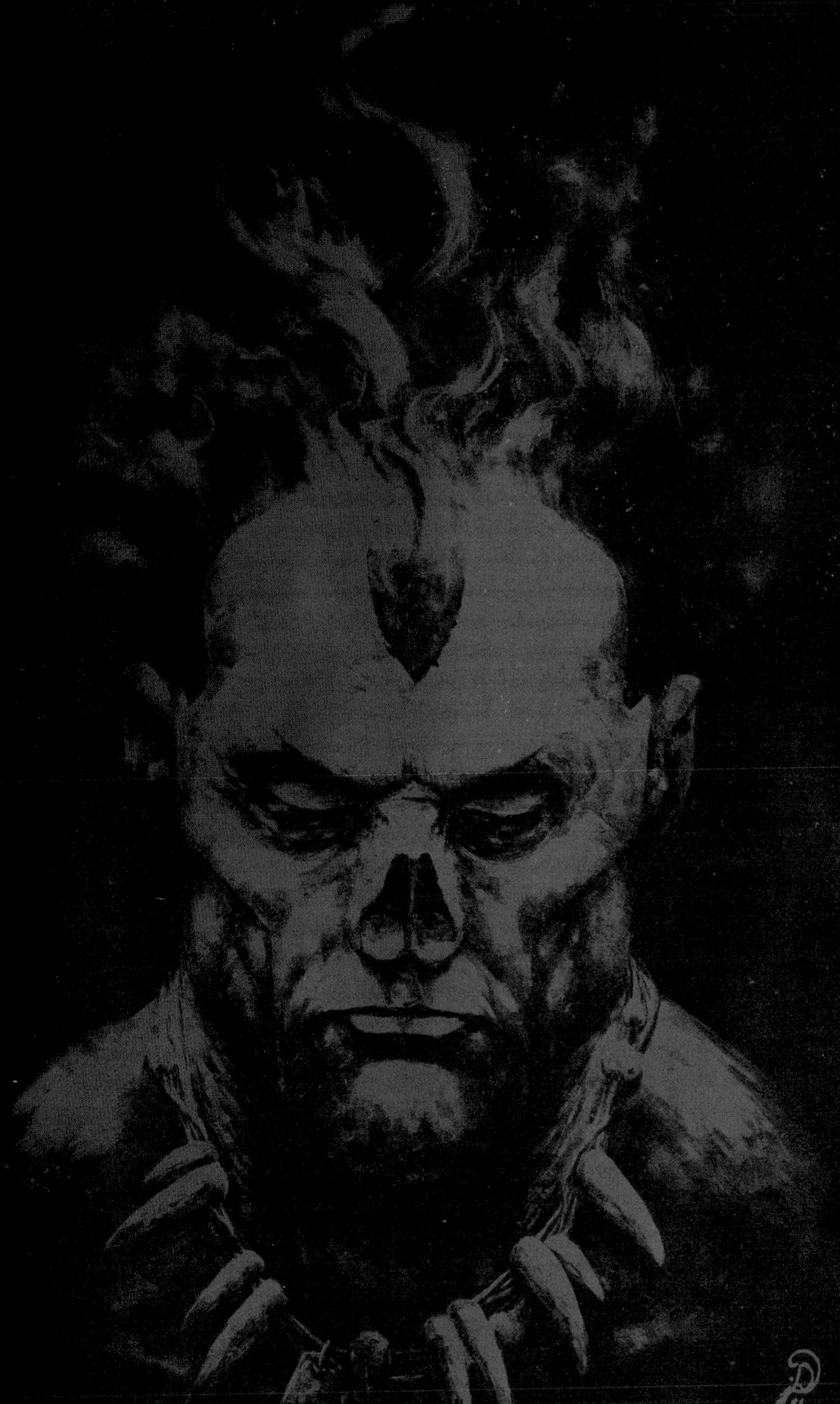

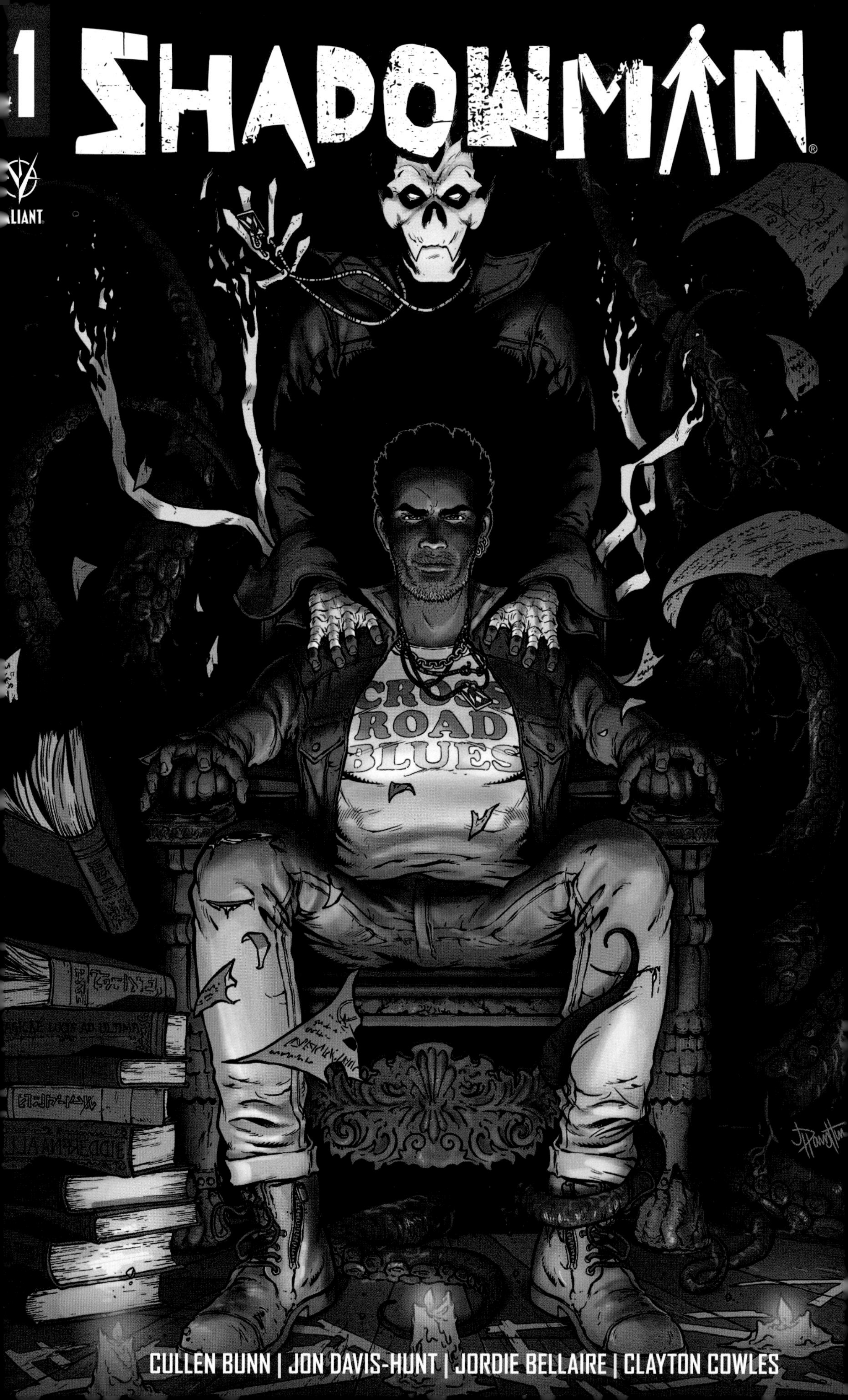
1
SHADOWMAN®
VALIANT
CROSS ROAD BLUES
CULLEN BUNN | JON DAVIS-HUNT | JORDIE BELLAIRE | CLAYTON COWLES

SHADOWMAN #1

WRITER: Cullen Bunn
ARTIST: Jon Davis-Hunt
COLORIST: Jordie Bellaire
LETTERER: Clayton Cowles
COVER ARTIST: Jon Davis-Hunt
ASSOCIATE EDITOR: David Menchel
SENIOR EDITOR: Heather Antos

A musician from New Orleans, Jack Boniface is Shadowman. With the help of the Shadow Loa, an immensely powerful voodoo spirit passed down through his lineage, Shadowman is one of few who can protect the Earth from the demons of the Deadside. Although the Shadow Loa has gifted him with incredible supernatural abilities, his powers come with a responsibility that's more than he bargained for...

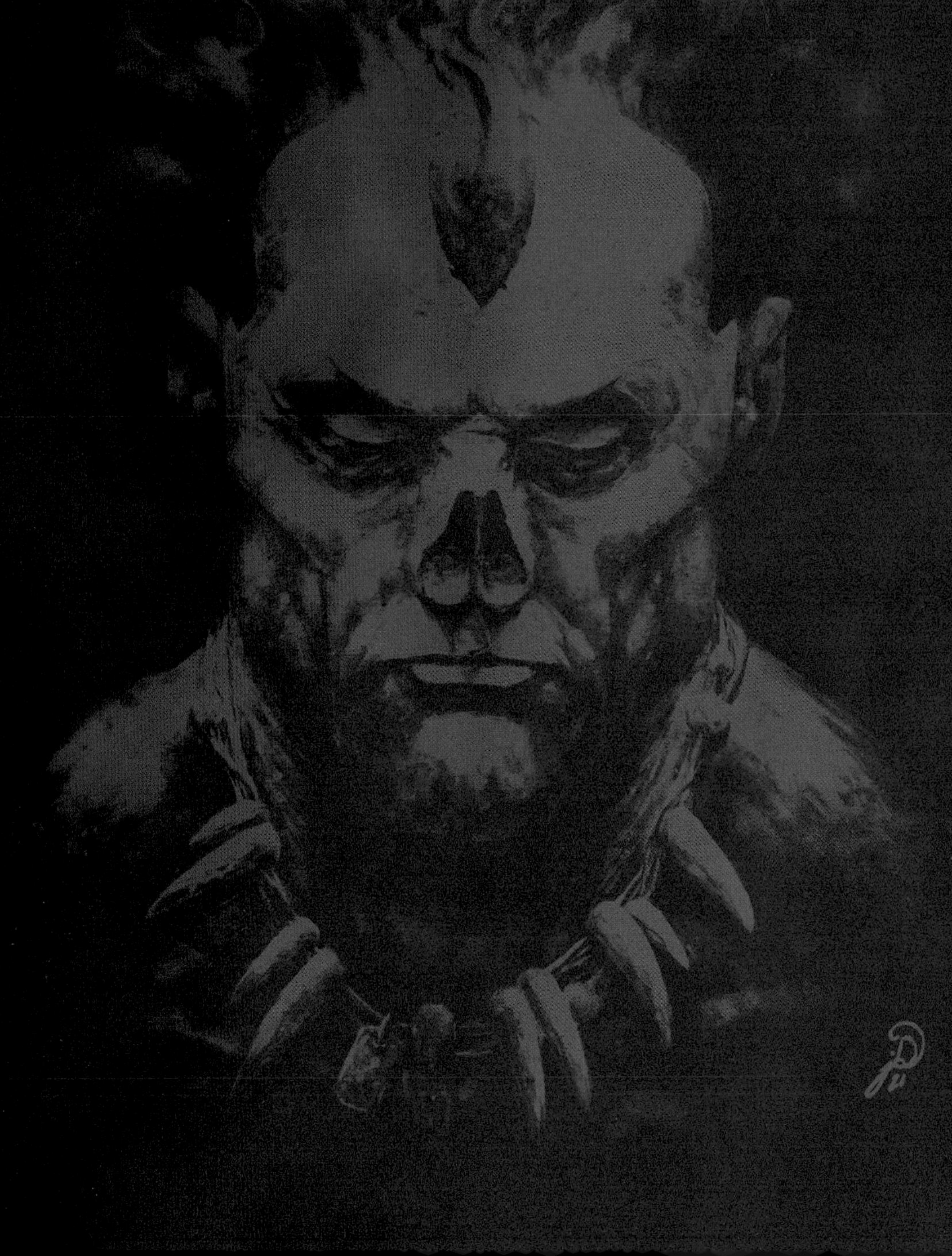

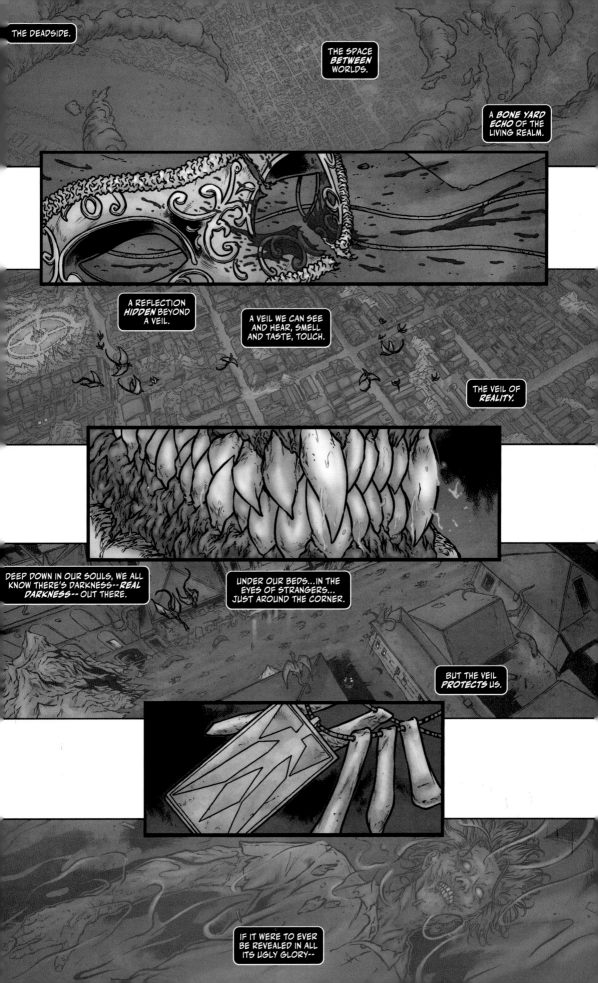

THE DEADSIDE.

THE SPACE *BETWEEN* WORLDS.

A *BONE YARD ECHO* OF THE LIVING REALM.

A REFLECTION *HIDDEN* BEYOND A VEIL.

A VEIL WE CAN SEE AND HEAR, SMELL AND TASTE, TOUCH.

THE VEIL OF *REALITY.*

DEEP DOWN IN OUR SOULS, WE ALL KNOW THERE'S DARKNESS--*REAL DARKNESS*-- OUT THERE.

UNDER OUR BEDS...IN THE EYES OF STRANGERS... JUST AROUND THE CORNER.

BUT THE VEIL *PROTECTS* US.

IF IT WERE TO EVER BE REVEALED IN ALL ITS UGLY GLORY--

THE *TRUTH* MIGHT *MURDER* US.

FOR NEARLY A WEEK, ONE OF THOSE TRUTHS HAS BEEN SLAUGHTERING PEOPLE ON THE STREETS OF NEW ORLEANS.

ALWAYS *MASQUERADERS.*

WHERE IS SHE? WHERE ARE YOU HIDING HER?

THWUD

I DON'T KNOW WHO YOU'RE TALKING ABOUT, BIG GUY.

AND I'M FAIRLY SURE...

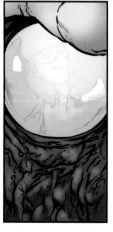

LIES! SHE WAS SUMMONED! SUMMONED TO THIS WORLD OF MEAT AND BLOOD!

YOU'RE HIDING HER FROM--

WUUUH?

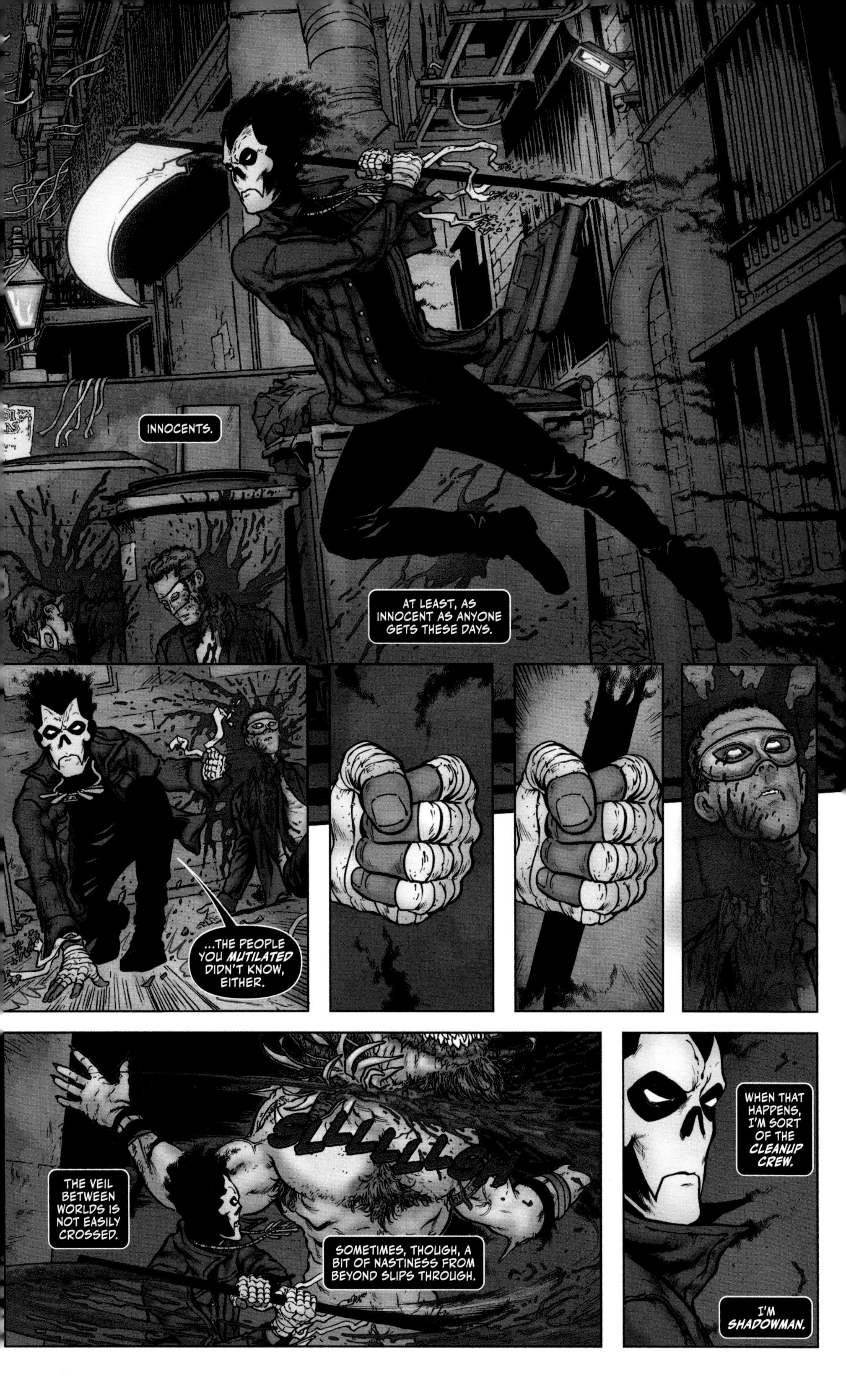
INNOCENTS.
AT LEAST, AS INNOCENT AS ANYONE GETS THESE DAYS.
...THE PEOPLE YOU MUTILATED DIDN'T KNOW, EITHER.
THE VEIL BETWEEN WORLDS IS NOT EASILY CROSSED.
SOMETIMES, THOUGH, A BIT OF NASTINESS FROM BEYOND SLIPS THROUGH.
SLLLLLSH
WHEN THAT HAPPENS, I'M SORT OF THE CLEANUP CREW.
I'M SHADOWMAN.

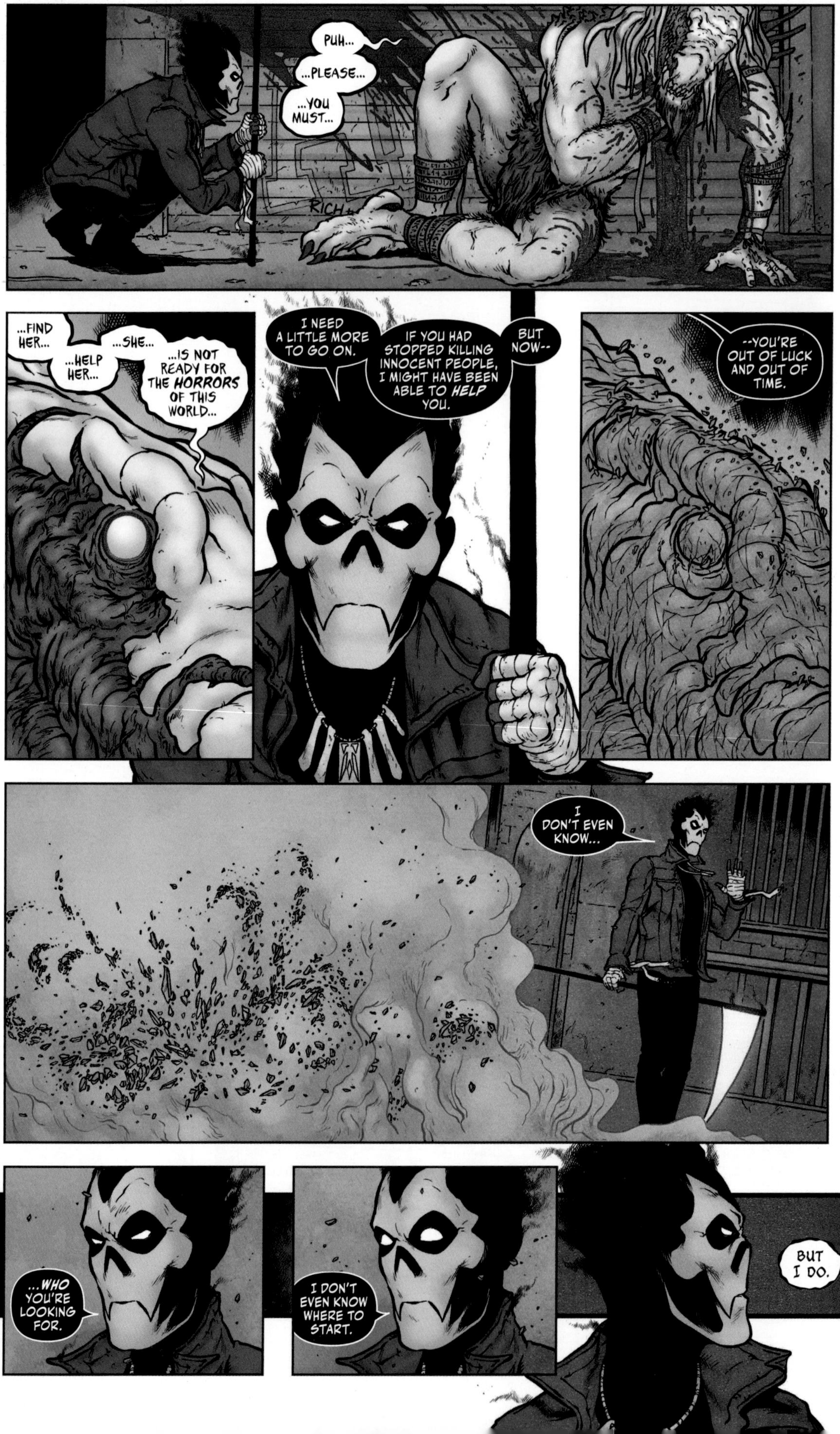
PUH...
...PLEASE...
...YOU MUST...
...FIND HER...
...HELP HER...
...SHE...
...IS NOT READY FOR THE HORRORS OF THIS WORLD...
I NEED A LITTLE MORE TO GO ON.
IF YOU HAD STOPPED KILLING INNOCENT PEOPLE, I MIGHT HAVE BEEN ABLE TO HELP YOU.
BUT NOW--
--YOU'RE OUT OF LUCK AND OUT OF TIME.
I DON'T EVEN KNOW...
...WHO YOU'RE LOOKING FOR.
I DON'T EVEN KNOW WHERE TO START.
BUT I DO.

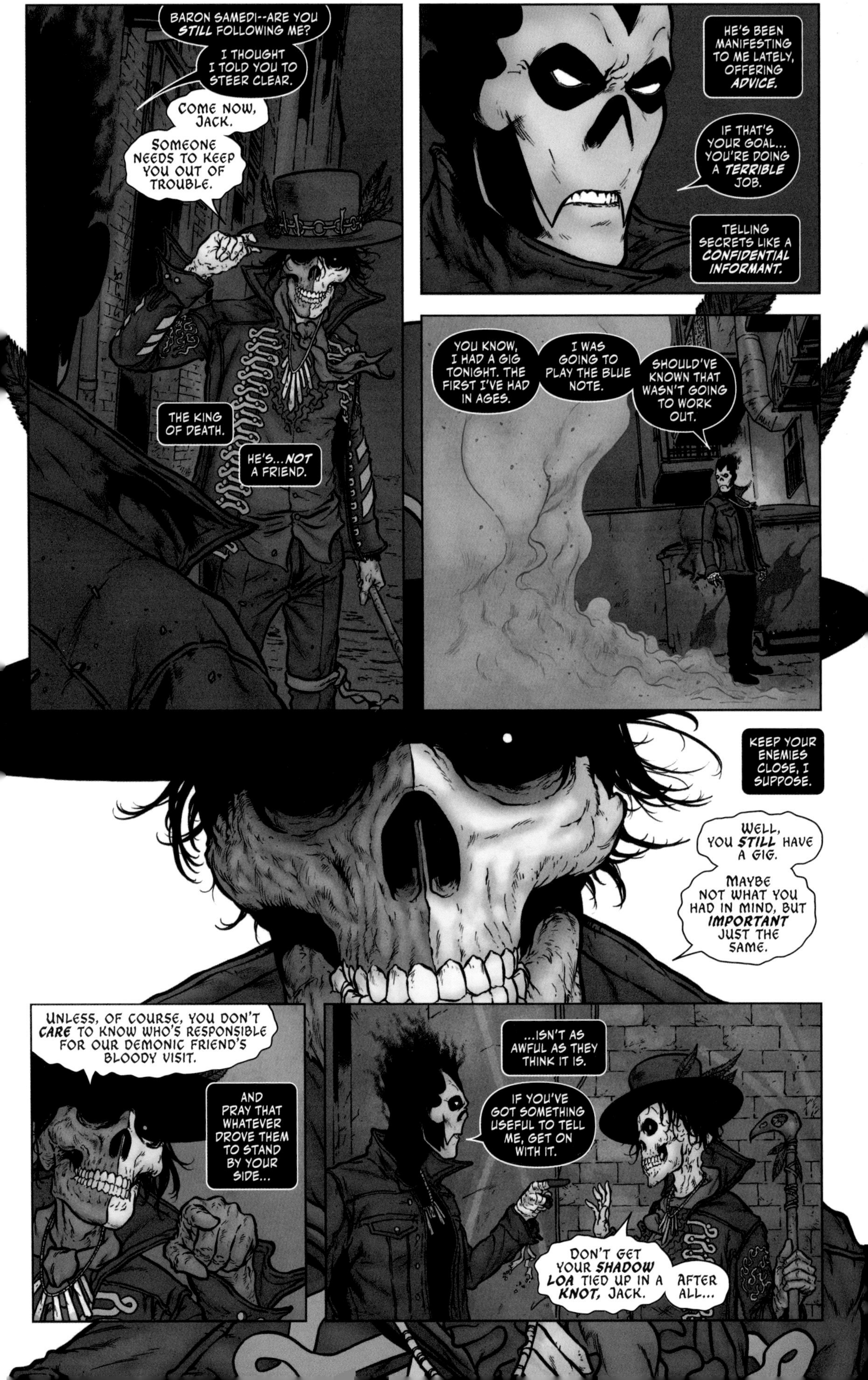
BARON SAMEDI--ARE YOU STILL FOLLOWING ME?
I THOUGHT I TOLD YOU TO STEER CLEAR.
COME NOW, JACK.
SOMEONE NEEDS TO KEEP YOU OUT OF TROUBLE.
THE KING OF DEATH.
HE'S...NOT A FRIEND.
HE'S BEEN MANIFESTING TO ME LATELY, OFFERING ADVICE.
IF THAT'S YOUR GOAL... YOU'RE DOING A TERRIBLE JOB.
TELLING SECRETS LIKE A CONFIDENTIAL INFORMANT.
YOU KNOW, I HAD A GIG TONIGHT. THE FIRST I'VE HAD IN AGES.
I WAS GOING TO PLAY THE BLUE NOTE.
SHOULD'VE KNOWN THAT WASN'T GOING TO WORK OUT.
KEEP YOUR ENEMIES CLOSE, I SUPPOSE.
WELL, YOU STILL HAVE A GIG.
MAYBE NOT WHAT YOU HAD IN MIND, BUT IMPORTANT JUST THE SAME.
UNLESS, OF COURSE, YOU DON'T CARE TO KNOW WHO'S RESPONSIBLE FOR OUR DEMONIC FRIEND'S BLOODY VISIT.
AND PRAY THAT WHATEVER DROVE THEM TO STAND BY YOUR SIDE...
...ISN'T AS AWFUL AS THEY THINK IT IS.
IF YOU'VE GOT SOMETHING USEFUL TO TELL ME, GET ON WITH IT.
DON'T GET YOUR SHADOW LOA TIED UP IN A KNOT, JACK.
AFTER ALL...

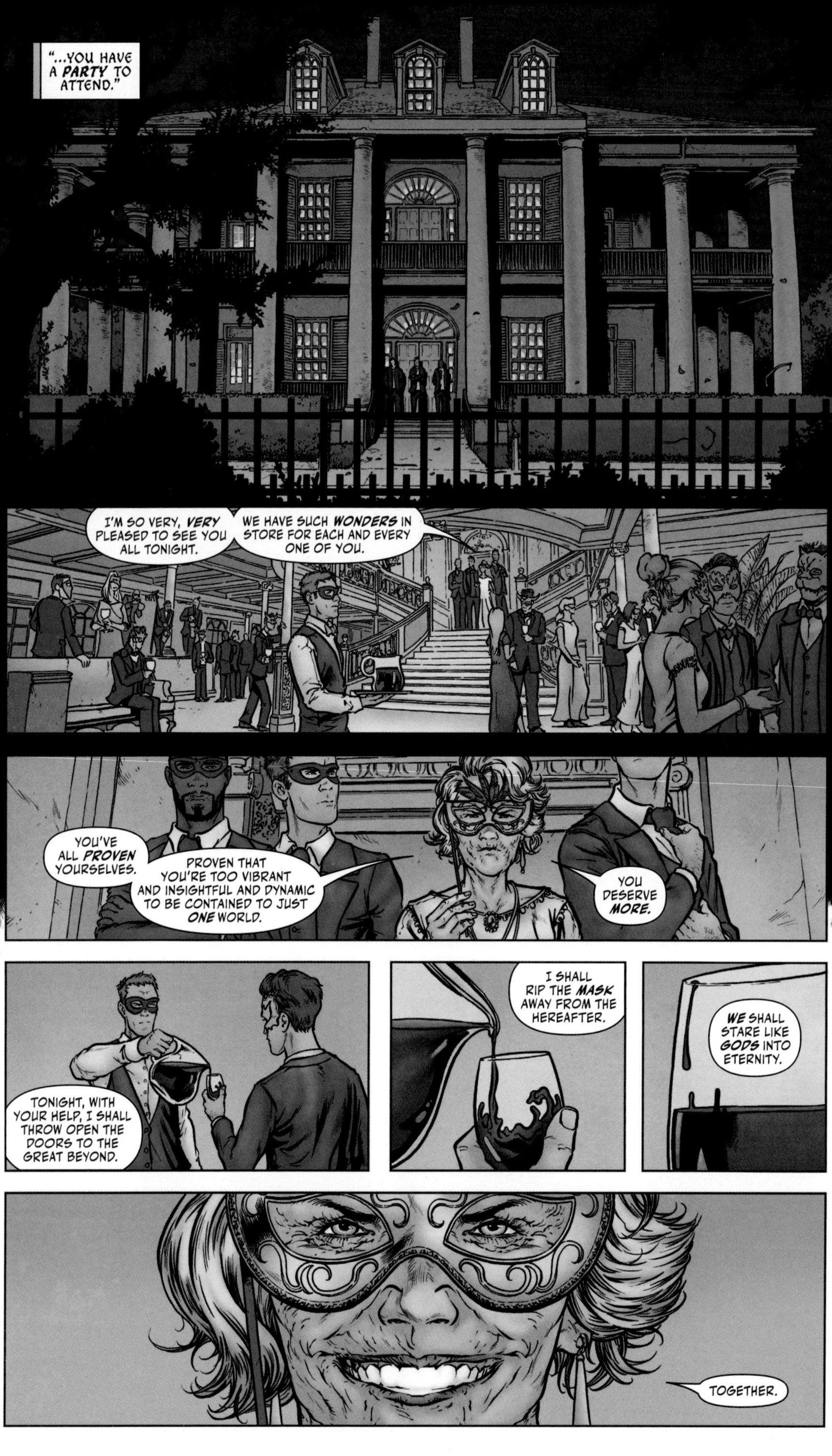
"...YOU HAVE A PARTY TO ATTEND."
I'M SO VERY, VERY PLEASED TO SEE YOU ALL TONIGHT.
WE HAVE SUCH WONDERS IN STORE FOR EACH AND EVERY ONE OF YOU.
YOU'VE ALL PROVEN YOURSELVES.
PROVEN THAT YOU'RE TOO VIBRANT AND INSIGHTFUL AND DYNAMIC TO BE CONTAINED TO JUST ONE WORLD.
YOU DESERVE MORE.
TONIGHT, WITH YOUR HELP, I SHALL THROW OPEN THE DOORS TO THE GREAT BEYOND.
I SHALL RIP THE MASK AWAY FROM THE HEREAFTER.
WE SHALL STARE LIKE GODS INTO ETERNITY.
TOGETHER.

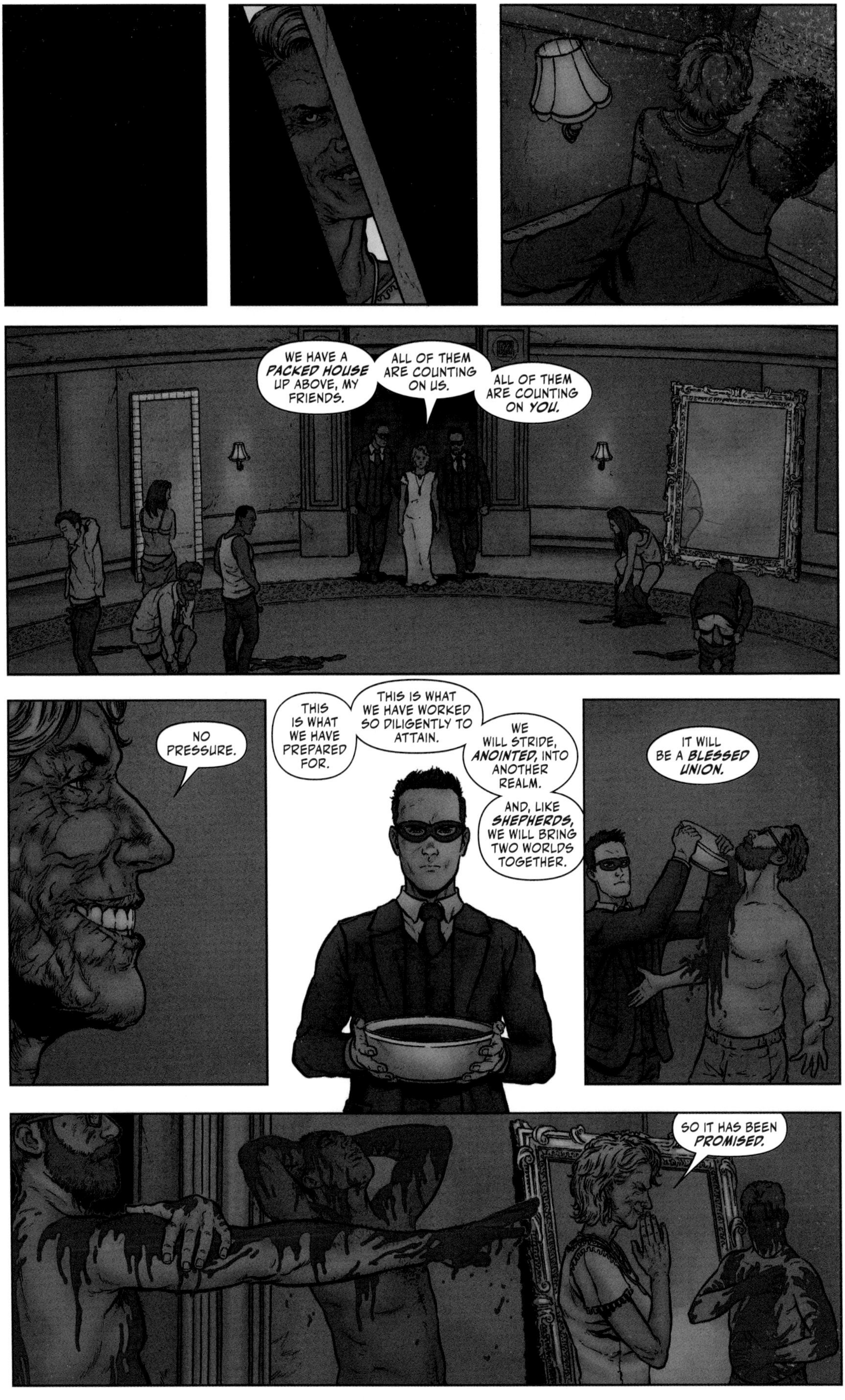

WE HAVE A PACKED HOUSE UP ABOVE, MY FRIENDS.
ALL OF THEM ARE COUNTING ON US.
ALL OF THEM ARE COUNTING ON YOU.
NO PRESSURE.
THIS IS WHAT WE HAVE PREPARED FOR.
THIS IS WHAT WE HAVE WORKED SO DILIGENTLY TO ATTAIN.
WE WILL STRIDE, ANOINTED, INTO ANOTHER REALM.
AND, LIKE SHEPHERDS, WE WILL BRING TWO WORLDS TOGETHER.
IT WILL BE A BLESSED UNION.
SO IT HAS BEEN PROMISED.

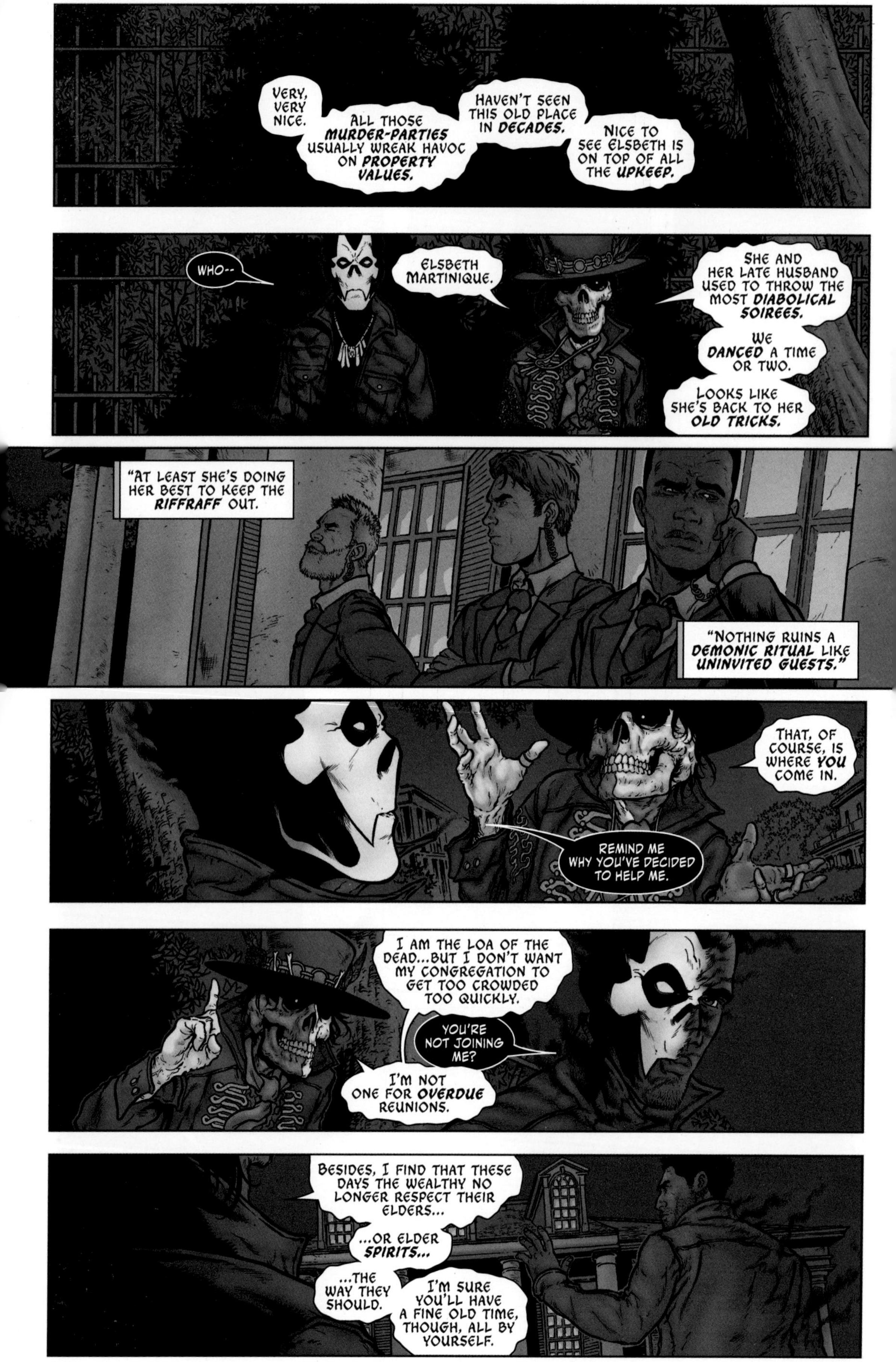

VERY, VERY NICE.
ALL THOSE MURDER-PARTIES USUALLY WREAK HAVOC ON PROPERTY VALUES.
HAVEN'T SEEN THIS OLD PLACE IN DECADES.
NICE TO SEE ELSBETH IS ON TOP OF ALL THE UPKEEP.
WHO--
ELSBETH MARTINIQUE.
SHE AND HER LATE HUSBAND USED TO THROW THE MOST DIABOLICAL SOIREES.
WE DANCED A TIME OR TWO.
LOOKS LIKE SHE'S BACK TO HER OLD TRICKS.
"AT LEAST SHE'S DOING HER BEST TO KEEP THE RIFFRAFF OUT.
"NOTHING RUINS A DEMONIC RITUAL LIKE UNINVITED GUESTS."
REMIND ME WHY YOU'VE DECIDED TO HELP ME.
THAT, OF COURSE, IS WHERE YOU COME IN.
I AM THE LOA OF THE DEAD...BUT I DON'T WANT MY CONGREGATION TO GET TOO CROWDED TOO QUICKLY.
YOU'RE NOT JOINING ME?
I'M NOT ONE FOR OVERDUE REUNIONS.
BESIDES, I FIND THAT THESE DAYS THE WEALTHY NO LONGER RESPECT THEIR ELDERS...
...OR ELDER SPIRITS...
...THE WAY THEY SHOULD.
I'M SURE YOU'LL HAVE A FINE OLD TIME, THOUGH, ALL BY YOURSELF.

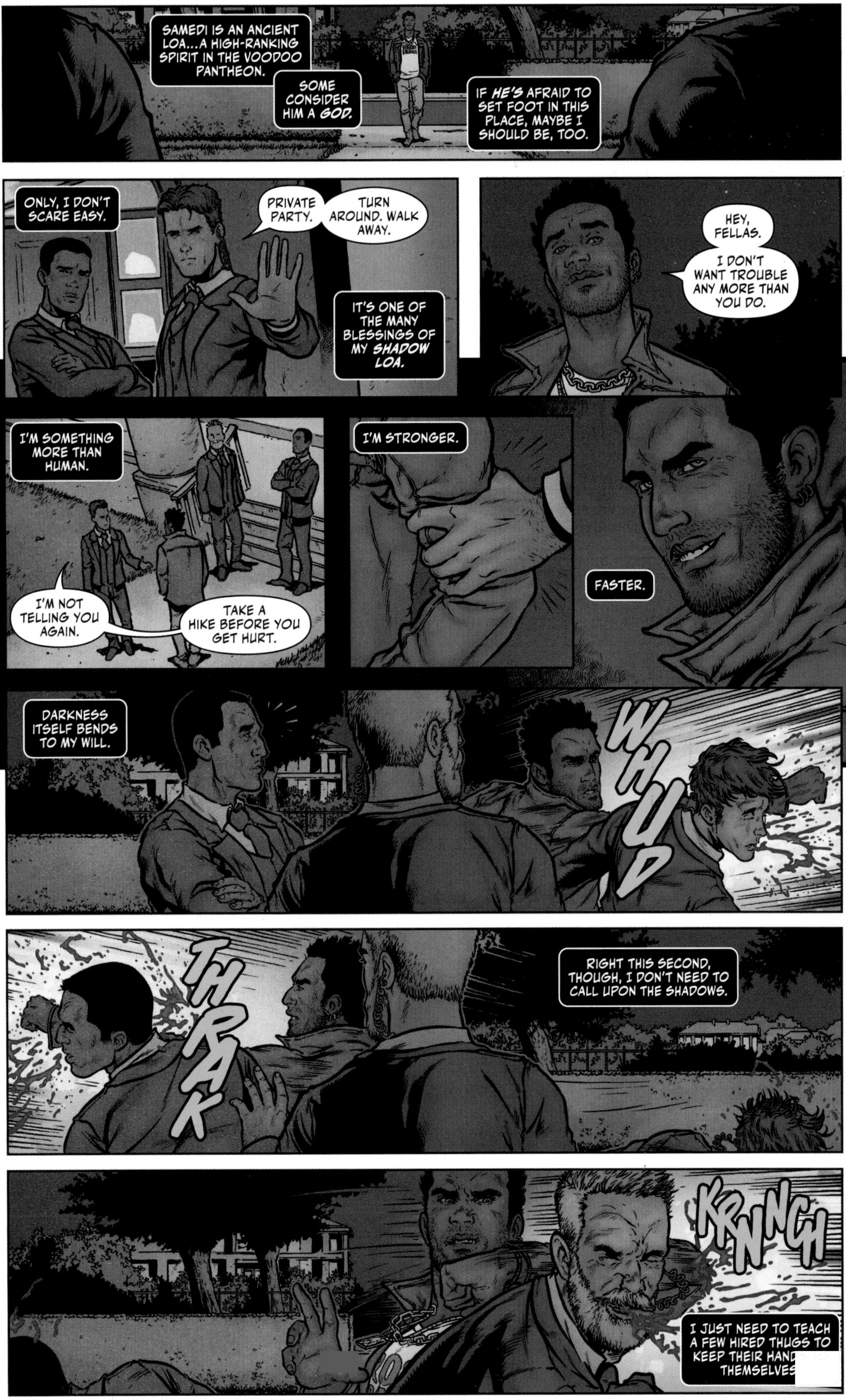
SAMEDI IS AN ANCIENT LOA...A HIGH-RANKING SPIRIT IN THE VOODOO PANTHEON.
SOME CONSIDER HIM A GOD.
IF HE'S AFRAID TO SET FOOT IN THIS PLACE, MAYBE I SHOULD BE, TOO.
ONLY, I DON'T SCARE EASY.
PRIVATE PARTY.
TURN AROUND. WALK AWAY.
IT'S ONE OF THE MANY BLESSINGS OF MY SHADOW LOA.
HEY, FELLAS.
I DON'T WANT TROUBLE ANY MORE THAN YOU DO.
I'M SOMETHING MORE THAN HUMAN.
I'M NOT TELLING YOU AGAIN.
TAKE A HIKE BEFORE YOU GET HURT.
I'M STRONGER.
FASTER.
DARKNESS ITSELF BENDS TO MY WILL.
WHUD
THRAK
RIGHT THIS SECOND, THOUGH, I DON'T NEED TO CALL UPON THE SHADOWS.
KRNNCH
I JUST NEED TO TEACH A FEW HIRED THUGS TO KEEP THEIR HAND
THEMSELVES

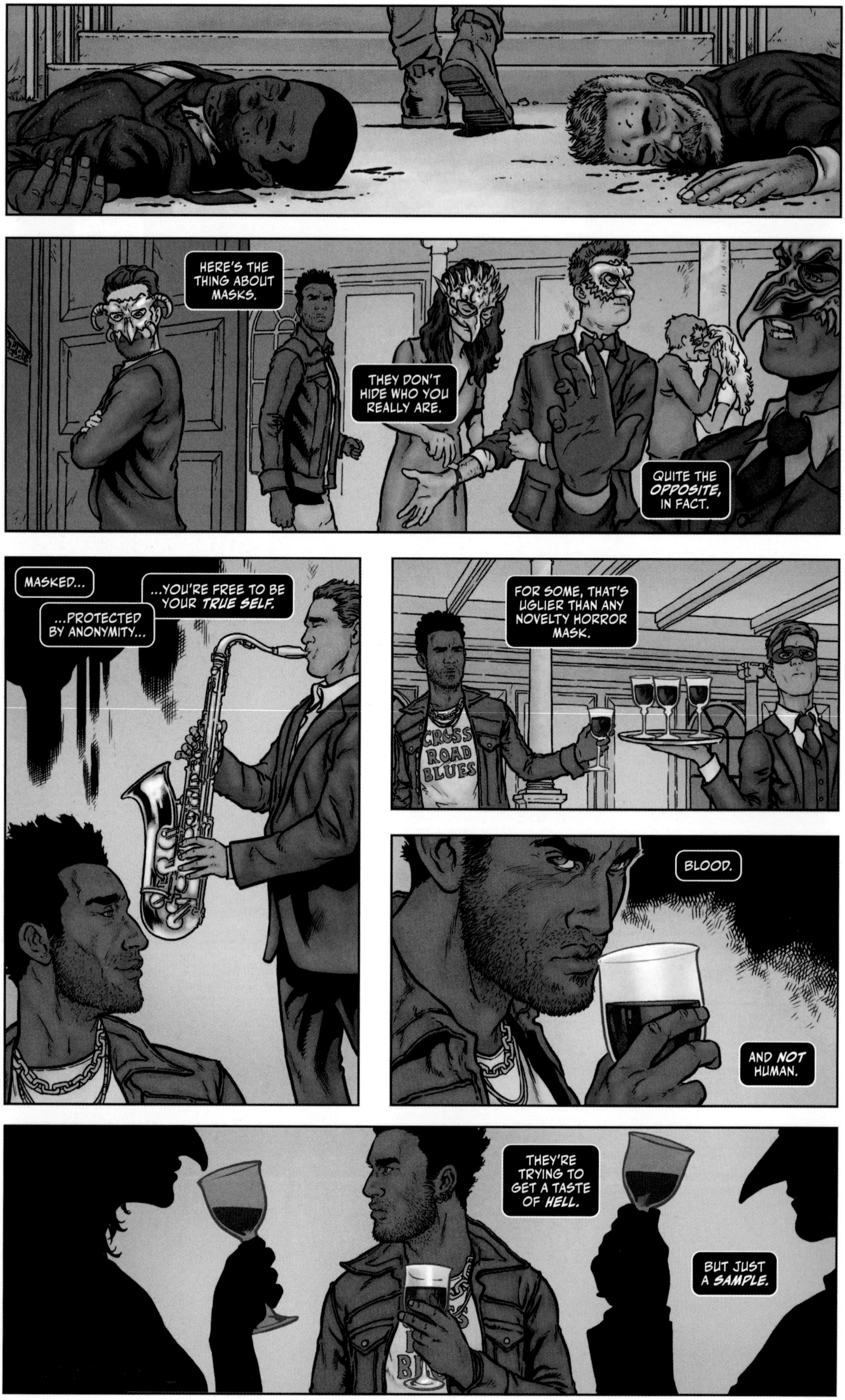
HERE'S THE THING ABOUT MASKS.
THEY DON'T HIDE WHO YOU REALLY ARE.
QUITE THE *OPPOSITE,* IN FACT.
MASKED...
...PROTECTED BY ANONYMITY...
...YOU'RE FREE TO BE YOUR *TRUE SELF.*
FOR SOME, THAT'S UGLIER THAN ANY NOVELTY HORROR MASK.
CROSS ROAD BLUES
BLOOD.
AND *NOT* HUMAN.
THEY'RE TRYING TO GET A TASTE OF *HELL.*
BUT JUST A *SAMPLE.*

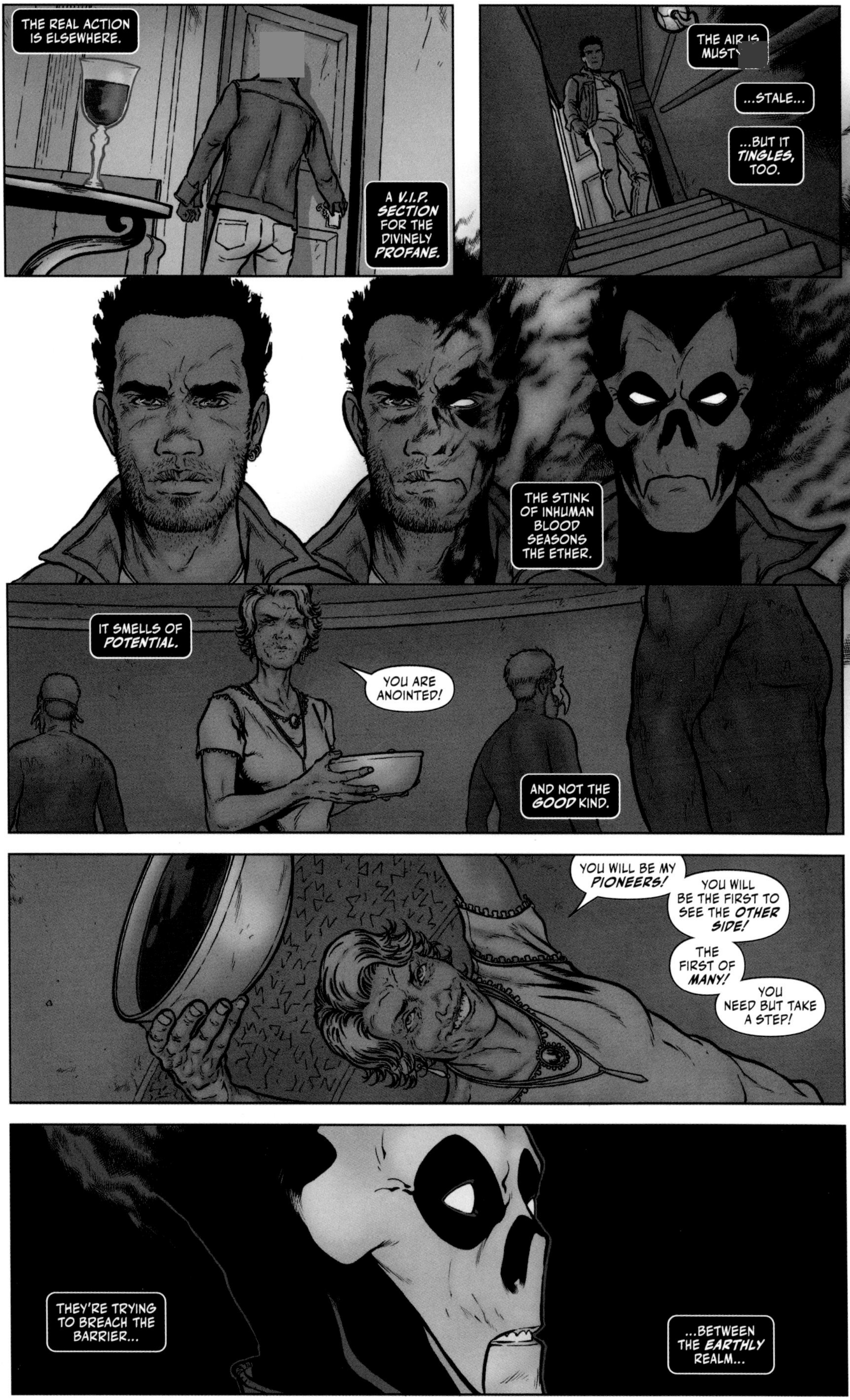
THE REAL ACTION IS ELSEWHERE.
A *V.I.P. SECTION* FOR THE DIVINELY *PROFANE.*
THE AIR IS MUSTY
...STALE...
...BUT IT *TINGLES,* TOO.
THE STINK OF INHUMAN BLOOD SEASONS THE ETHER.
IT SMELLS OF *POTENTIAL.*
YOU ARE ANOINTED!
AND NOT THE *GOOD* KIND.
YOU WILL BE MY *PIONEERS!*
YOU WILL BE THE FIRST TO SEE THE *OTHER SIDE!*
THE FIRST OF *MANY!*
YOU NEED BUT TAKE A STEP!
THEY'RE TRYING TO BREACH THE BARRIER...
...BETWEEN THE *EARTHLY* REALM...

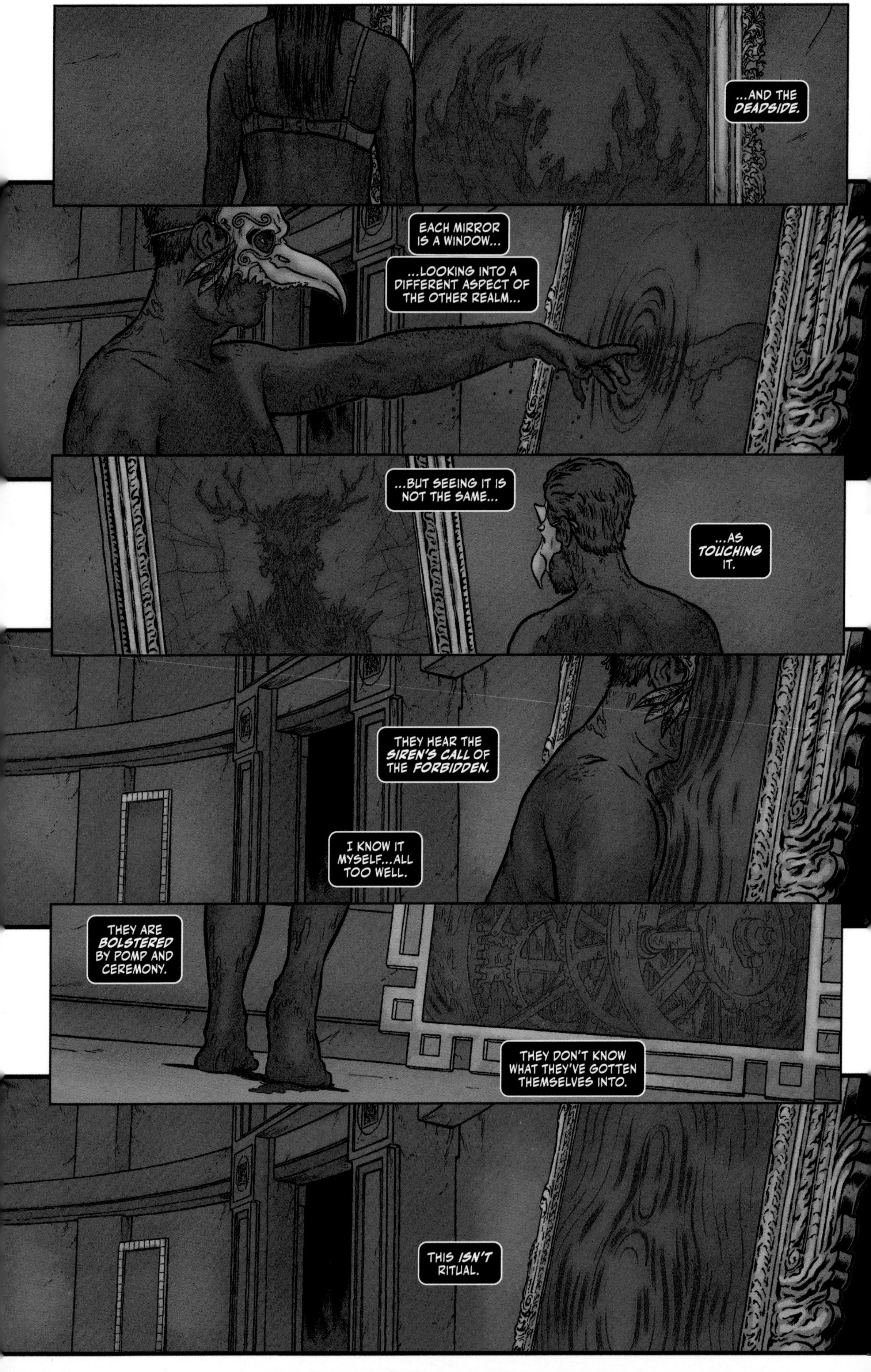
...AND THE DEADSIDE.
EACH MIRROR IS A WINDOW...
...LOOKING INTO A DIFFERENT ASPECT OF THE OTHER REALM...
...BUT SEEING IT IS NOT THE SAME...
...AS TOUCHING IT.
THEY HEAR THE SIREN'S CALL OF THE FORBIDDEN.
I KNOW IT MYSELF...ALL TOO WELL.
THEY ARE BOLSTERED BY POMP AND CEREMONY.
THEY DON'T KNOW WHAT THEY'VE GOTTEN THEMSELVES INTO.
THIS ISN'T RITUAL.

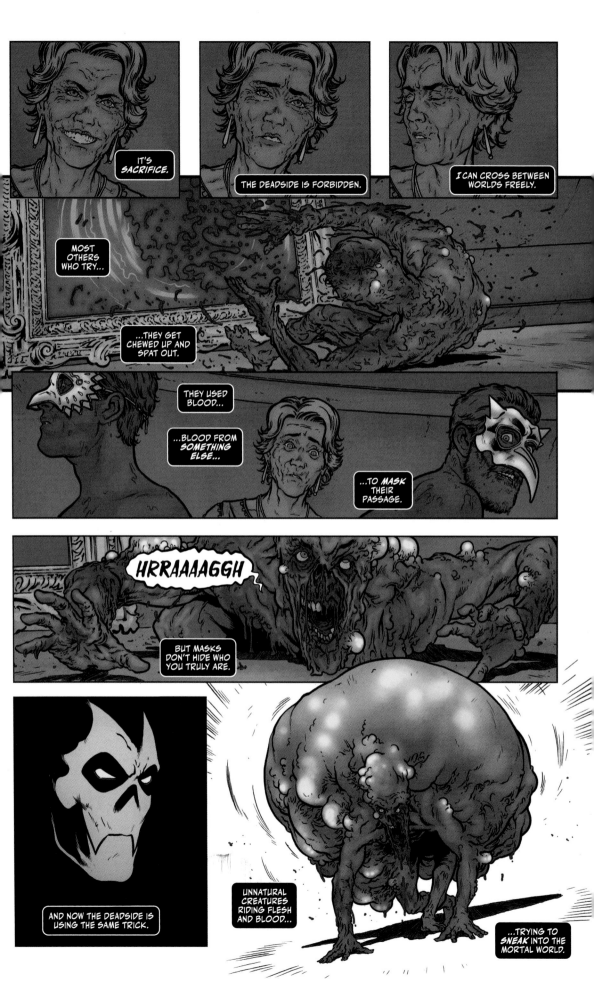

IT'S SACRIFICE.

THE DEADSIDE IS FORBIDDEN.

I CAN CROSS BETWEEN WORLDS FREELY.

MOST OTHERS WHO TRY...

...THEY GET CHEWED UP AND SPAT OUT.

THEY USED BLOOD...

...BLOOD FROM *SOMETHING ELSE*...

...TO *MASK* THEIR PASSAGE.

HRRAAAAGGH

BUT MASKS DON'T HIDE WHO YOU TRULY ARE.

AND NOW THE DEADSIDE IS USING THE SAME TRICK.

UNNATURAL CREATURES RIDING FLESH AND BLOOD...

...TRYING TO *SNEAK* INTO THE MORTAL WORLD.

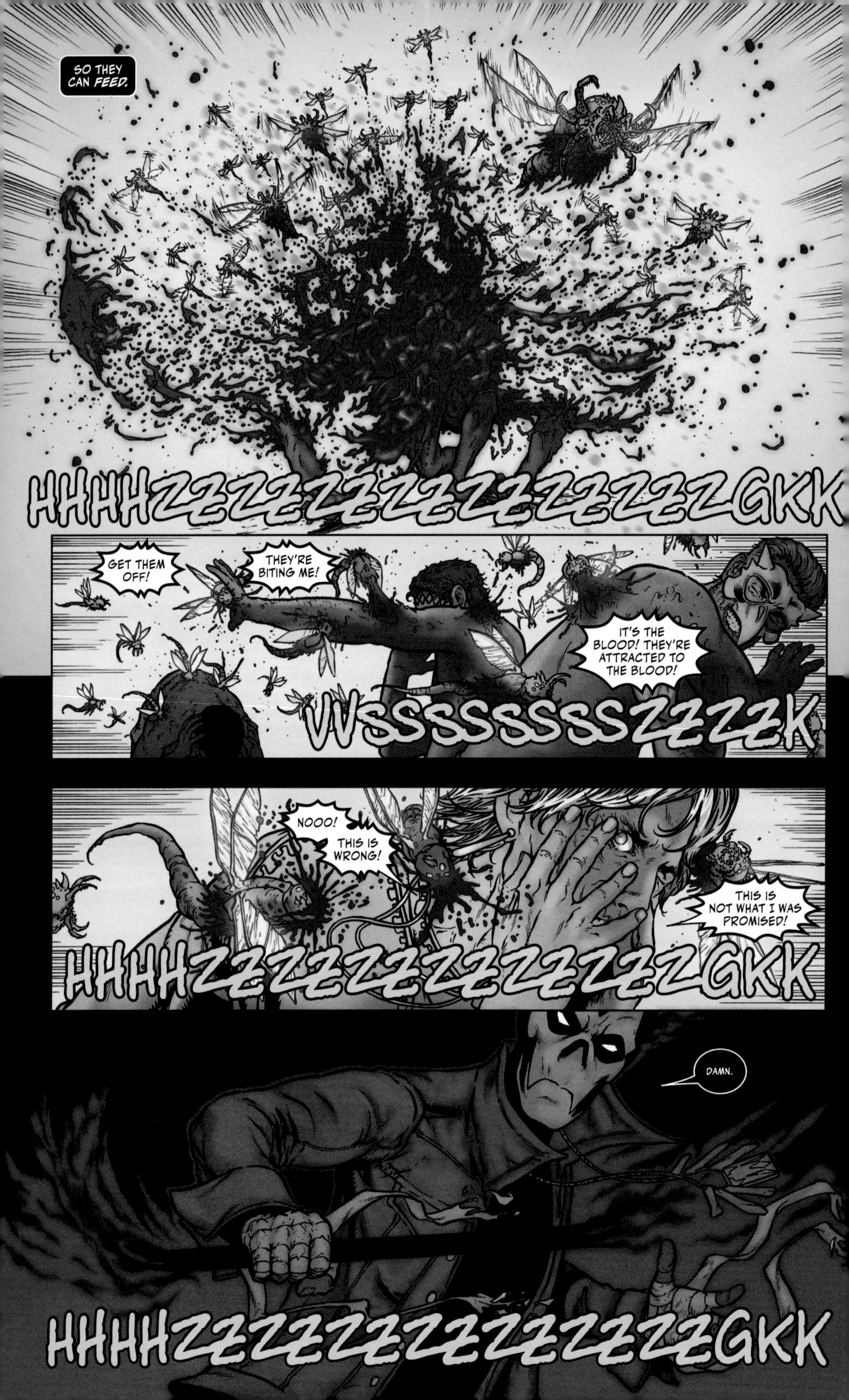
SO THEY CAN FEED.
HHHHZZZZZZZZZZZZZZZZGKK
GET THEM OFF!
THEY'RE BITING ME!
IT'S THE BLOOD! THEY'RE ATTRACTED TO THE BLOOD!
VVSSSSSSSSZZZZK
NOOO!
THIS IS WRONG!
THIS IS NOT WHAT I WAS PROMISED!
HHHHZZZZZZZZZZZZZZZZGKK
DAMN.
HHHHZZZZZZZZZZZZZZZZGKK

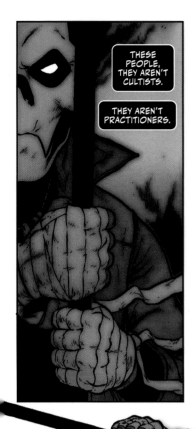

THESE PEOPLE, THEY AREN'T CULTISTS.

THEY AREN'T PRACTITIONERS.

THEY'RE *SIGHTSEERS.*

THEY'RE DEPRAVED RICH FOLK LOOKING FOR A *BIG THRILL.*

FOOLS AT A ZOO, DARING EACH OTHER TO JUMP THE FENCE INTO THE LION'S DOMAIN.

FOOD FOR THE DEADSIDE.

RUN.

THAT BEGS THE QUESTION.

WHO *TAUGHT* THESE NITWITS HOW TO PUNCH A *HOLE* IN REALITY?

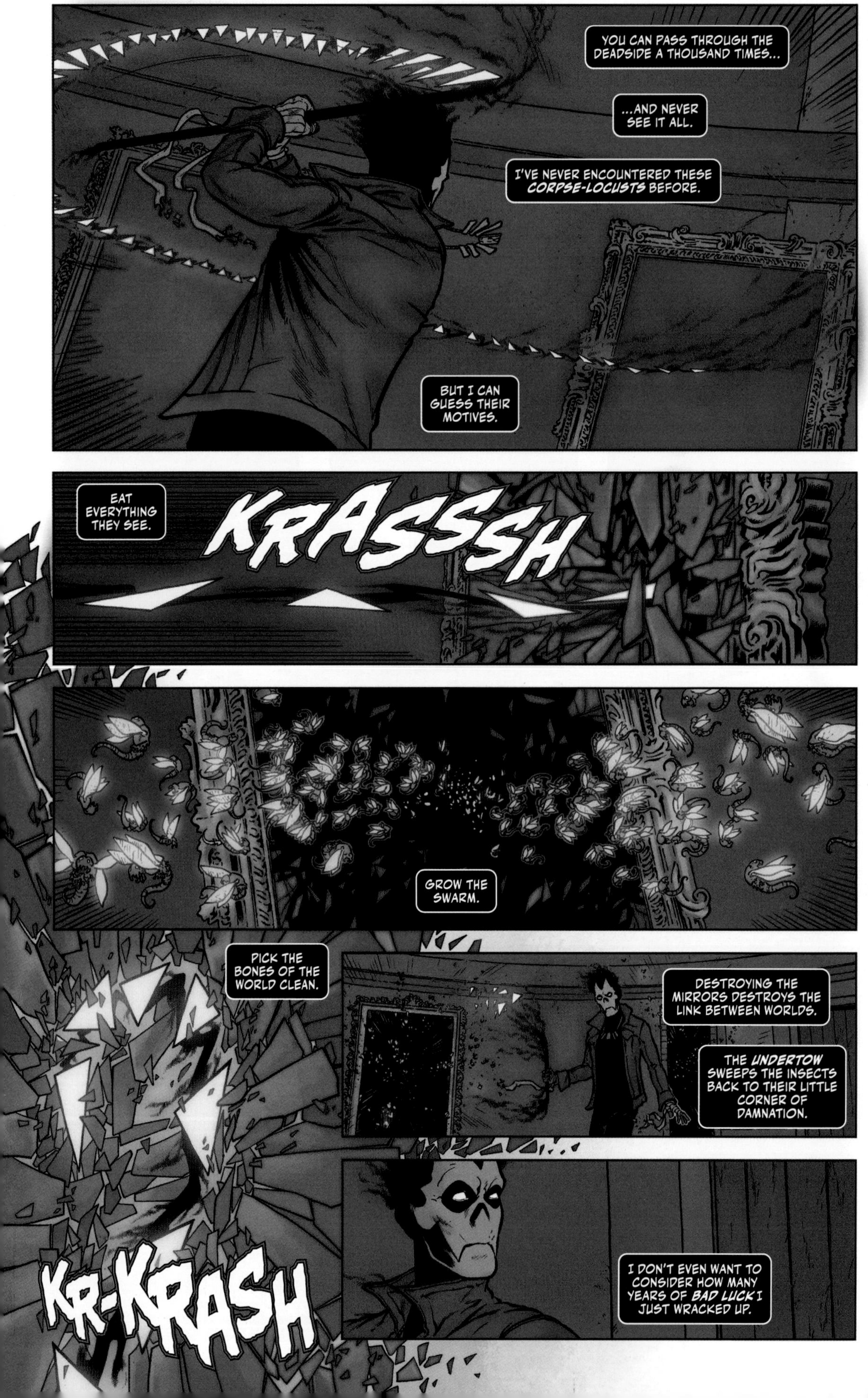

YOU CAN PASS THROUGH THE DEADSIDE A THOUSAND TIMES...
...AND NEVER SEE IT ALL.
I'VE NEVER ENCOUNTERED THESE CORPSE-LOCUSTS BEFORE.
BUT I CAN GUESS THEIR MOTIVES.
EAT EVERYTHING THEY SEE.
KRASSSH
GROW THE SWARM.
PICK THE BONES OF THE WORLD CLEAN.
DESTROYING THE MIRRORS DESTROYS THE LINK BETWEEN WORLDS.
THE UNDERTOW SWEEPS THE INSECTS BACK TO THEIR LITTLE CORNER OF DAMNATION.
KR-KRASH
I DON'T EVEN WANT TO CONSIDER HOW MANY YEARS OF BAD LUCK I JUST WRACKED UP.

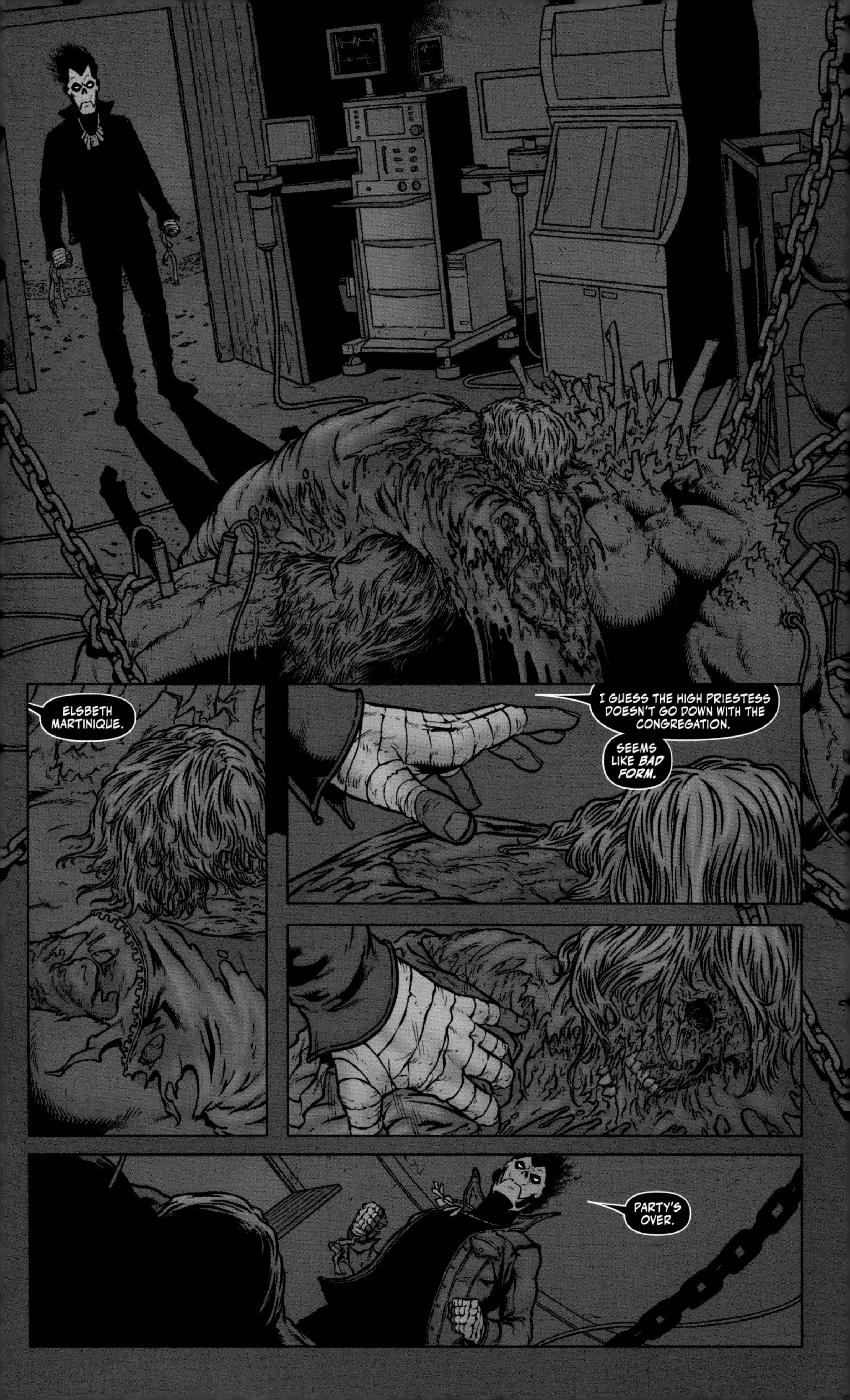
ELSBETH MARTINIQUE.
I GUESS THE HIGH PRIESTESS DOESN'T GO DOWN WITH THE CONGREGATION.
SEEMS LIKE *BAD FORM.*
PARTY'S OVER.

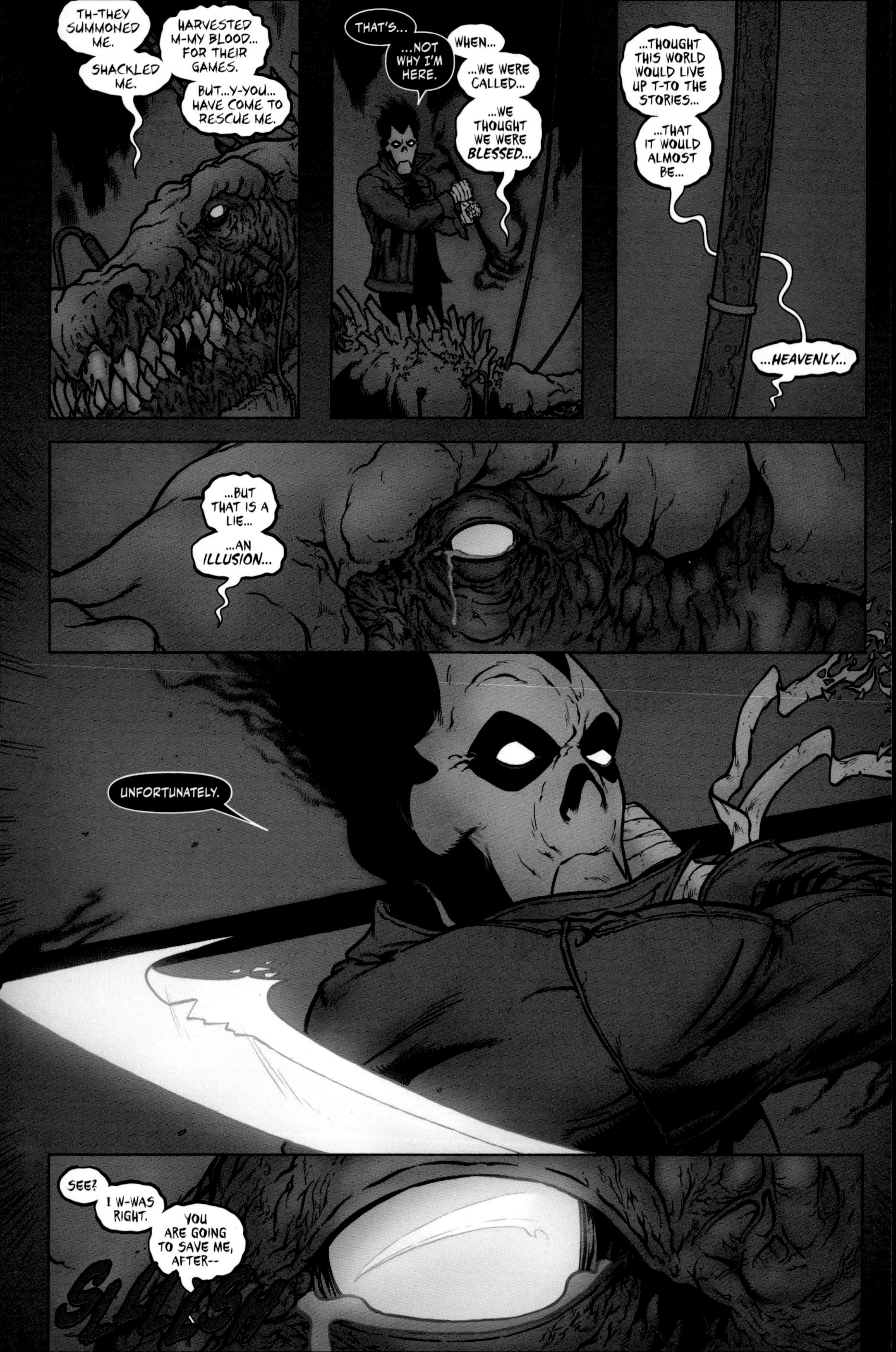
TH-THEY SUMMONED ME.
SHACKLED ME.
HARVESTED M-MY BLOOD... FOR THEIR GAMES.
BUT...Y-YOU... HAVE COME TO RESCUE ME.
THAT'S...
...NOT WHY I'M HERE.
WHEN...
...WE WERE CALLED...
...WE THOUGHT WE WERE BLESSED...
...THOUGHT THIS WORLD WOULD LIVE UP T-TO THE STORIES...
...THAT IT WOULD ALMOST BE...
...HEAVENLY...
...BUT THAT IS A LIE...
...AN ILLUSION...
UNFORTUNATELY.
SEE?
I W-WAS RIGHT.
YOU ARE GOING TO SAVE ME, AFTER--

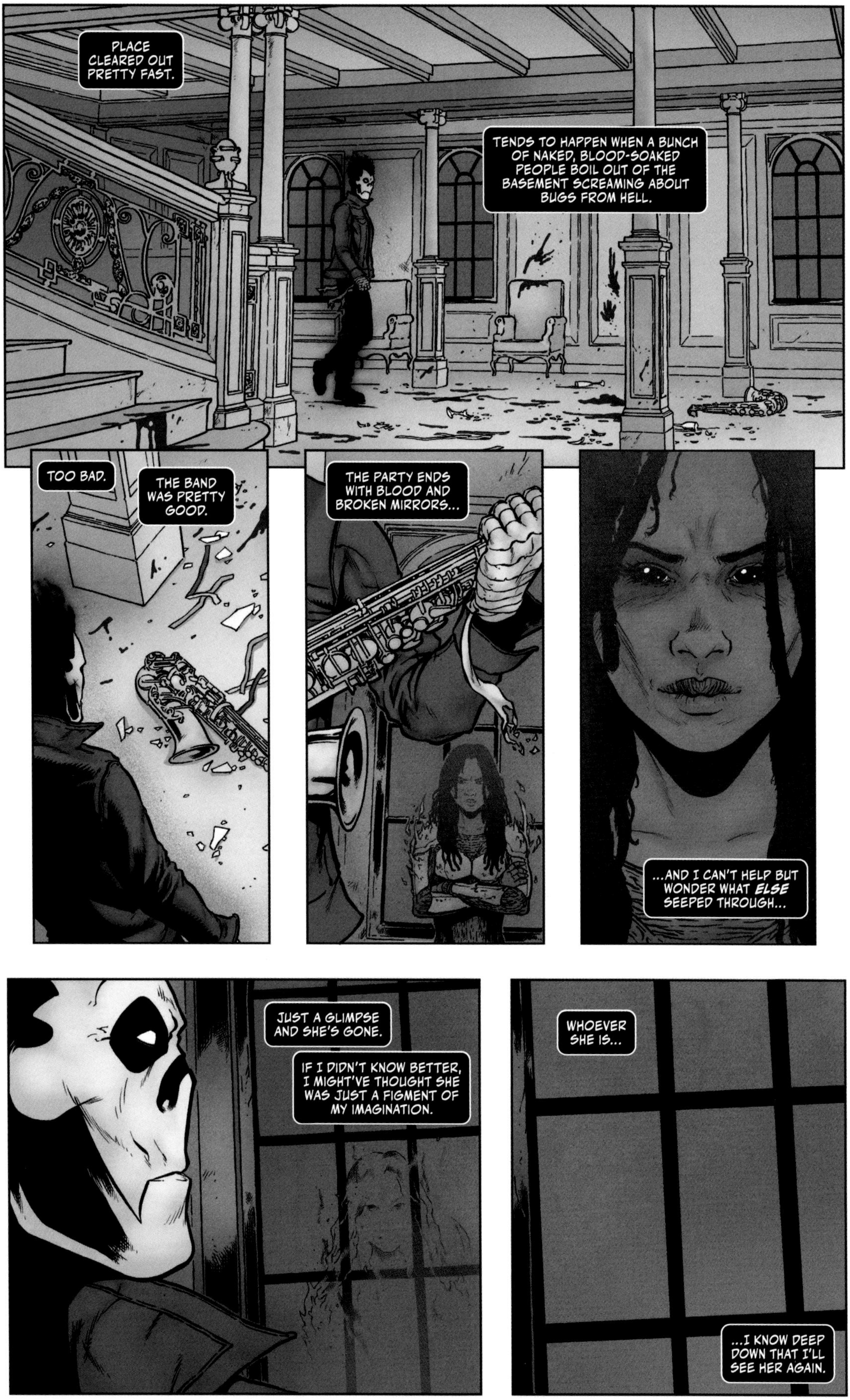
PLACE CLEARED OUT PRETTY FAST.
TENDS TO HAPPEN WHEN A BUNCH OF NAKED, BLOOD-SOAKED PEOPLE BOIL OUT OF THE BASEMENT SCREAMING ABOUT BUGS FROM HELL.
TOO BAD.
THE BAND WAS PRETTY GOOD.
THE PARTY ENDS WITH BLOOD AND BROKEN MIRRORS...
...AND I CAN'T HELP BUT WONDER WHAT *ELSE* SEEPED THROUGH...
JUST A GLIMPSE AND SHE'S GONE.
IF I DIDN'T KNOW BETTER, I MIGHT'VE THOUGHT SHE WAS JUST A FIGMENT OF MY IMAGINATION.
WHOEVER SHE IS...
...I KNOW DEEP DOWN THAT I'LL SEE HER AGAIN.

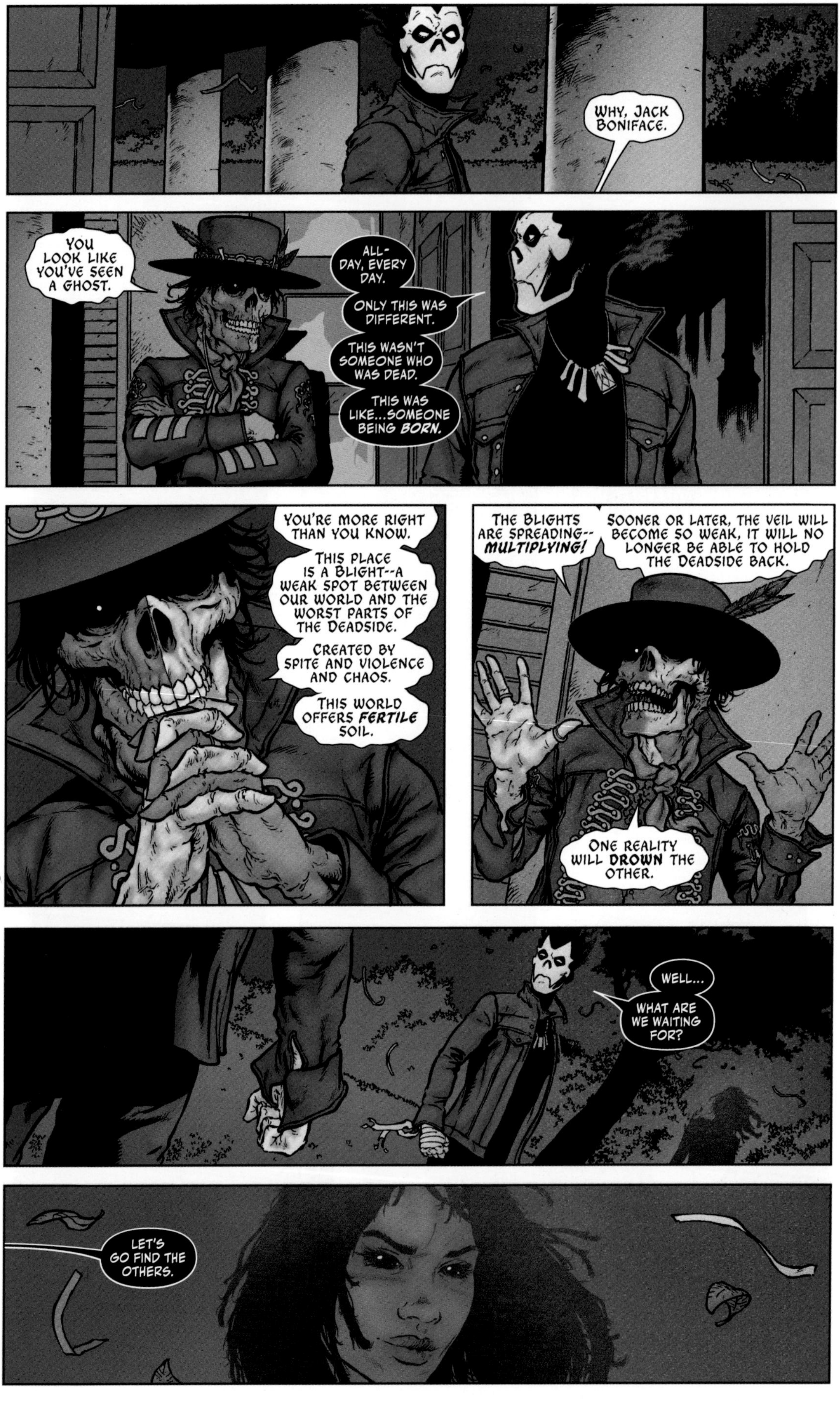
WHY, JACK BONIFACE.
YOU LOOK LIKE YOU'VE SEEN A GHOST.
ALL-DAY, EVERY DAY.
ONLY THIS WAS DIFFERENT.
THIS WASN'T SOMEONE WHO WAS DEAD.
THIS WAS LIKE...SOMEONE BEING *BORN.*
YOU'RE MORE RIGHT THAN YOU KNOW.
THIS PLACE IS A BLIGHT--A WEAK SPOT BETWEEN OUR WORLD AND THE WORST PARTS OF THE DEADSIDE.
CREATED BY SPITE AND VIOLENCE AND CHAOS.
THIS WORLD OFFERS **FERTILE** SOIL.
THE BLIGHTS ARE SPREADING--**MULTIPLYING!**
SOONER OR LATER, THE VEIL WILL BECOME SO WEAK, IT WILL NO LONGER BE ABLE TO HOLD THE DEADSIDE BACK.
ONE REALITY WILL **DROWN** THE OTHER.
WELL...
WHAT ARE WE WAITING FOR?
LET'S GO FIND THE OTHERS.

2
SHADOWMAN®
VALIANT
CULLEN BUNN | JON DAVIS-HUNT | JORDIE BELLAIRE | CLAYTON COWLES

SHADOWMAN #2

WRITER: Cullen Bunn
ARTIST: Jon Davis-Hunt
COLORIST: Jordie Bellaire
LETTERER: Clayton Cowles
COVER ARTIST: Jon Davis-Hunt
ASSOCIATE EDITOR: David Menchel
SENIOR EDITOR: Heather Antos

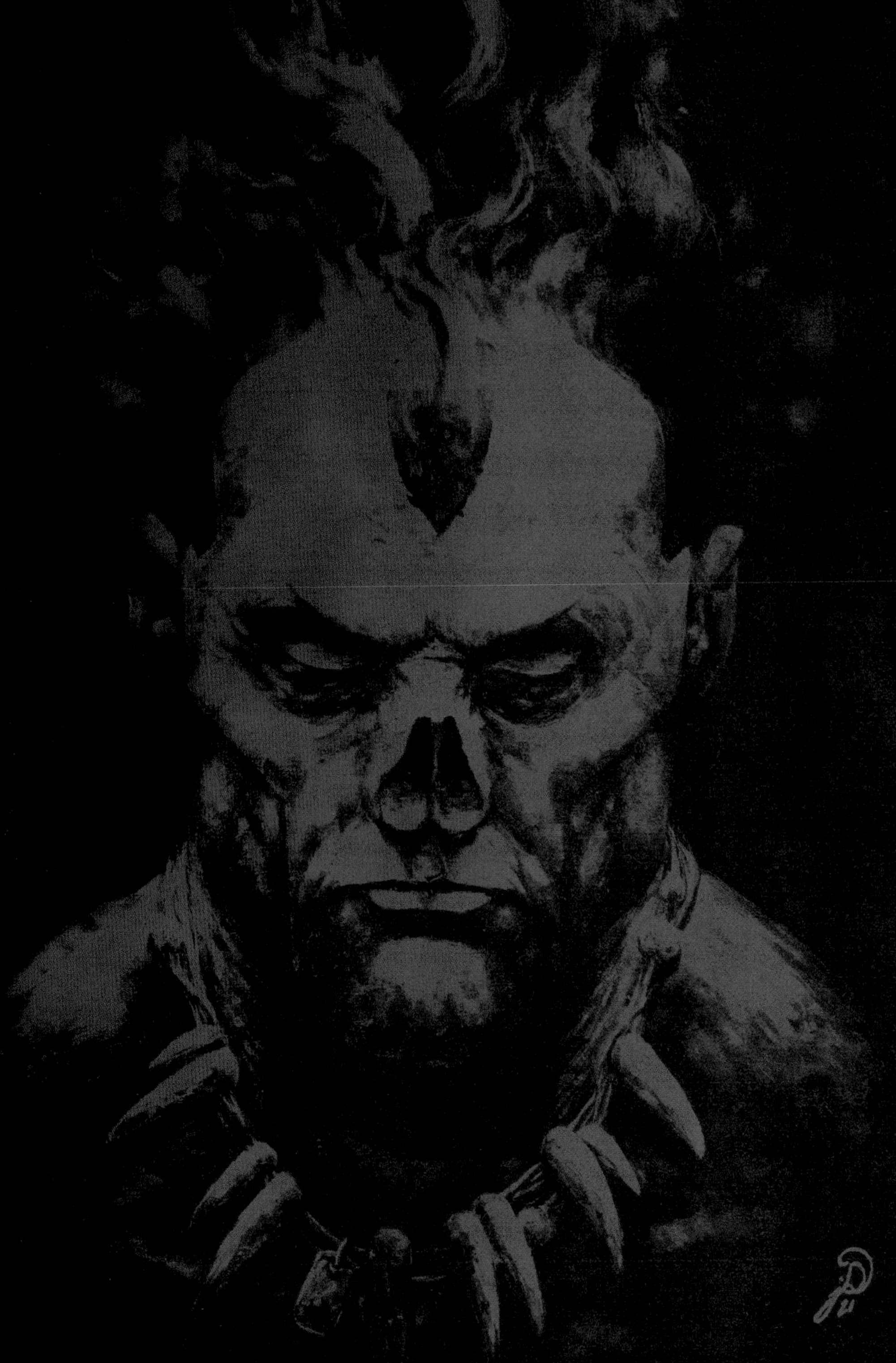

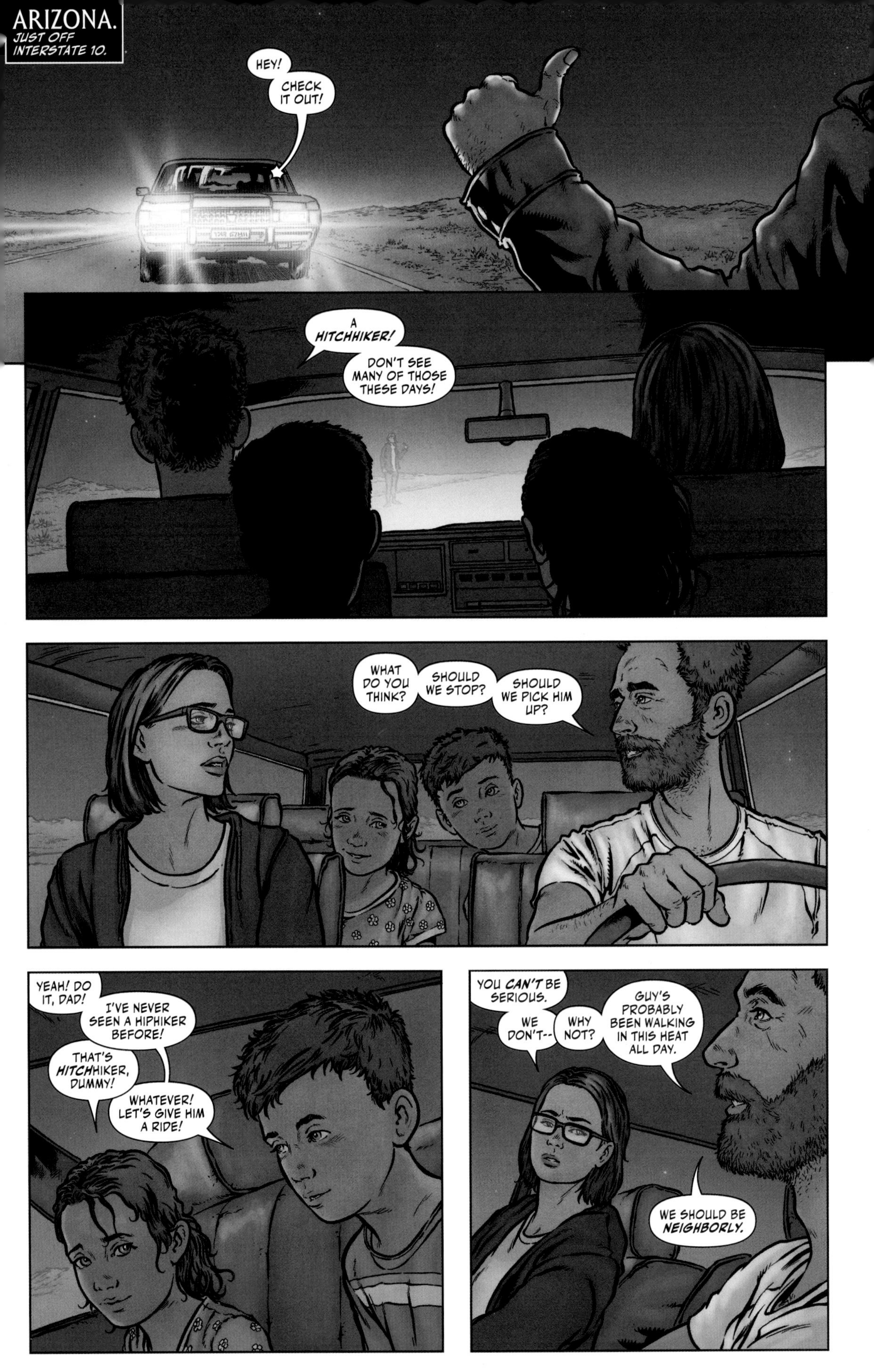
ARIZONA. JUST OFF INTERSTATE 10.
HEY!
CHECK IT OUT!
A HITCHHIKER!
DON'T SEE MANY OF THOSE THESE DAYS!
WHAT DO YOU THINK?
SHOULD WE STOP?
SHOULD WE PICK HIM UP?
YEAH! DO IT, DAD!
I'VE NEVER SEEN A HIPHIKER BEFORE!
THAT'S HITCHHIKER, DUMMY!
WHATEVER! LET'S GIVE HIM A RIDE!
YOU CAN'T BE SERIOUS.
WE DON'T--
WHY NOT?
GUY'S PROBABLY BEEN WALKING IN THIS HEAT ALL DAY.
WE SHOULD BE NEIGHBORLY.

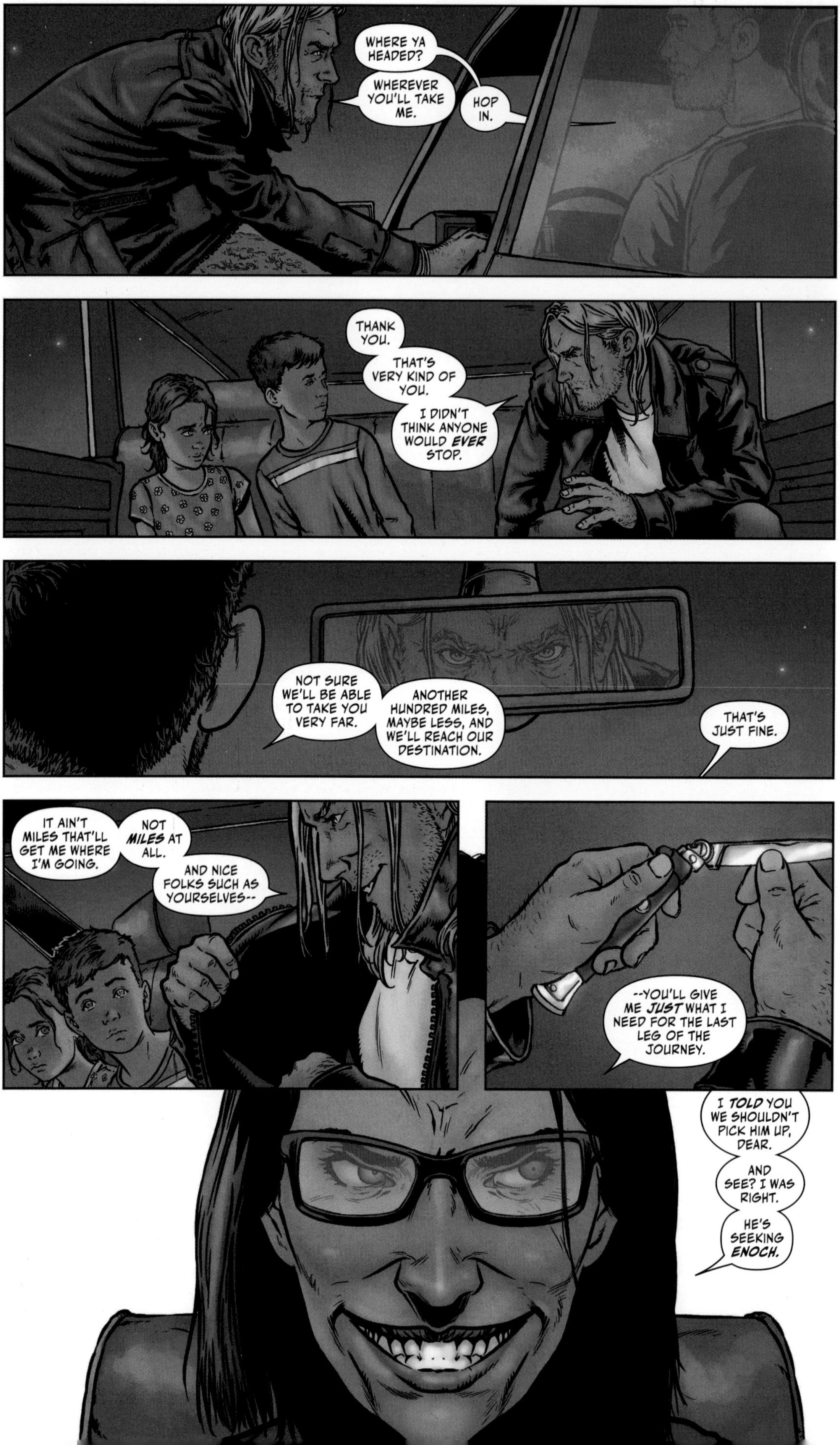
WHERE YA HEADED?
WHEREVER YOU'LL TAKE ME.
HOP IN.
THANK YOU.
THAT'S VERY KIND OF YOU.
I DIDN'T THINK ANYONE WOULD EVER STOP.
NOT SURE WE'LL BE ABLE TO TAKE YOU VERY FAR.
ANOTHER HUNDRED MILES, MAYBE LESS, AND WE'LL REACH OUR DESTINATION.
THAT'S JUST FINE.
IT AIN'T MILES THAT'LL GET ME WHERE I'M GOING.
NOT MILES AT ALL.
AND NICE FOLKS SUCH AS YOURSELVES--
--YOU'LL GIVE ME JUST WHAT I NEED FOR THE LAST LEG OF THE JOURNEY.
I TOLD YOU WE SHOULDN'T PICK HIM UP, DEAR.
AND SEE? I WAS RIGHT.
HE'S SEEKING ENOCH.

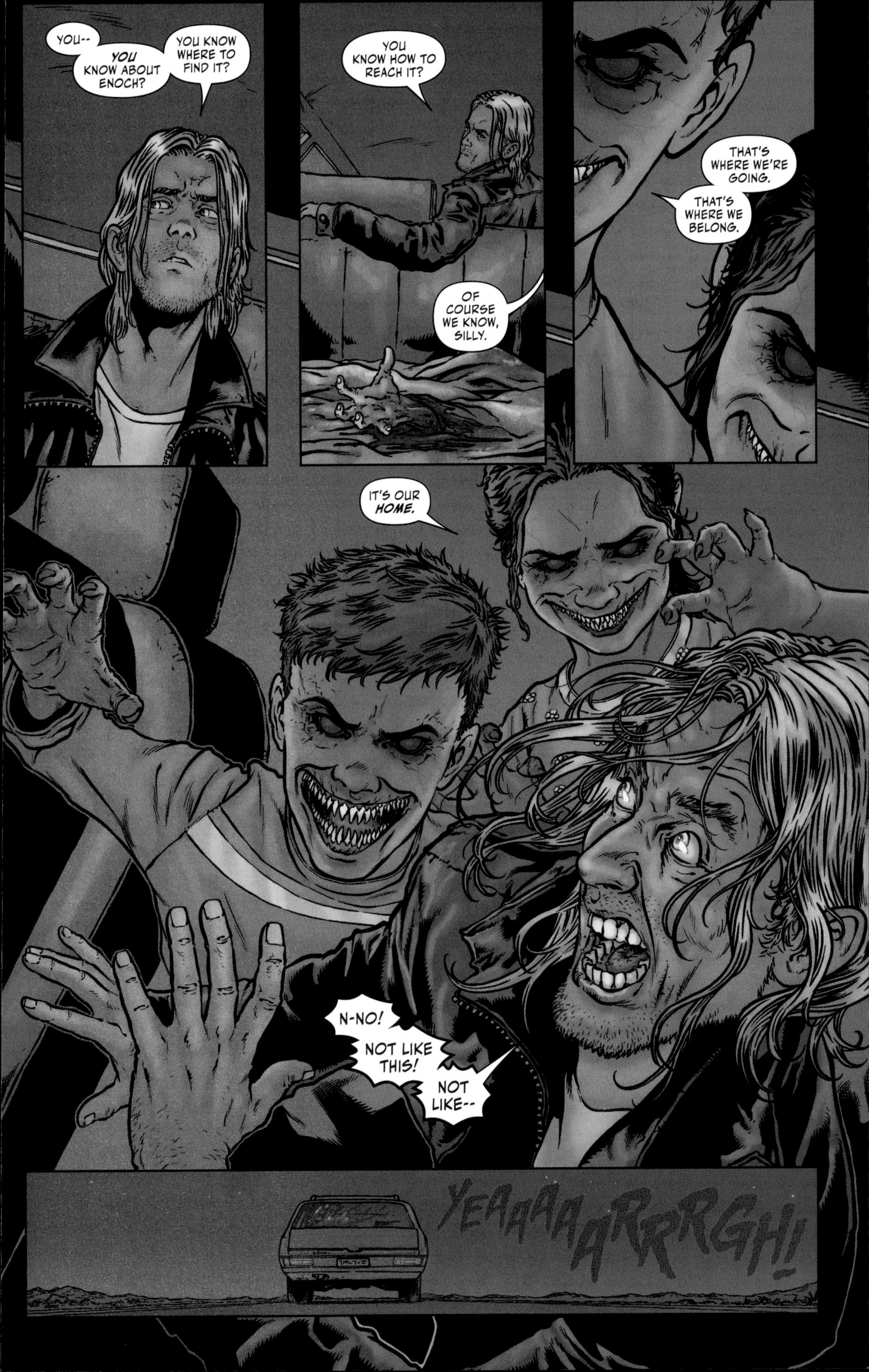
YOU--
YOU KNOW ABOUT ENOCH?
YOU KNOW WHERE TO FIND IT?
YOU KNOW HOW TO REACH IT?
OF COURSE WE KNOW, SILLY.
THAT'S WHERE WE'RE GOING.
THAT'S WHERE WE BELONG.
IT'S OUR ***HOME.***
N-NO!
NOT LIKE THIS!
NOT LIKE--
YEAAAAARRRRGH!

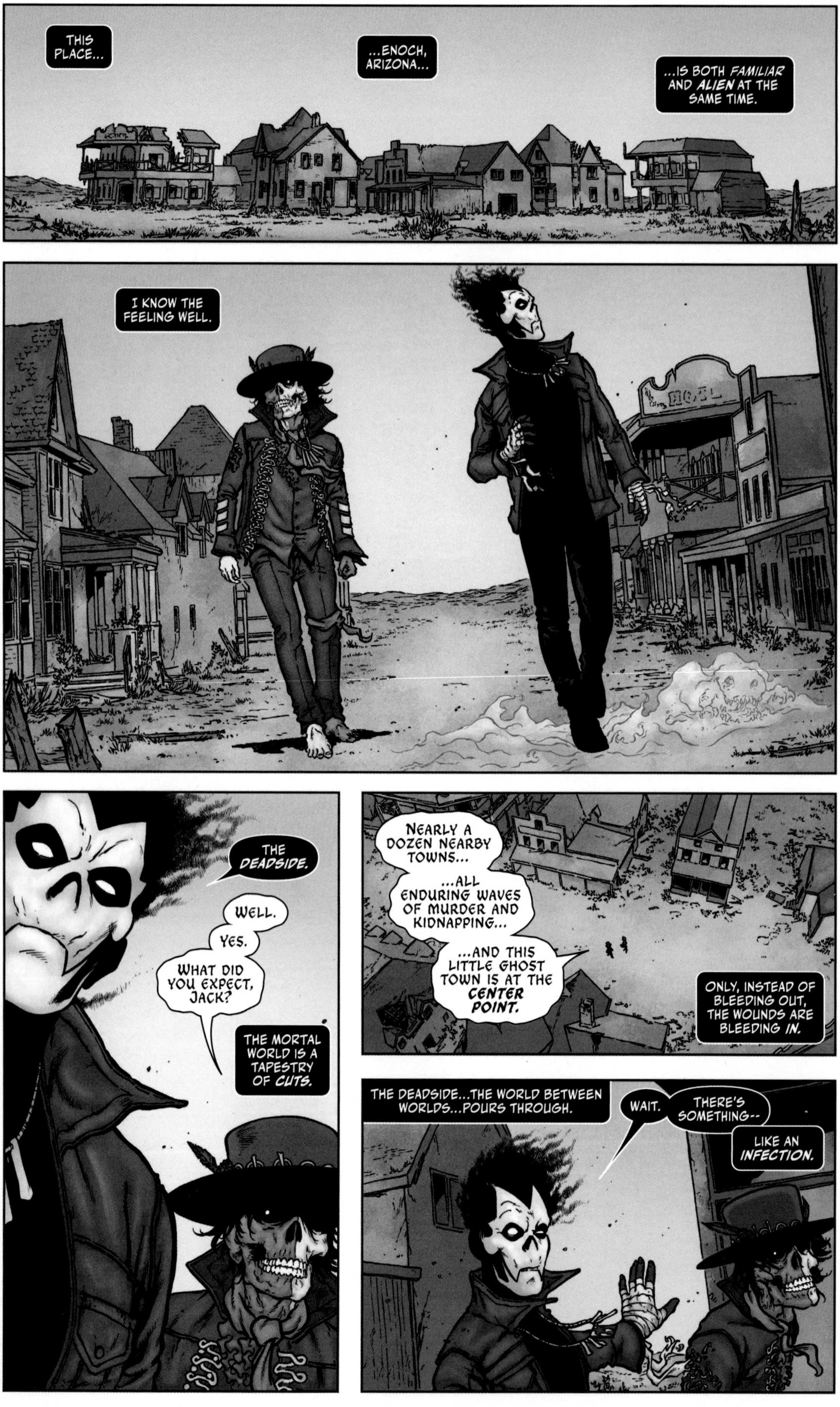
THIS PLACE...
...ENOCH, ARIZONA...
...IS BOTH FAMILIAR AND ALIEN AT THE SAME TIME.
I KNOW THE FEELING WELL.
THE DEADSIDE.
WELL.
YES.
WHAT DID YOU EXPECT, JACK?
THE MORTAL WORLD IS A TAPESTRY OF CUTS.
NEARLY A DOZEN NEARBY TOWNS...
...ALL ENDURING WAVES OF MURDER AND KIDNAPPING...
...AND THIS LITTLE GHOST TOWN IS AT THE CENTER POINT.
ONLY, INSTEAD OF BLEEDING OUT, THE WOUNDS ARE BLEEDING IN.
THE DEADSIDE...THE WORLD BETWEEN WORLDS...POURS THROUGH.
WAIT.
THERE'S SOMETHING--
LIKE AN INFECTION.

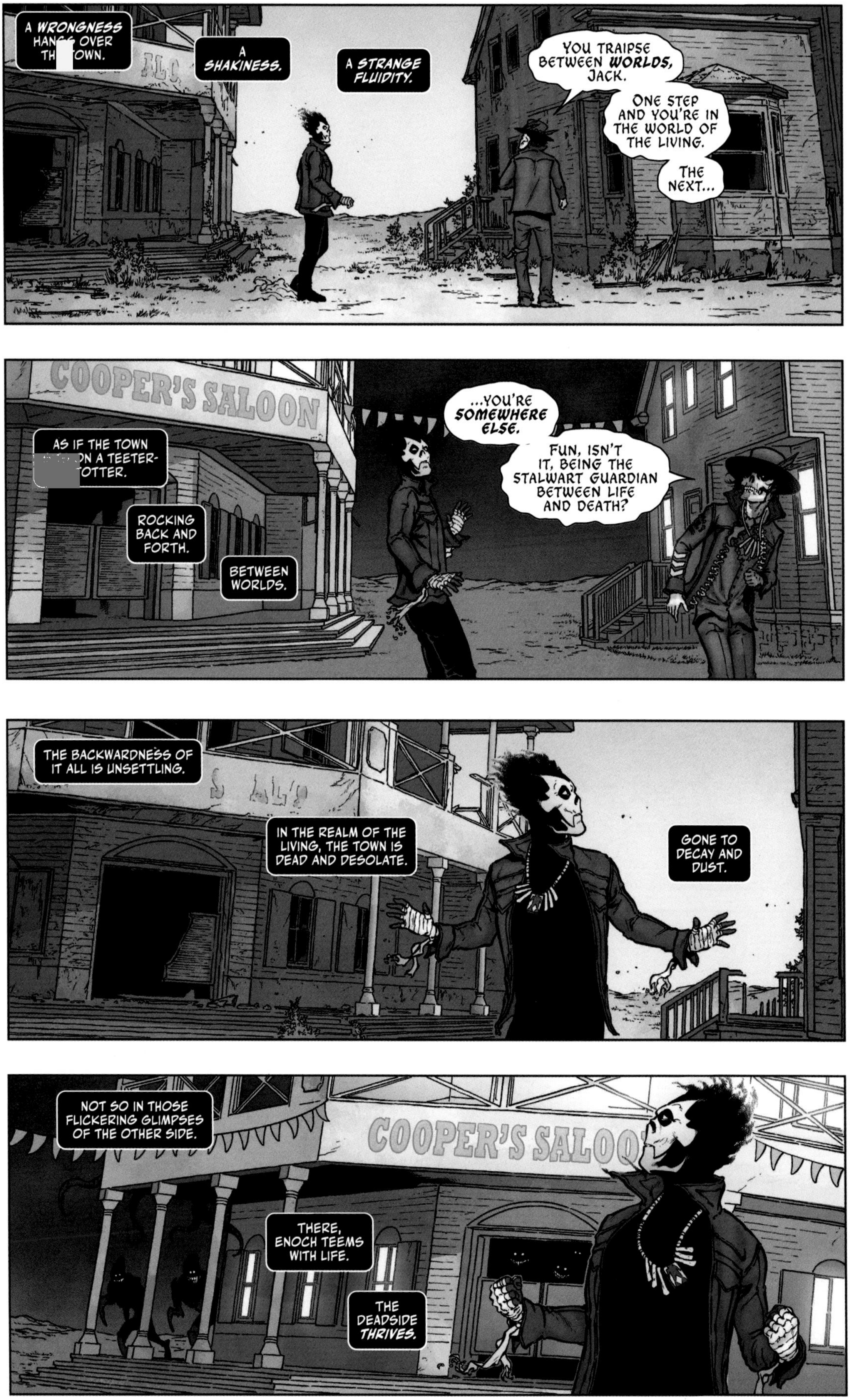
A WRONGNESS HANGS OVER THE TOWN.
A SHAKINESS.
A STRANGE FLUIDITY.
YOU TRAIPSE BETWEEN WORLDS, JACK.
ONE STEP AND YOU'RE IN THE WORLD OF THE LIVING.
THE NEXT...
COOPER'S SALOON
AS IF THE TOWN ON A TEETER-TOTTER.
ROCKING BACK AND FORTH.
BETWEEN WORLDS.
...YOU'RE SOMEWHERE ELSE.
FUN, ISN'T IT, BEING THE STALWART GUARDIAN BETWEEN LIFE AND DEATH?
THE BACKWARDNESS OF IT ALL IS UNSETTLING.
IN THE REALM OF THE LIVING, THE TOWN IS DEAD AND DESOLATE.
GONE TO DECAY AND DUST.
NOT SO IN THOSE FLICKERING GLIMPSES OF THE OTHER SIDE.
COOPER'S SALOO
THERE, ENOCH TEEMS WITH LIFE.
THE DEADSIDE THRIVES.

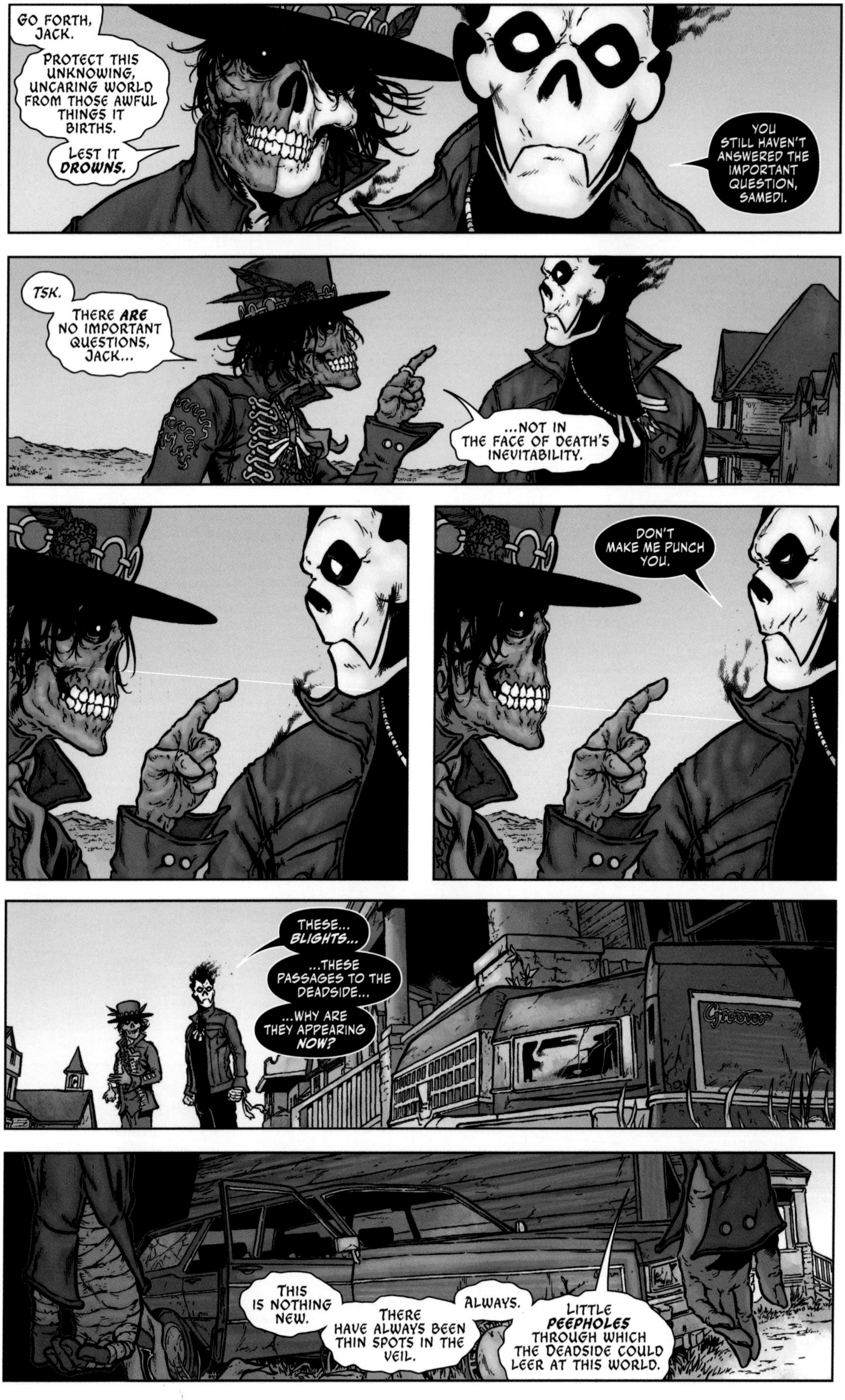
GO FORTH, JACK.
PROTECT THIS UNKNOWING, UNCARING WORLD FROM THOSE AWFUL THINGS IT BIRTHS.
LEST IT DROWNS.
YOU STILL HAVEN'T ANSWERED THE IMPORTANT QUESTION, SAMEDI.
TSK.
THERE ARE NO IMPORTANT QUESTIONS, JACK...
...NOT IN THE FACE OF DEATH'S INEVITABILITY.
DON'T MAKE ME PUNCH YOU.
THESE... BLIGHTS...
...THESE PASSAGES TO THE DEADSIDE...
...WHY ARE THEY APPEARING NOW?
Groover
THIS IS NOTHING NEW.
THERE HAVE ALWAYS BEEN THIN SPOTS IN THE VEIL.
ALWAYS.
LITTLE PEEPHOLES THROUGH WHICH THE DEADSIDE COULD LEER AT THIS WORLD.

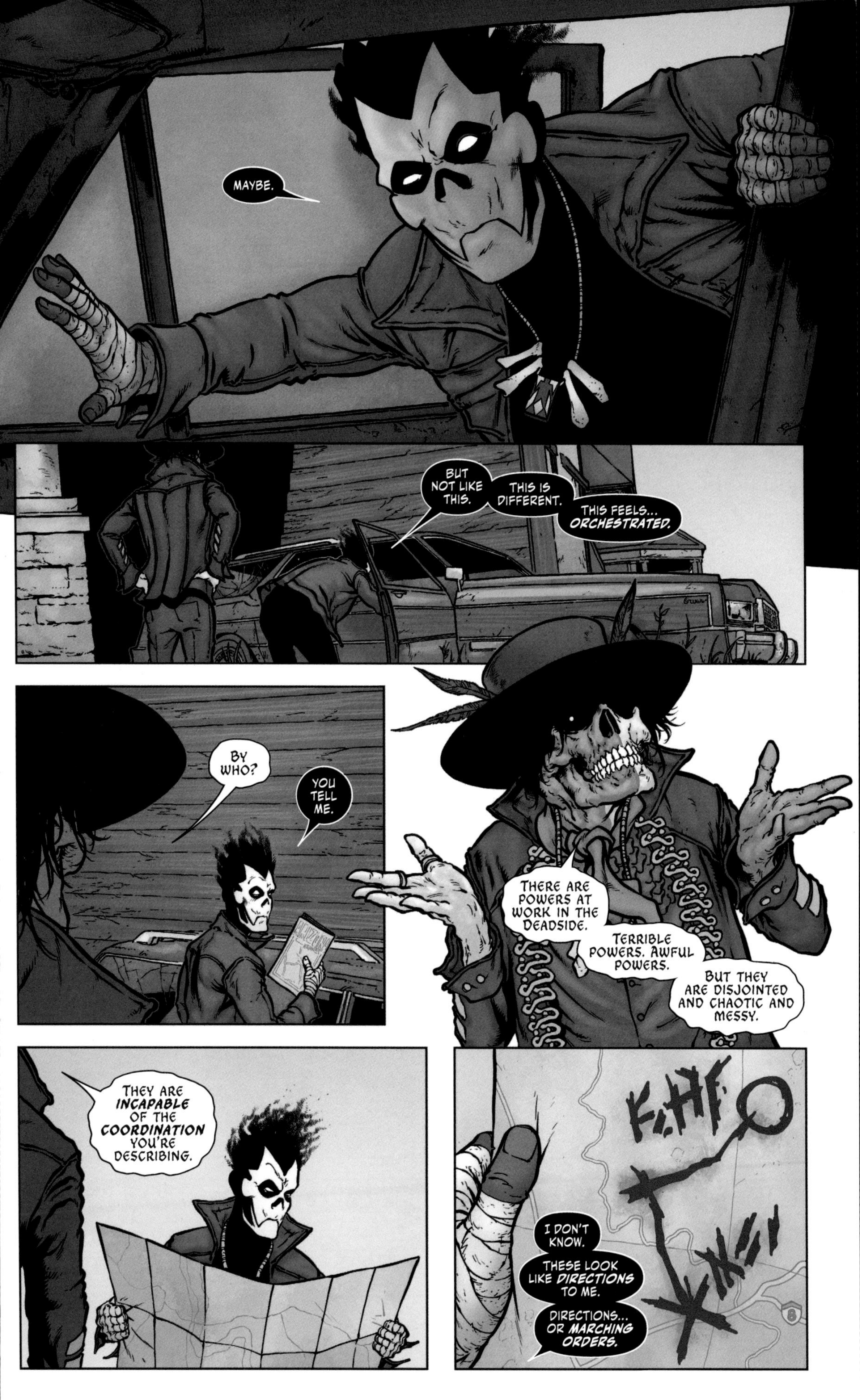
MAYBE.
BUT NOT LIKE THIS.
THIS IS DIFFERENT.
THIS FEELS... ORCHESTRATED.
BY WHO?
YOU TELL ME.
THERE ARE POWERS AT WORK IN THE DEADSIDE.
TERRIBLE POWERS. AWFUL POWERS.
BUT THEY ARE DISJOINTED AND CHAOTIC AND MESSY.
THEY ARE INCAPABLE OF THE COORDINATION YOU'RE DESCRIBING.
I DON'T KNOW.
THESE LOOK LIKE DIRECTIONS TO ME.
DIRECTIONS... OR MARCHING ORDERS.

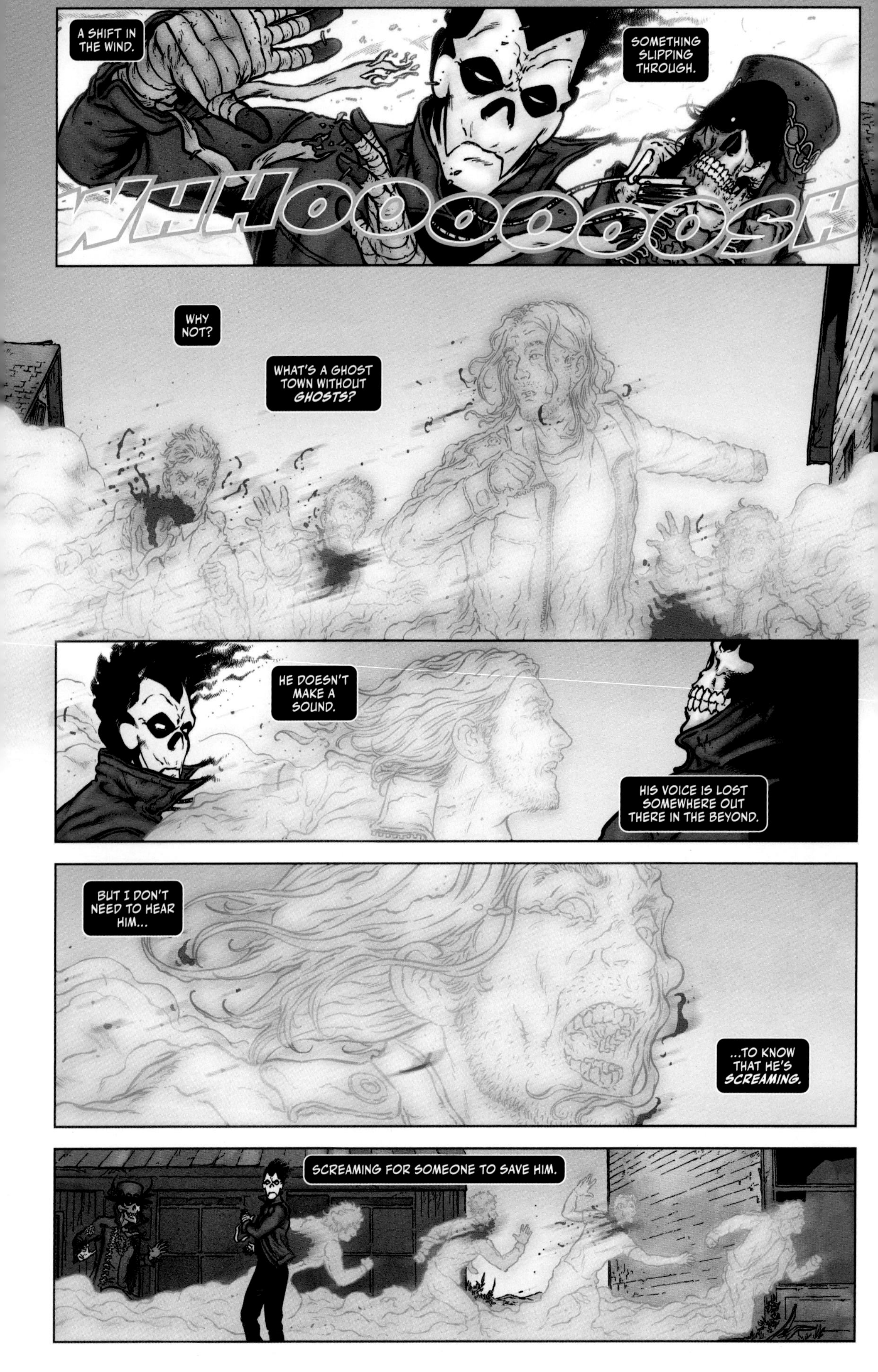
A SHIFT IN THE WIND.
SOMETHING SLIPPING THROUGH.
WHHOOOOOOOSH
WHY NOT?
WHAT'S A GHOST TOWN WITHOUT *GHOSTS?*
HE DOESN'T MAKE A SOUND.
HIS VOICE IS LOST SOMEWHERE OUT THERE IN THE BEYOND.
BUT I DON'T NEED TO HEAR HIM...
...TO KNOW THAT HE'S *SCREAMING.*
SCREAMING FOR SOMEONE TO SAVE HIM.

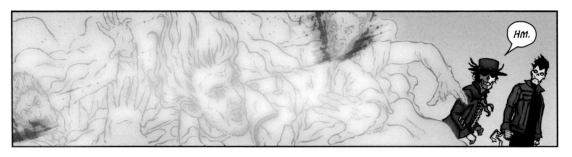

HM.

YOU'RE NOT GOING TO HELP?

I DON'T SEE YOU JUMPING TO HIS DEFENSE, EITHER. YOU COULD STOP THEM.

"YOU'RE THE LOA OF THE DEAD, AFTER ALL."

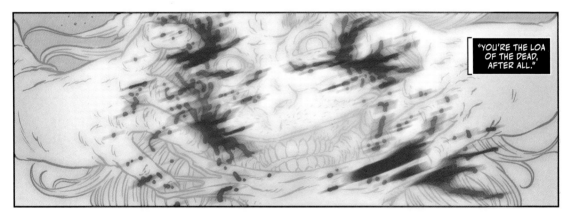

THESE SPIRITS-- I HAVE NO CONTROL OVER THEM. DIDN'T YOU SEE THEIR WOUNDS?

THEY WERE OFFERED UP-- SACRIFICED.

"THEY BELONG TO SOMETHING ELSE NOW."

THERE'S MORE. THE PHANTOM THE OTHERS WERE CHASING...I GET THIS SENSE THAT--

HE DESERVES IT.

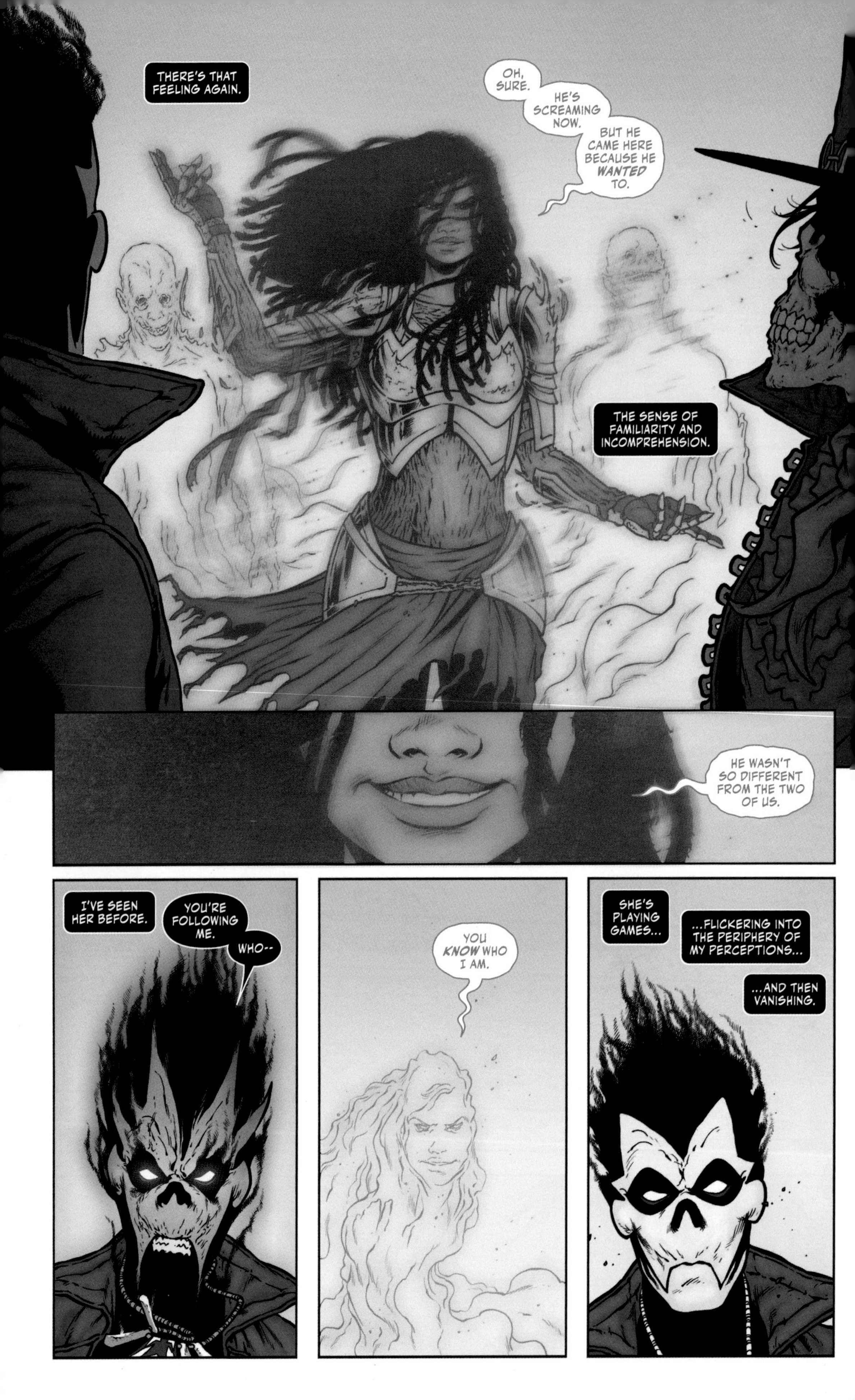
THERE'S THAT FEELING AGAIN.
OH, SURE.
HE'S SCREAMING NOW.
BUT HE CAME HERE BECAUSE HE WANTED TO.
THE SENSE OF FAMILIARITY AND INCOMPREHENSION.
HE WASN'T SO DIFFERENT FROM THE TWO OF US.
I'VE SEEN HER BEFORE.
YOU'RE FOLLOWING ME.
WHO--
YOU KNOW WHO I AM.
SHE'S PLAYING GAMES...
...FLICKERING INTO THE PERIPHERY OF MY PERCEPTIONS...
...AND THEN VANISHING.

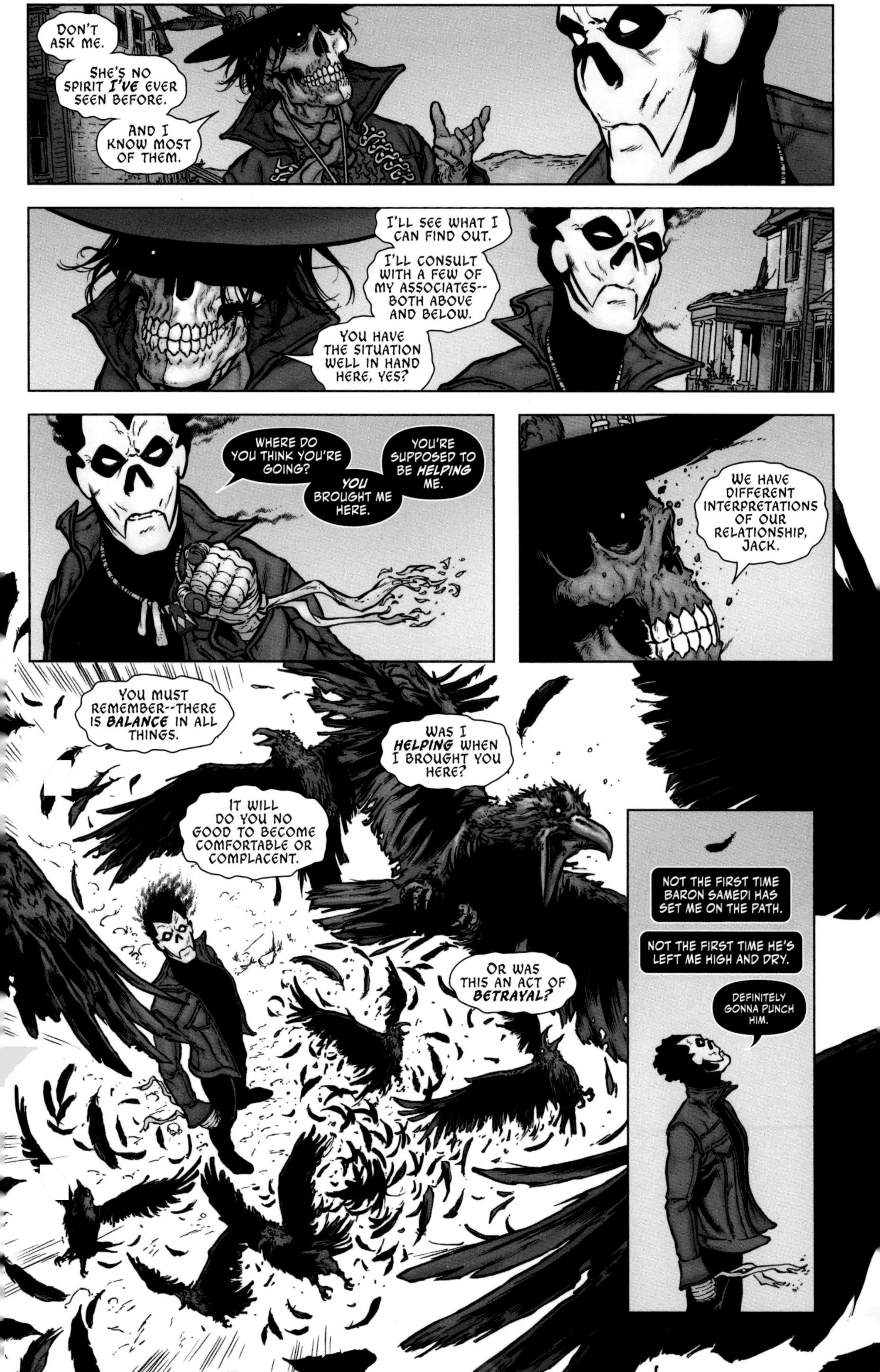

DON'T ASK ME.
SHE'S NO SPIRIT I'VE EVER SEEN BEFORE.
AND I KNOW MOST OF THEM.
I'LL SEE WHAT I CAN FIND OUT.
I'LL CONSULT WITH A FEW OF MY ASSOCIATES-- BOTH ABOVE AND BELOW.
YOU HAVE THE SITUATION WELL IN HAND HERE, YES?
WHERE DO YOU THINK YOU'RE GOING?
YOU BROUGHT ME HERE.
YOU'RE SUPPOSED TO BE HELPING ME.
WE HAVE DIFFERENT INTERPRETATIONS OF OUR RELATIONSHIP, JACK.
YOU MUST REMEMBER--THERE IS BALANCE IN ALL THINGS.
WAS I HELPING WHEN I BROUGHT YOU HERE?
IT WILL DO YOU NO GOOD TO BECOME COMFORTABLE OR COMPLACENT.
OR WAS THIS AN ACT OF BETRAYAL?
NOT THE FIRST TIME BARON SAMEDI HAS SET ME ON THE PATH.
NOT THE FIRST TIME HE'S LEFT ME HIGH AND DRY.
DEFINITELY GONNA PUNCH HIM.

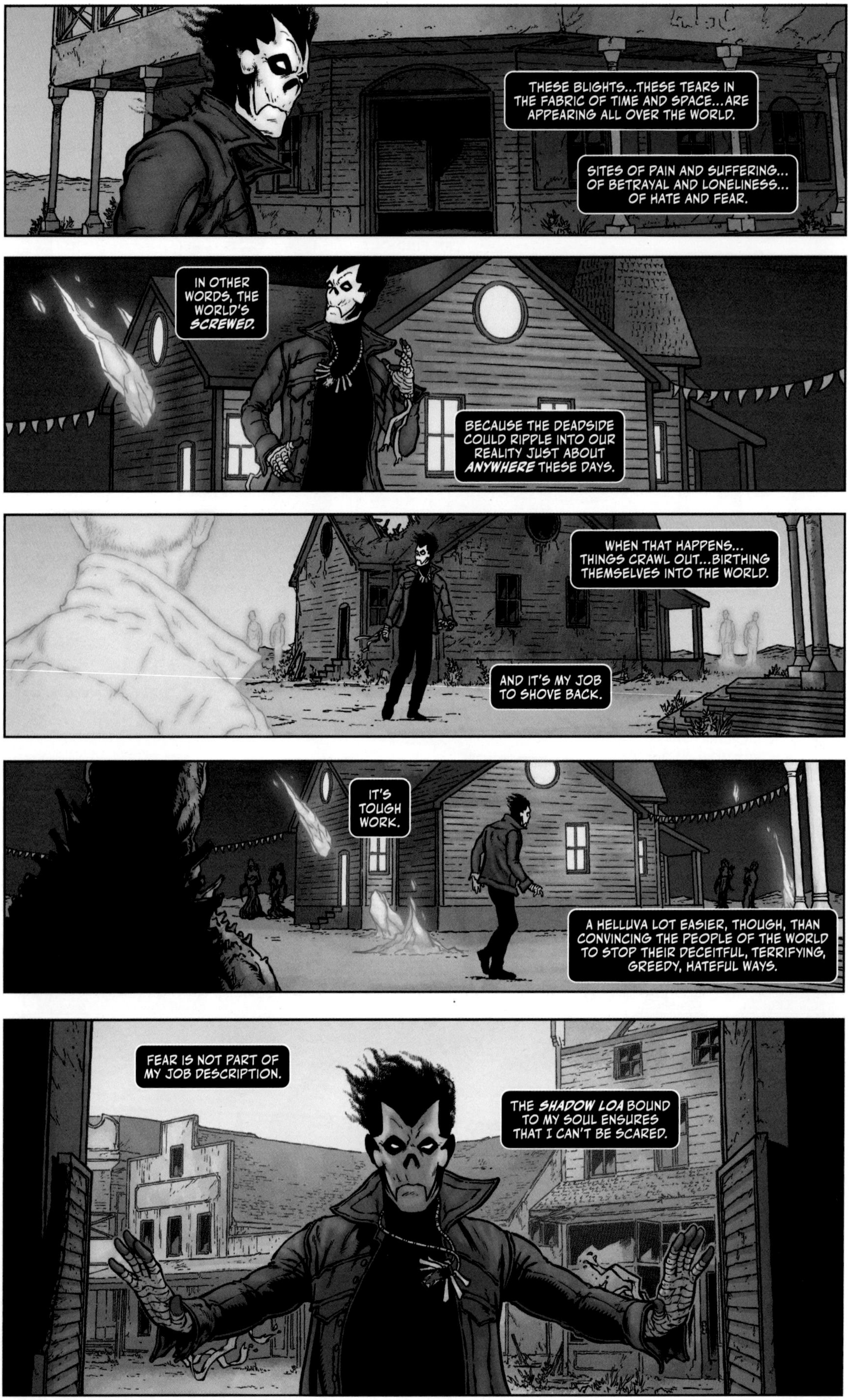
THESE BLIGHTS...THESE TEARS IN THE FABRIC OF TIME AND SPACE...ARE APPEARING ALL OVER THE WORLD.
SITES OF PAIN AND SUFFERING... OF BETRAYAL AND LONELINESS... OF HATE AND FEAR.
IN OTHER WORDS, THE WORLD'S *SCREWED.*
BECAUSE THE DEADSIDE COULD RIPPLE INTO OUR REALITY JUST ABOUT *ANYWHERE* THESE DAYS.
WHEN THAT HAPPENS... THINGS CRAWL OUT...BIRTHING THEMSELVES INTO THE WORLD.
AND IT'S MY JOB TO SHOVE BACK.
IT'S TOUGH WORK.
A HELLUVA LOT EASIER, THOUGH, THAN CONVINCING THE PEOPLE OF THE WORLD TO STOP THEIR DECEITFUL, TERRIFYING, GREEDY, HATEFUL WAYS.
FEAR IS NOT PART OF MY JOB DESCRIPTION.
THE *SHADOW LOA* BOUND TO MY SOUL ENSURES THAT I CAN'T BE SCARED.

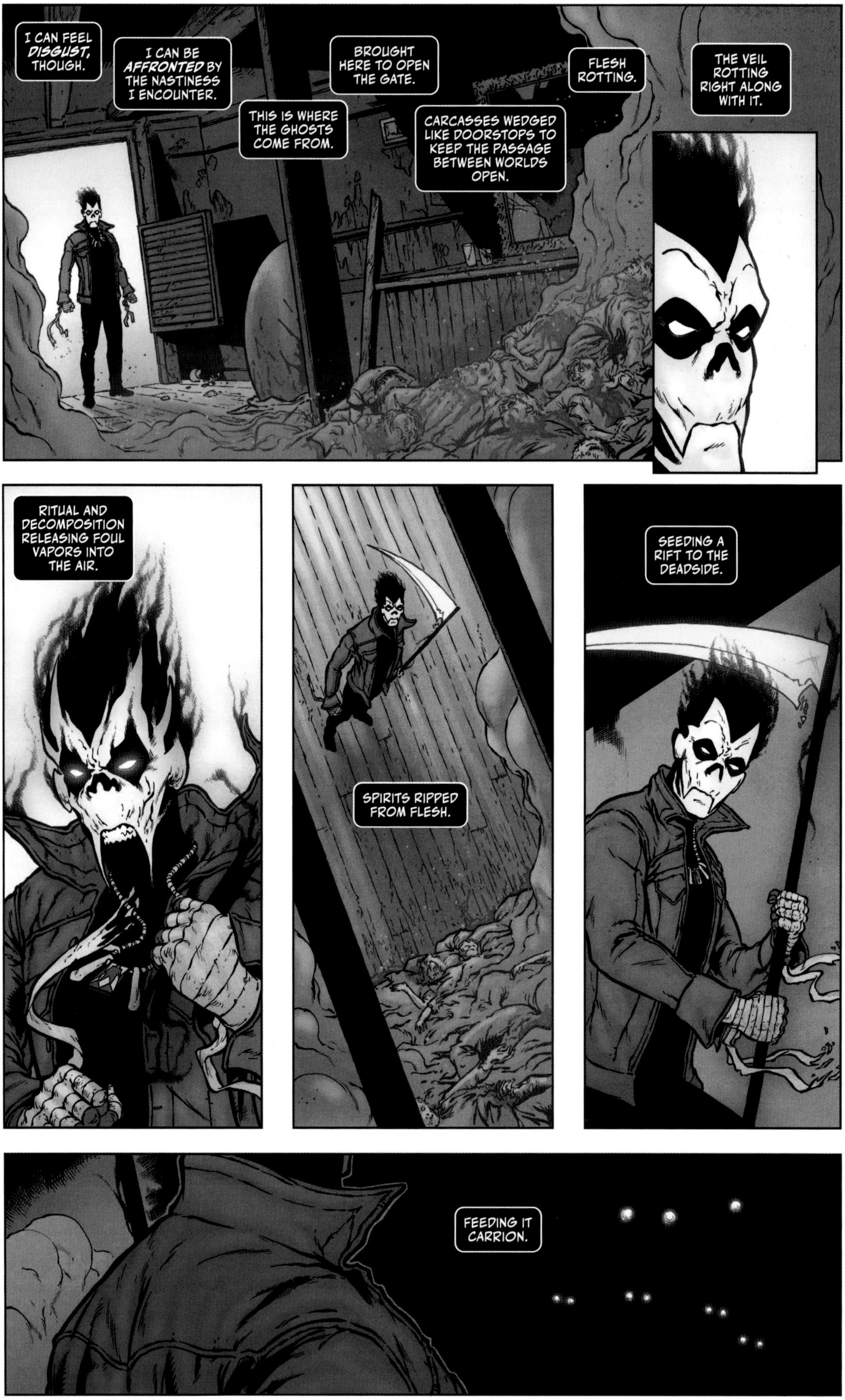
I CAN FEEL DISGUST, THOUGH.
I CAN BE AFFRONTED BY THE NASTINESS I ENCOUNTER.
THIS IS WHERE THE GHOSTS COME FROM.
BROUGHT HERE TO OPEN THE GATE.
CARCASSES WEDGED LIKE DOORSTOPS TO KEEP THE PASSAGE BETWEEN WORLDS OPEN.
FLESH ROTTING.
THE VEIL ROTTING RIGHT ALONG WITH IT.
RITUAL AND DECOMPOSITION RELEASING FOUL VAPORS INTO THE AIR.
SPIRITS RIPPED FROM FLESH.
SEEDING A RIFT TO THE DEADSIDE.
FEEDING IT CARRION.

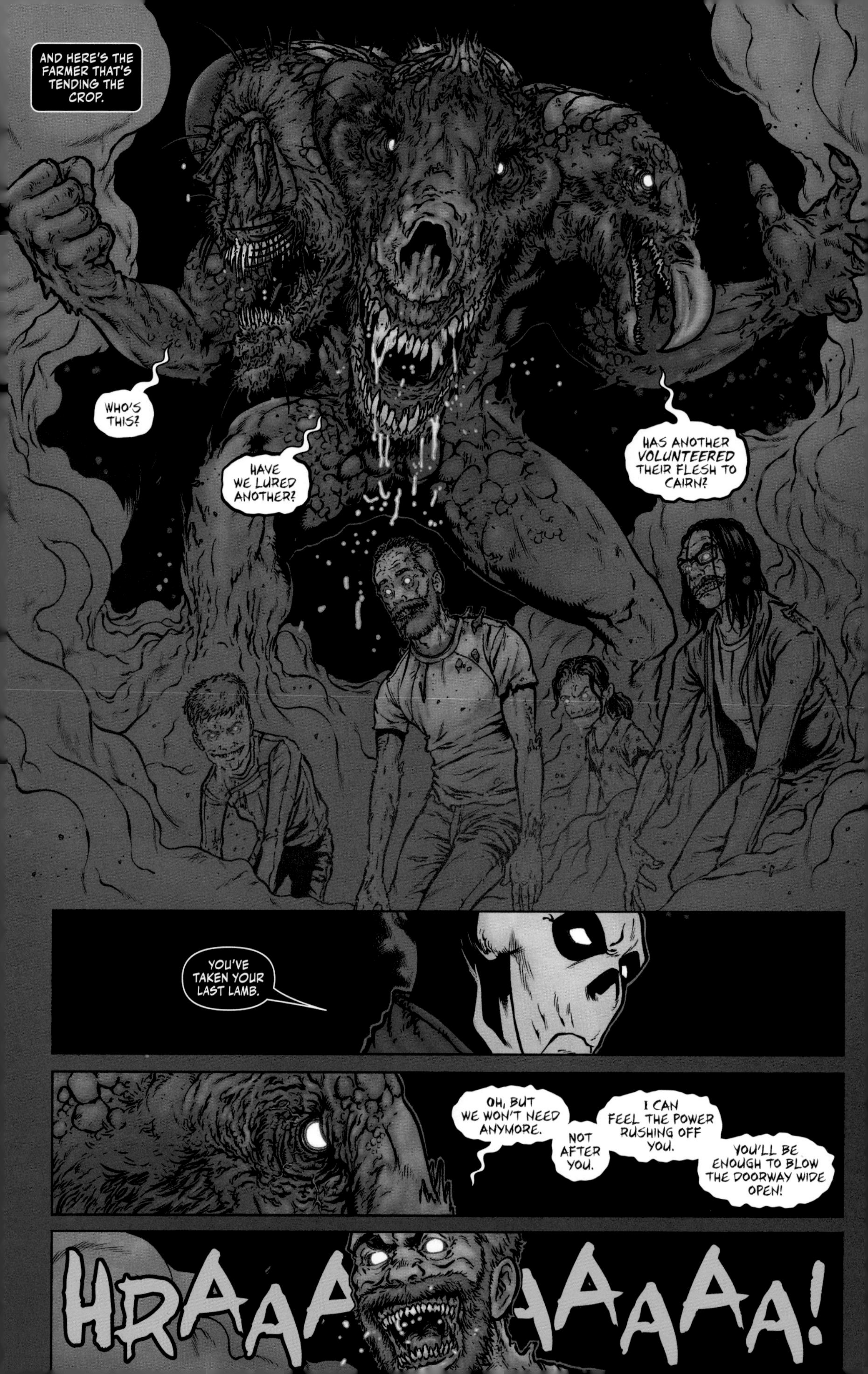
AND HERE'S THE FARMER THAT'S TENDING THE CROP.
WHO'S THIS?
HAVE WE LURED ANOTHER?
HAS ANOTHER VOLUNTEERED THEIR FLESH TO CAIRN?
YOU'VE TAKEN YOUR LAST LAMB.
OH, BUT WE WON'T NEED ANYMORE.
NOT AFTER YOU.
I CAN FEEL THE POWER RUSHING OFF YOU.
YOU'LL BE ENOUGH TO BLOW THE DOORWAY WIDE OPEN!
HRAAAAAAAAA!

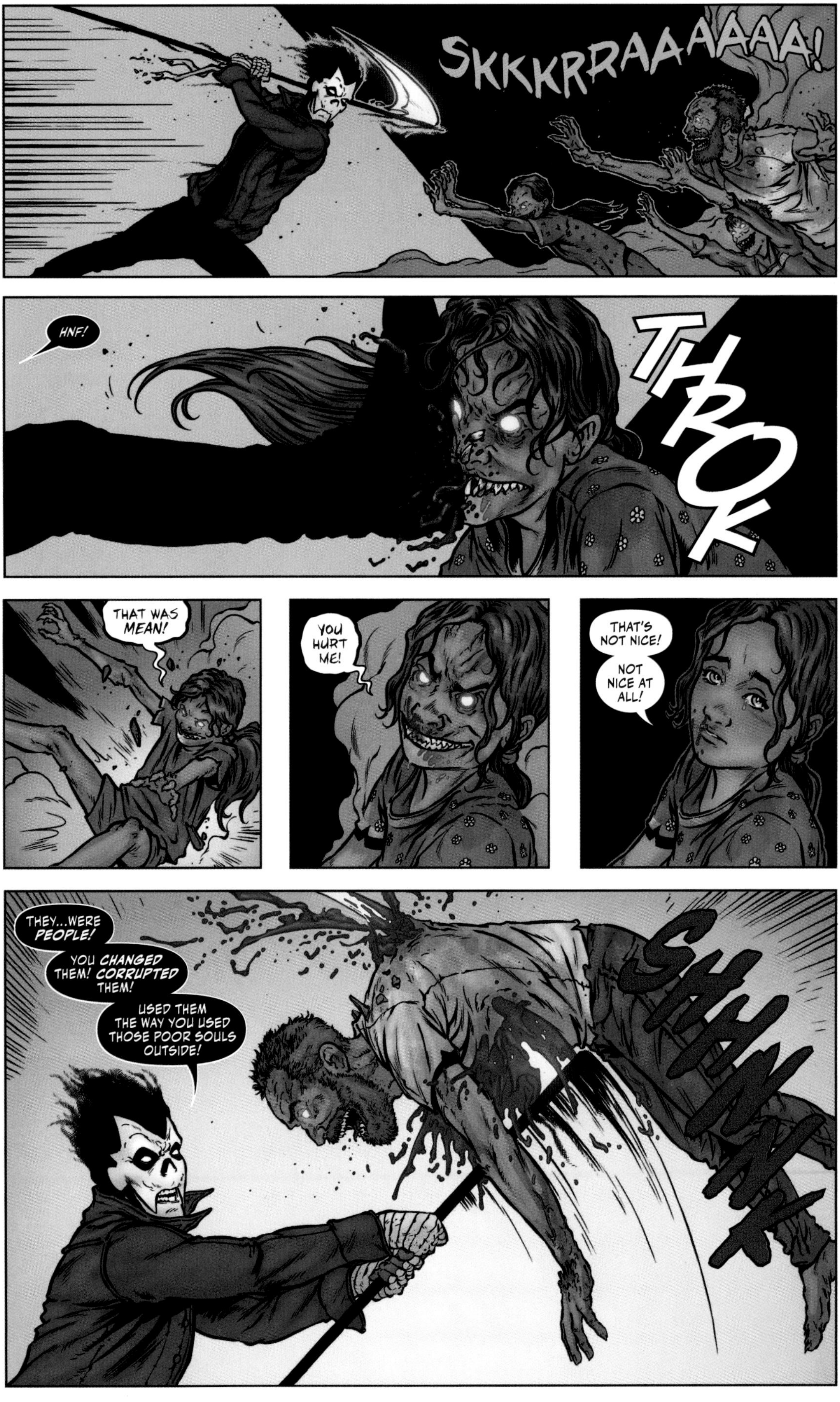
SKKKRRAAAAAAA!
HNF!
THROK
THAT WAS MEAN!
YOU HURT ME!
THAT'S NOT NICE!
NOT NICE AT ALL!
THEY...WERE PEOPLE!
YOU CHANGED THEM! CORRUPTED THEM!
USED THEM THE WAY YOU USED THOSE POOR SOULS OUTSIDE!
SHHNNK

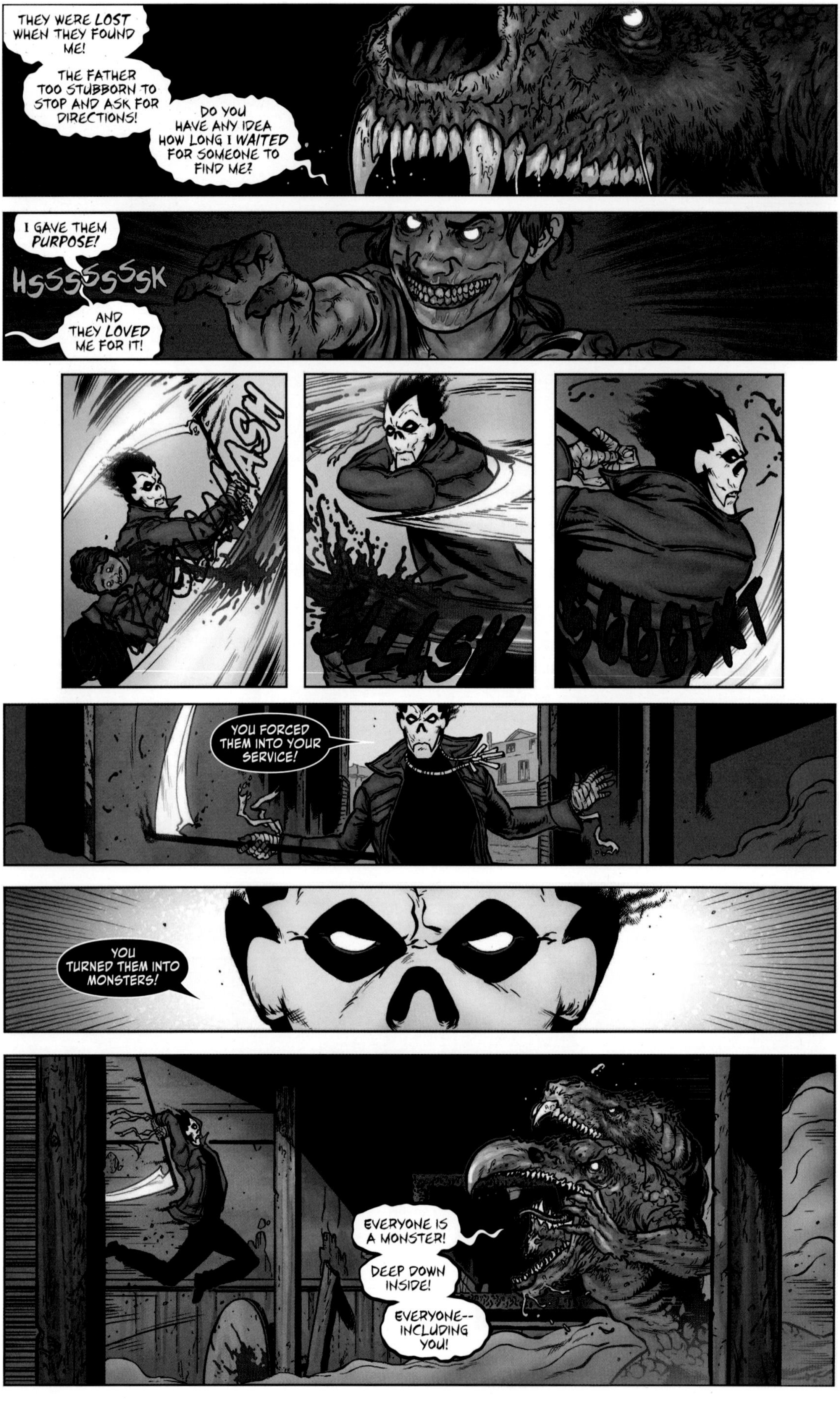
THEY WERE LOST WHEN THEY FOUND ME!
THE FATHER TOO STUBBORN TO STOP AND ASK FOR DIRECTIONS!
DO YOU HAVE ANY IDEA HOW LONG I WAITED FOR SOMEONE TO FIND ME?
I GAVE THEM PURPOSE!
HSSSSSSSK
AND THEY LOVED ME FOR IT!
YOU FORCED THEM INTO YOUR SERVICE!
YOU TURNED THEM INTO MONSTERS!
EVERYONE IS A MONSTER!
DEEP DOWN INSIDE!
EVERYONE-- INCLUDING YOU!

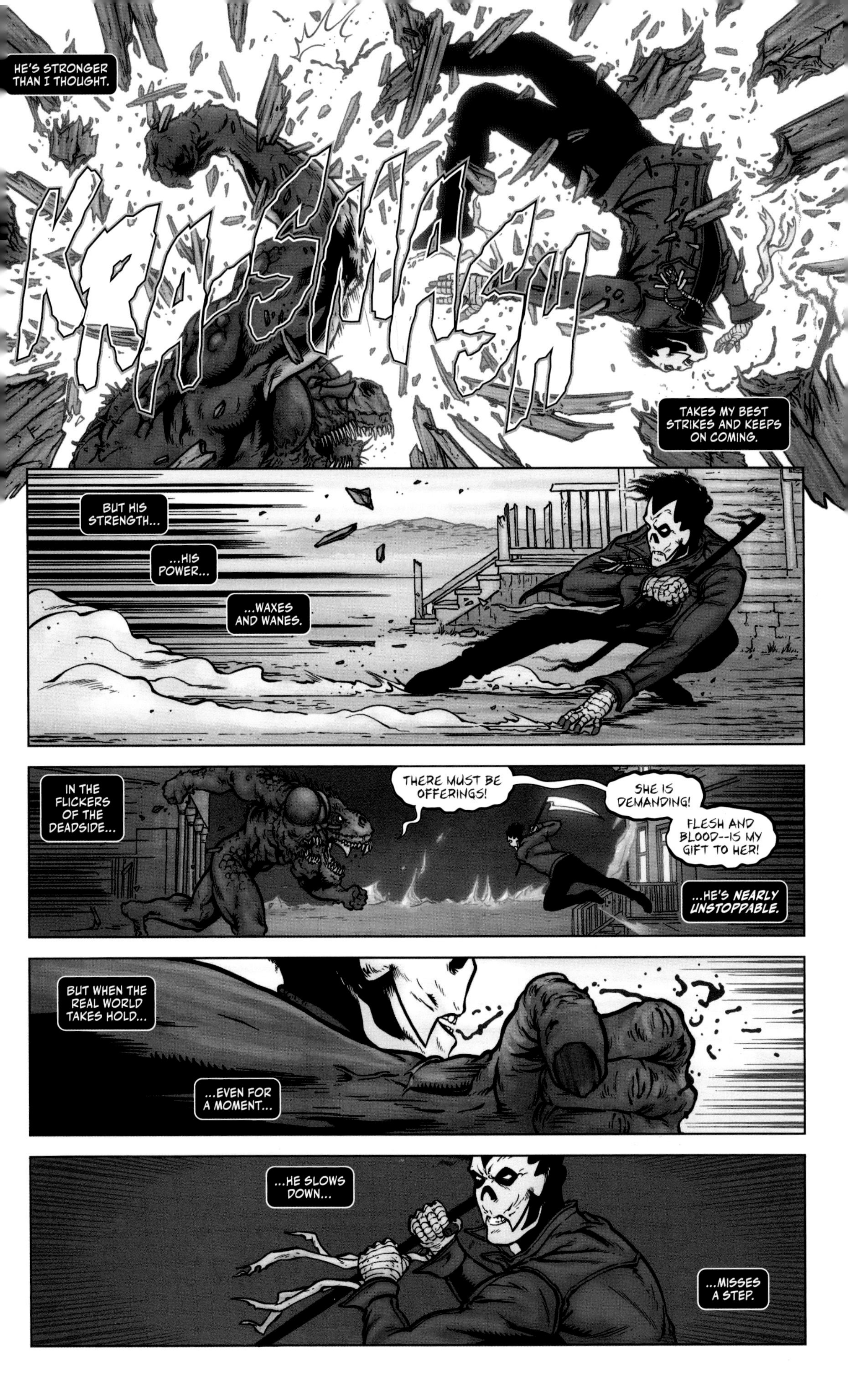
HE'S STRONGER THAN I THOUGHT.
KRA-SMASH
TAKES MY BEST STRIKES AND KEEPS ON COMING.
BUT HIS STRENGTH...
...HIS POWER...
...WAXES AND WANES.
IN THE FLICKERS OF THE DEADSIDE...
THERE MUST BE OFFERINGS!
SHE IS DEMANDING!
FLESH AND BLOOD--IS MY GIFT TO HER!
...HE'S NEARLY UNSTOPPABLE.
BUT WHEN THE REAL WORLD TAKES HOLD...
...EVEN FOR A MOMENT...
...HE SLOWS DOWN...
...MISSES A STEP.

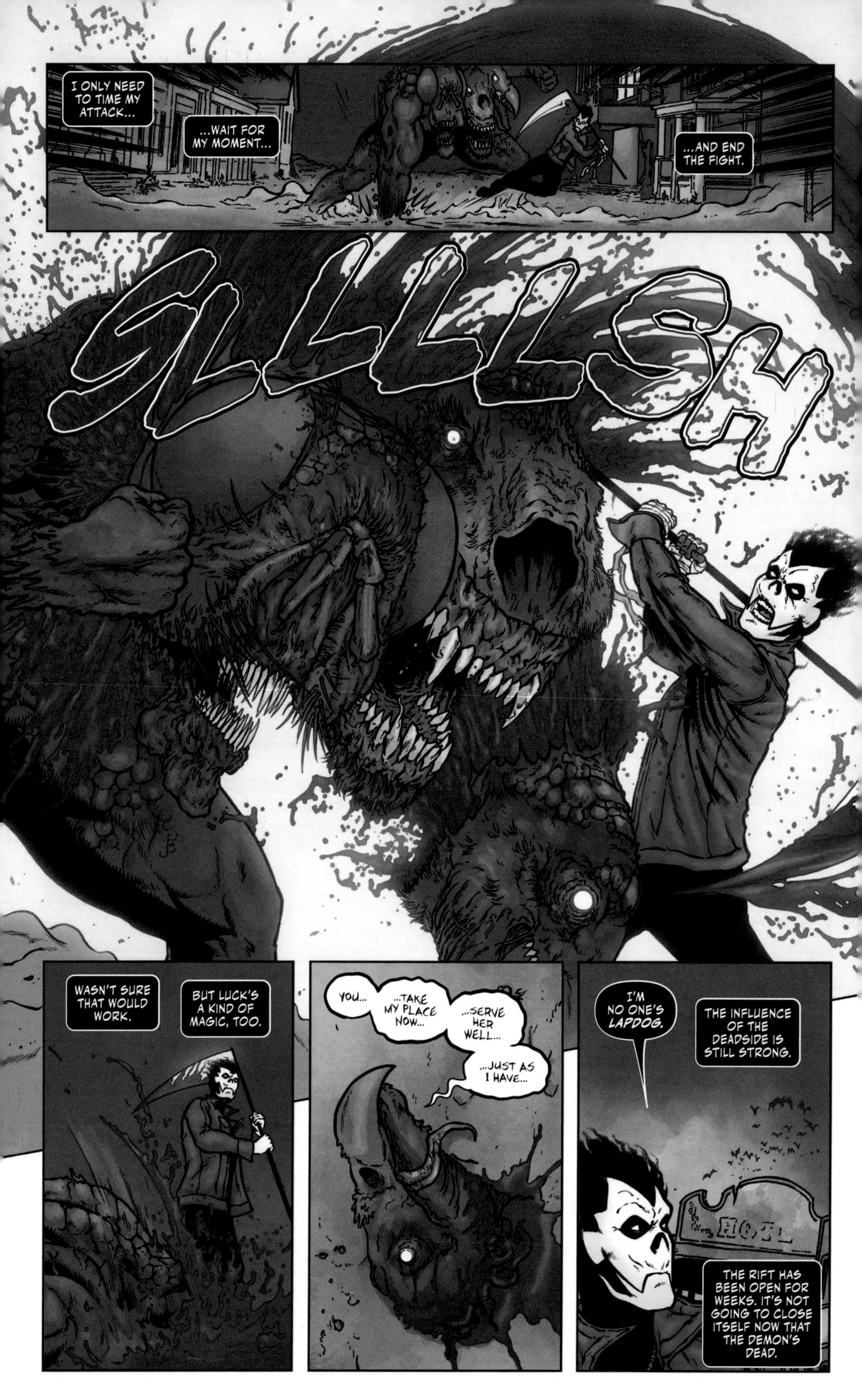
I ONLY NEED TO TIME MY ATTACK...
...WAIT FOR MY MOMENT...
...AND END THE FIGHT.
GLLLLSH
WASN'T SURE THAT WOULD WORK.
BUT LUCK'S A KIND OF MAGIC, TOO.
YOU...
...TAKE MY PLACE NOW...
...SERVE HER WELL...
...JUST AS I HAVE...
I'M NO ONE'S *LAPDOG.*
THE INFLUENCE OF THE DEADSIDE IS STILL STRONG.
THE RIFT HAS BEEN OPEN FOR WEEKS. IT'S NOT GOING TO CLOSE ITSELF NOW THAT THE DEMON'S DEAD.

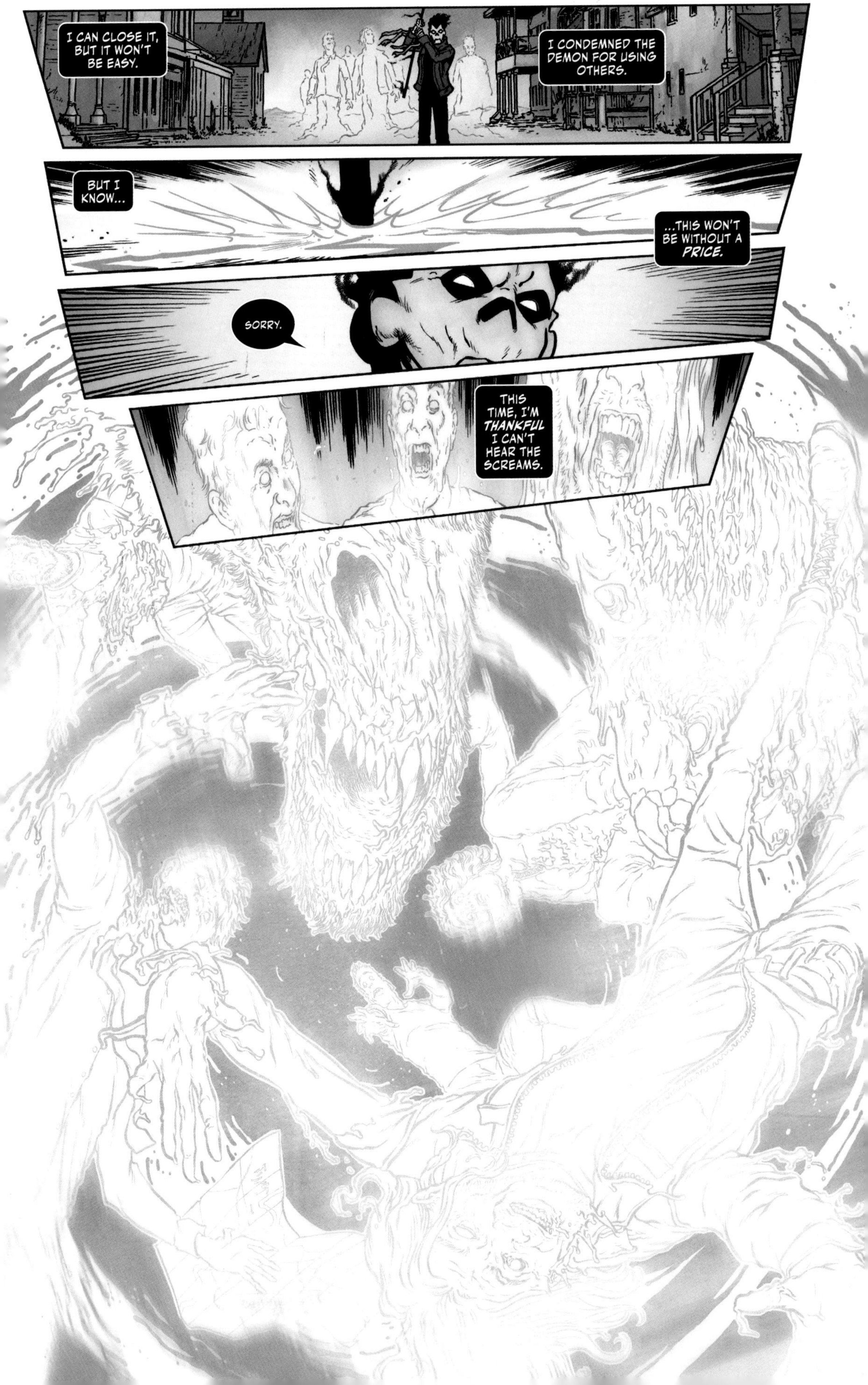
I CAN CLOSE IT, BUT IT WON'T BE EASY.
I CONDEMNED THE DEMON FOR USING OTHERS.
BUT I KNOW...
...THIS WON'T BE WITHOUT A *PRICE.*
SORRY.
THIS TIME, I'M *THANKFUL* I CAN'T HEAR THE SCREAMS.

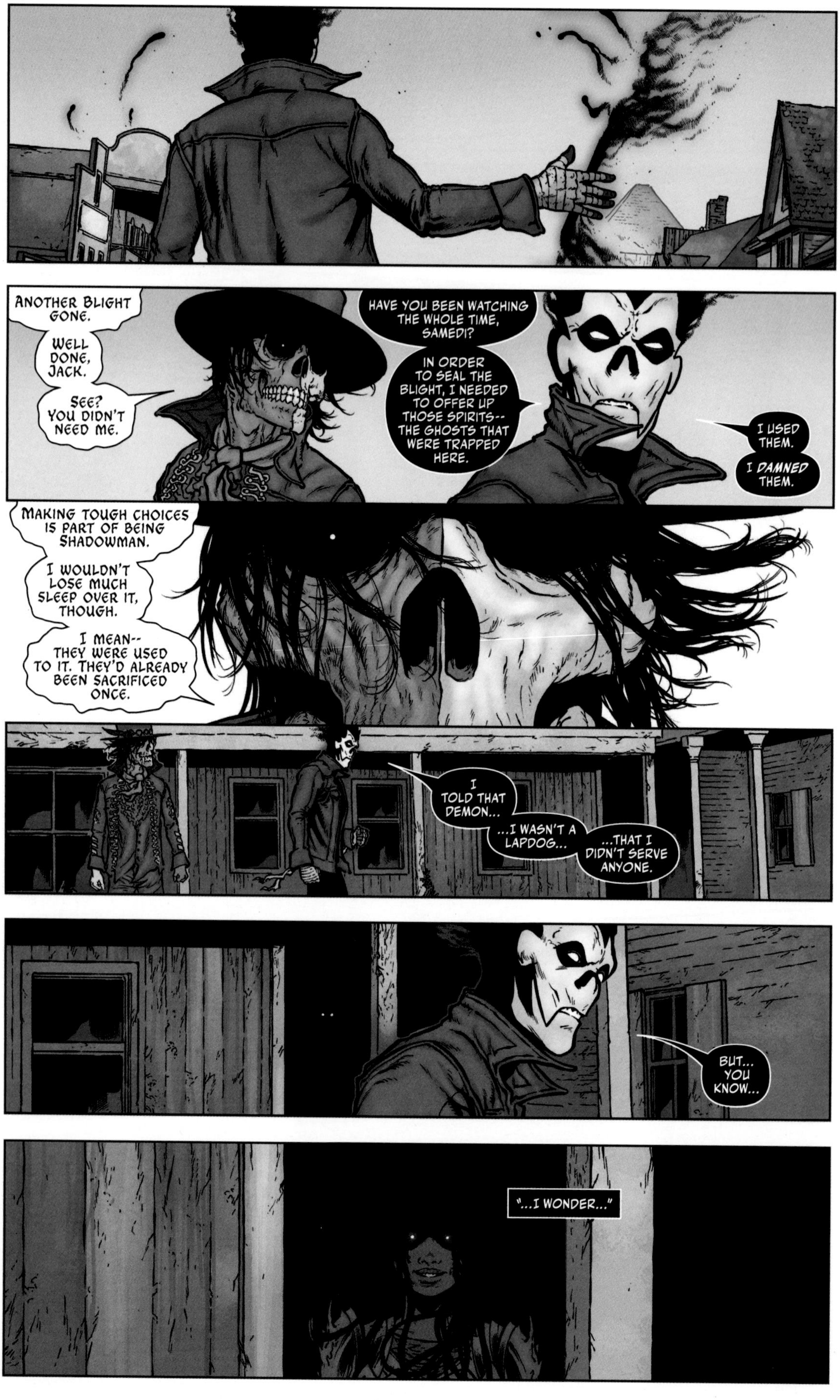
ANOTHER BLIGHT GONE.
WELL DONE, JACK.
SEE? YOU DIDN'T NEED ME.
HAVE YOU BEEN WATCHING THE WHOLE TIME, SAMEDI?
IN ORDER TO SEAL THE BLIGHT, I NEEDED TO OFFER UP THOSE SPIRITS-- THE GHOSTS THAT WERE TRAPPED HERE.
I USED THEM.
I *DAMNED* THEM.
MAKING TOUGH CHOICES IS PART OF BEING SHADOWMAN.
I WOULDN'T LOSE MUCH SLEEP OVER IT, THOUGH.
I MEAN-- THEY WERE USED TO IT. THEY'D ALREADY BEEN SACRIFICED ONCE.
I TOLD THAT DEMON...
...I WASN'T A LAPDOG...
...THAT I DIDN'T SERVE ANYONE.
BUT... YOU KNOW...
"...I WONDER..."

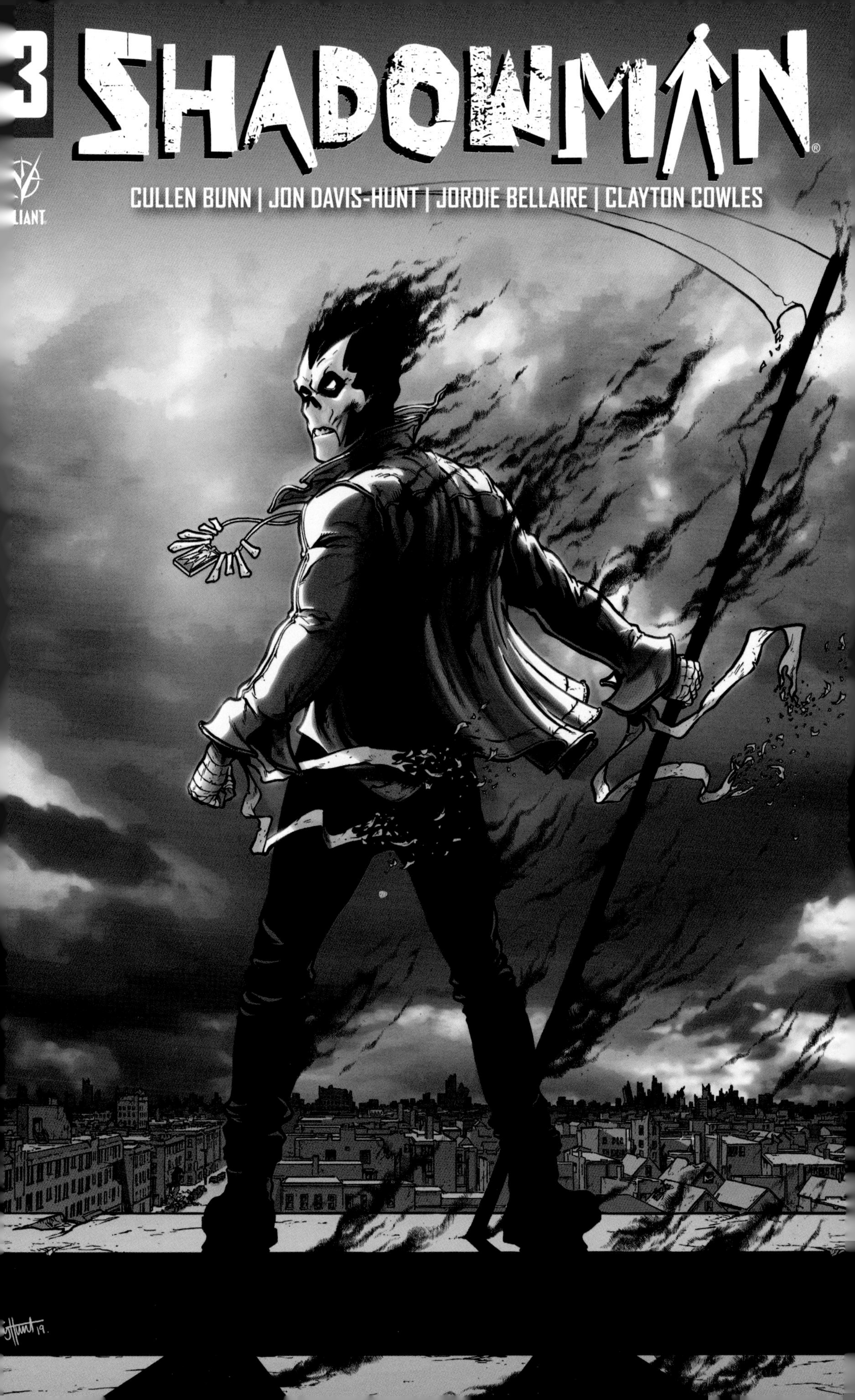
3
SHADOWMAN
CULLEN BUNN | JON DAVIS-HUNT | JORDIE BELLAIRE | CLAYTON COWLES

SHADOWMAN #3

WRITER: Cullen Bunn
ARTIST: Jon Davis-Hunt
COLORIST: Jordie Bellaire
LETTERER: Clayton Cowles
COVER ARTIST: Jon Davis-Hunt
EDITORIAL ASSISTANT: Audrey Meeker
ASSOCIATE EDITOR: David Menchel
SENIOR EDITOR: Heather Antos

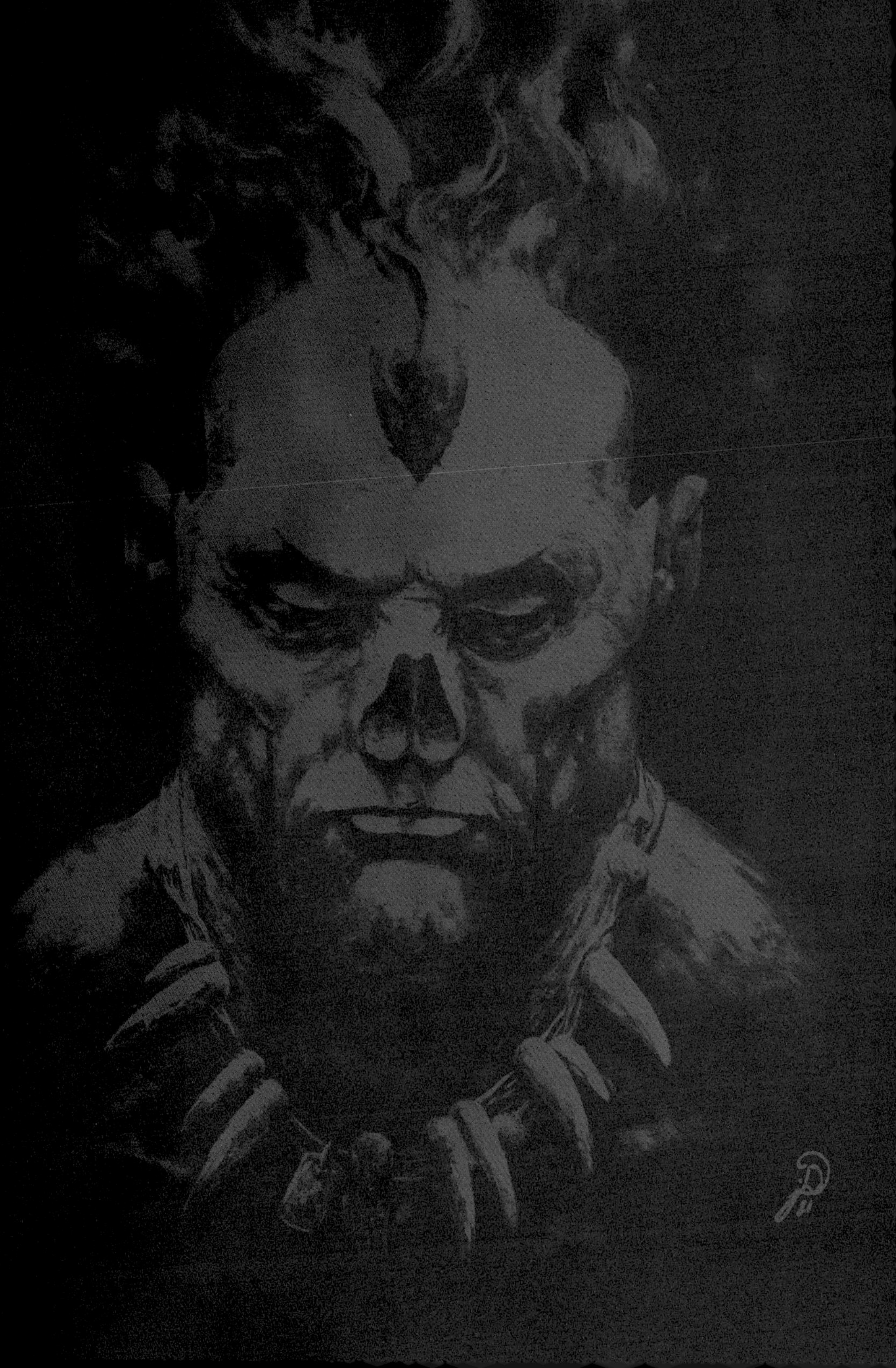

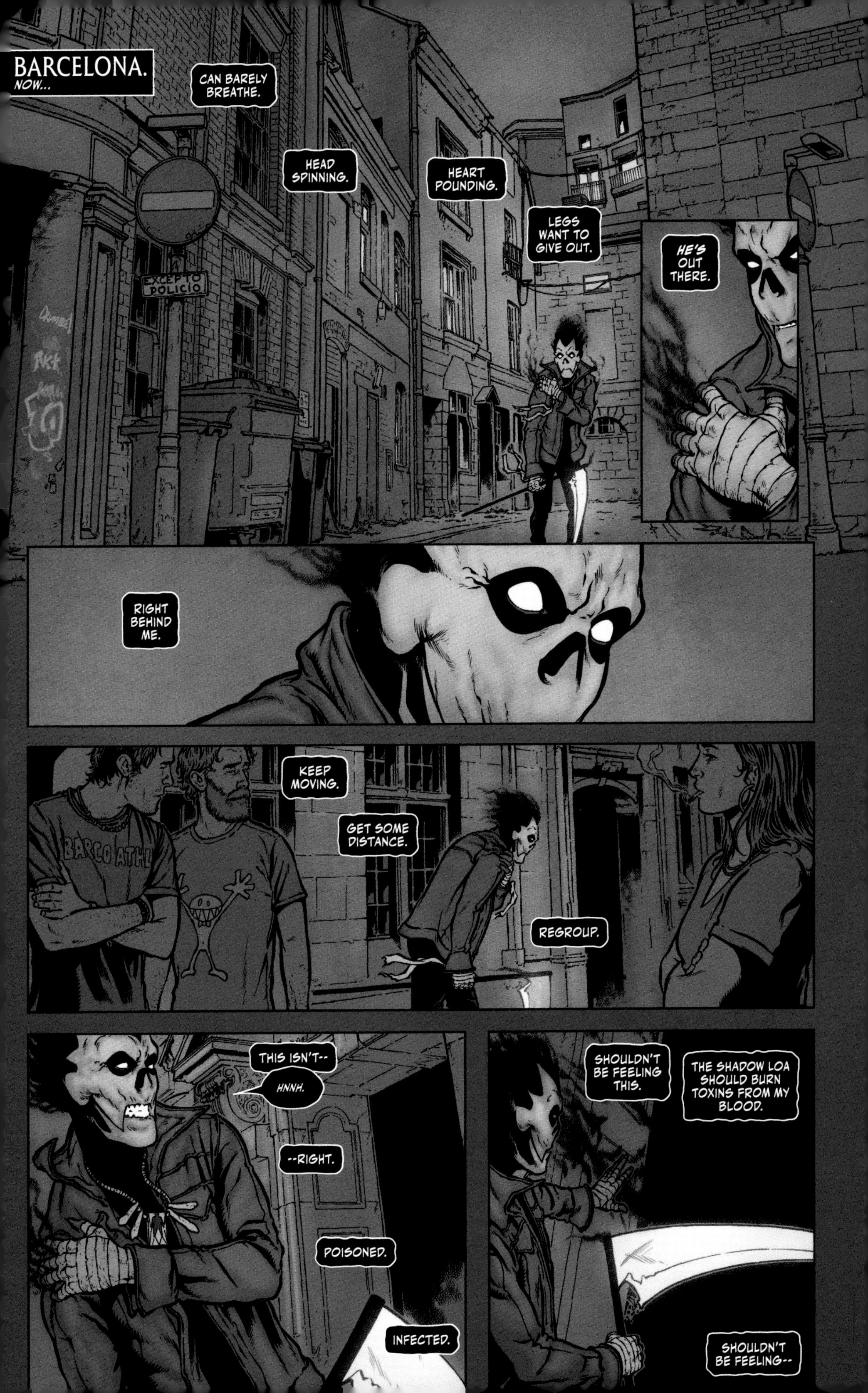
BARCELONA.
NOW...
CAN BARELY BREATHE.
HEAD SPINNING.
HEART POUNDING.
LEGS WANT TO GIVE OUT.
EXCEPTO POLICIA
HE'S OUT THERE.
RIGHT BEHIND ME.
KEEP MOVING.
GET SOME DISTANCE.
REGROUP.
THIS ISN'T--
HNNH.
--RIGHT.
POISONED.
INFECTED.
SHOULDN'T BE FEELING THIS.
THE SHADOW LOA SHOULD BURN TOXINS FROM MY BLOOD.
SHOULDN'T BE FEELING--

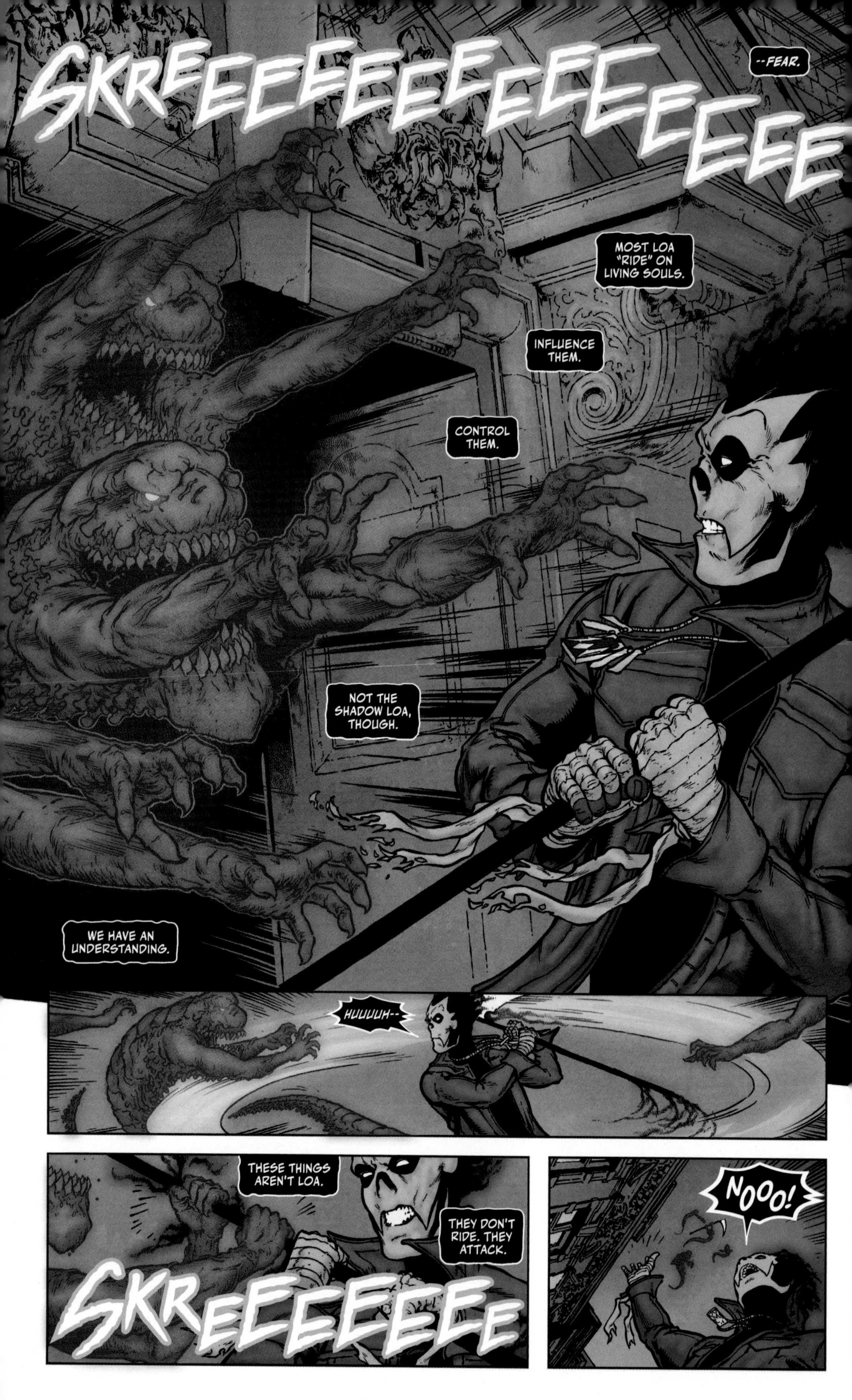
SKREEEEEEEEEEEEEEE
--FEAR.
MOST LOA "RIDE" ON LIVING SOULS.
INFLUENCE THEM.
CONTROL THEM.
NOT THE SHADOW LOA, THOUGH.
WE HAVE AN UNDERSTANDING.
HUUUUH--
THESE THINGS AREN'T LOA.
THEY DON'T RIDE. THEY ATTACK.
SKREEEEEEEE
NOOO!

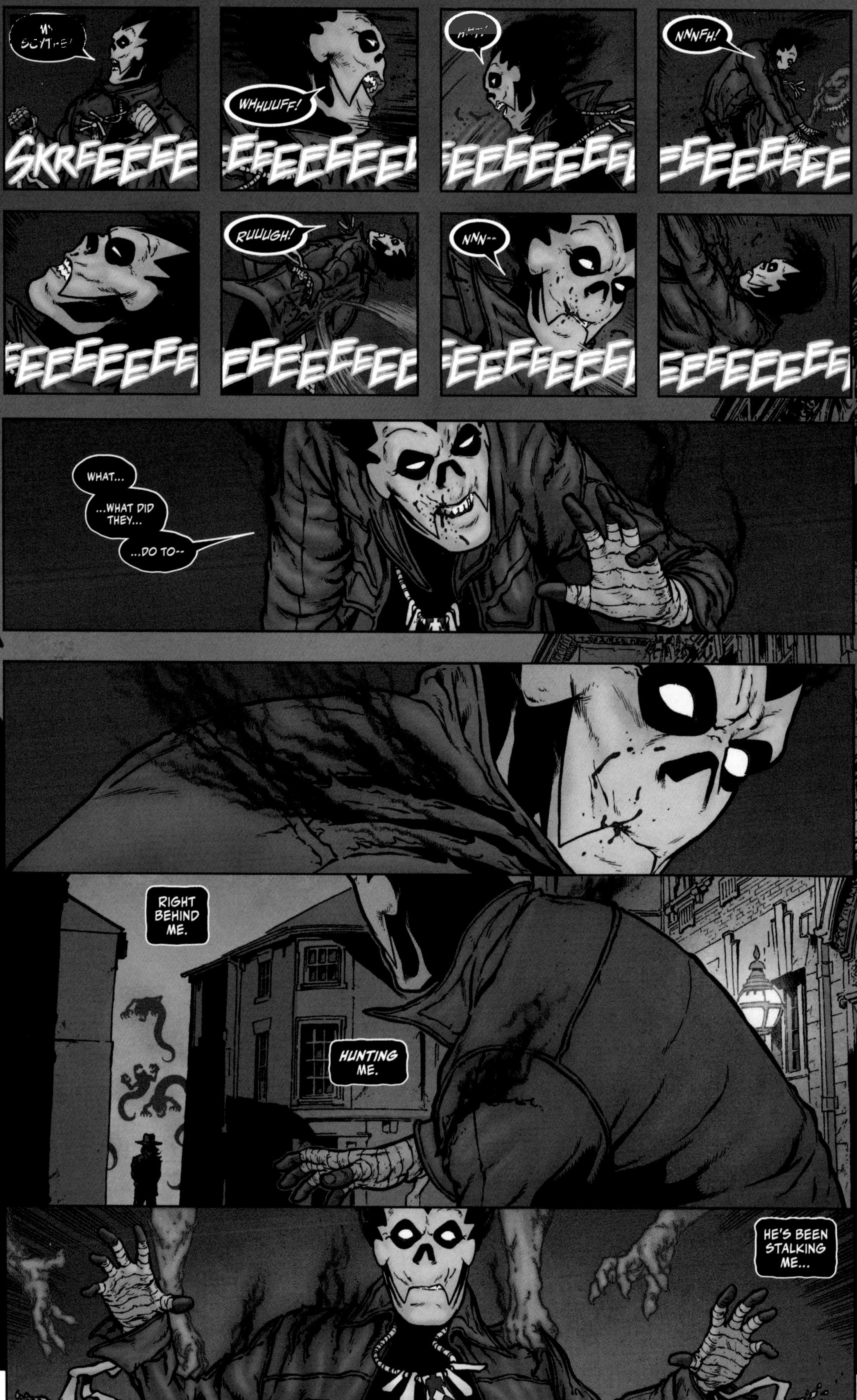
MY SCYTHE!
SKREEEEEEE
WHHUUFF!
EEEEEEEEE
EEEEEEEEE
NNNFH!
EEEEEEEEE
EEEEEEEEE
RUUUGH!
EEEEEEEEE
NNN--
EEEEEEEEE
EEEEEEEEE
WHAT...
...WHAT DID THEY...
...DO TO--
RIGHT BEHIND ME.
HUNTING ME.
HE'S BEEN STALKING ME...

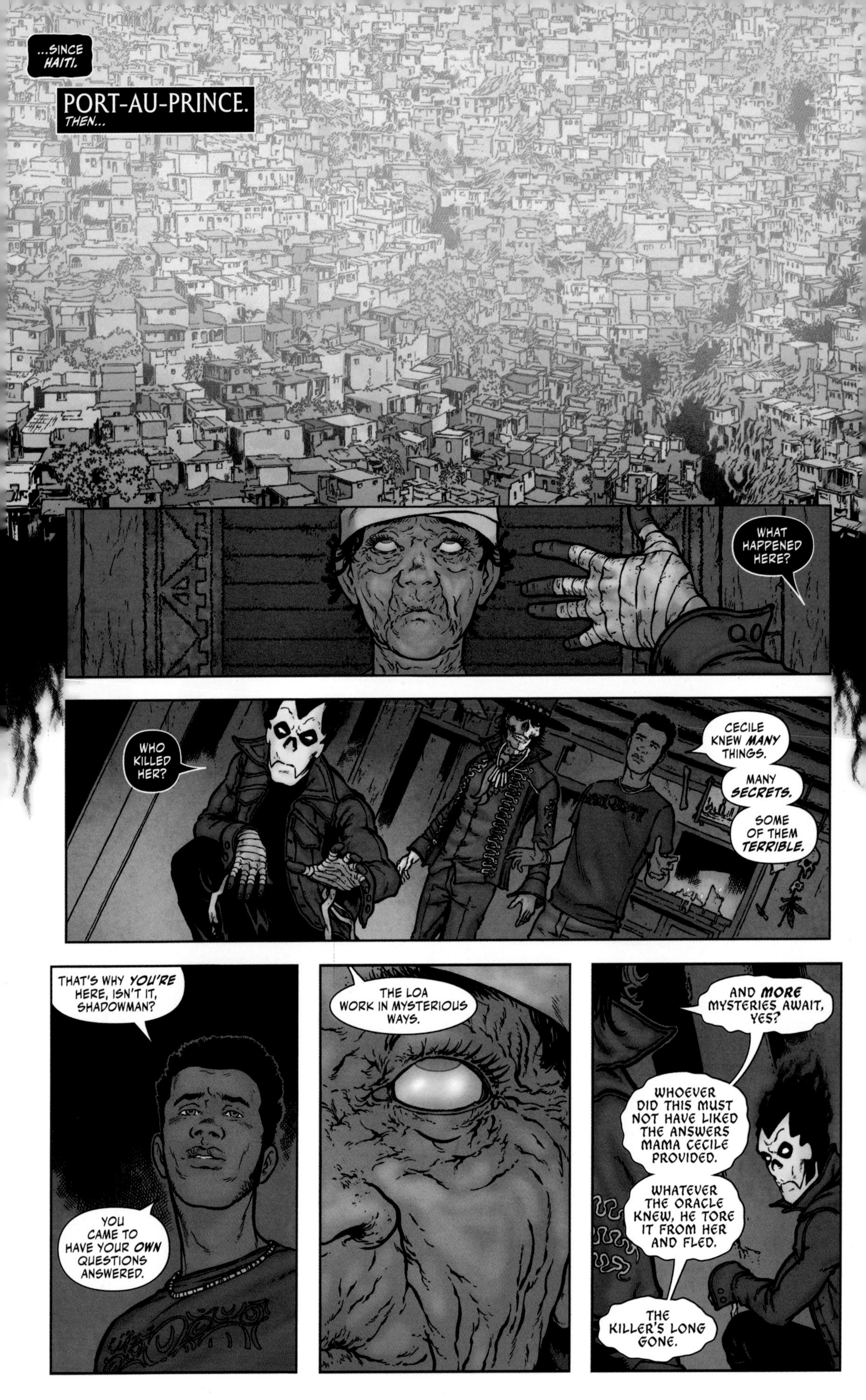
...SINCE HAITI.
PORT-AU-PRINCE.
THEN...
WHAT HAPPENED HERE?
WHO KILLED HER?
CECILE KNEW MANY THINGS.
MANY SECRETS.
SOME OF THEM TERRIBLE.
THAT'S WHY YOU'RE HERE, ISN'T IT, SHADOWMAN?
YOU CAME TO HAVE YOUR OWN QUESTIONS ANSWERED.
THE LOA WORK IN MYSTERIOUS WAYS.
AND MORE MYSTERIES AWAIT, YES?
WHOEVER DID THIS MUST NOT HAVE LIKED THE ANSWERS MAMA CECILE PROVIDED.
WHATEVER THE ORACLE KNEW, HE TORE IT FROM HER AND FLED.
THE KILLER'S LONG GONE.

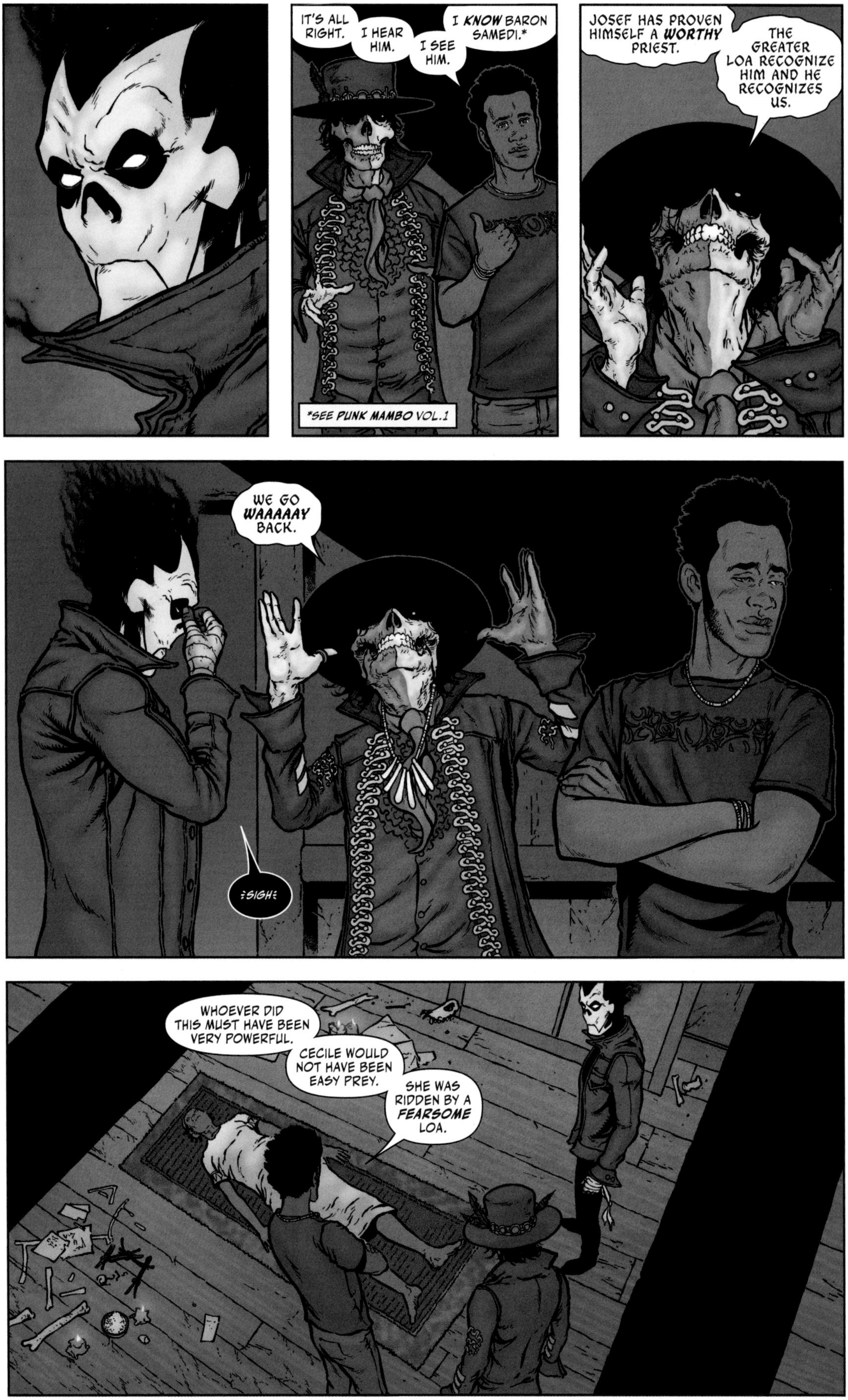
IT'S ALL RIGHT.
I HEAR HIM.
I SEE HIM.
I KNOW BARON SAMEDI.*
*SEE PUNK MAMBO VOL.1
JOSEF HAS PROVEN HIMSELF A WORTHY PRIEST.
THE GREATER LOA RECOGNIZE HIM AND HE RECOGNIZES US.
WE GO WAAAAAY BACK.
:SIGH:
WHOEVER DID THIS MUST HAVE BEEN VERY POWERFUL.
CECILE WOULD NOT HAVE BEEN EASY PREY.
SHE WAS RIDDEN BY A FEARSOME LOA.

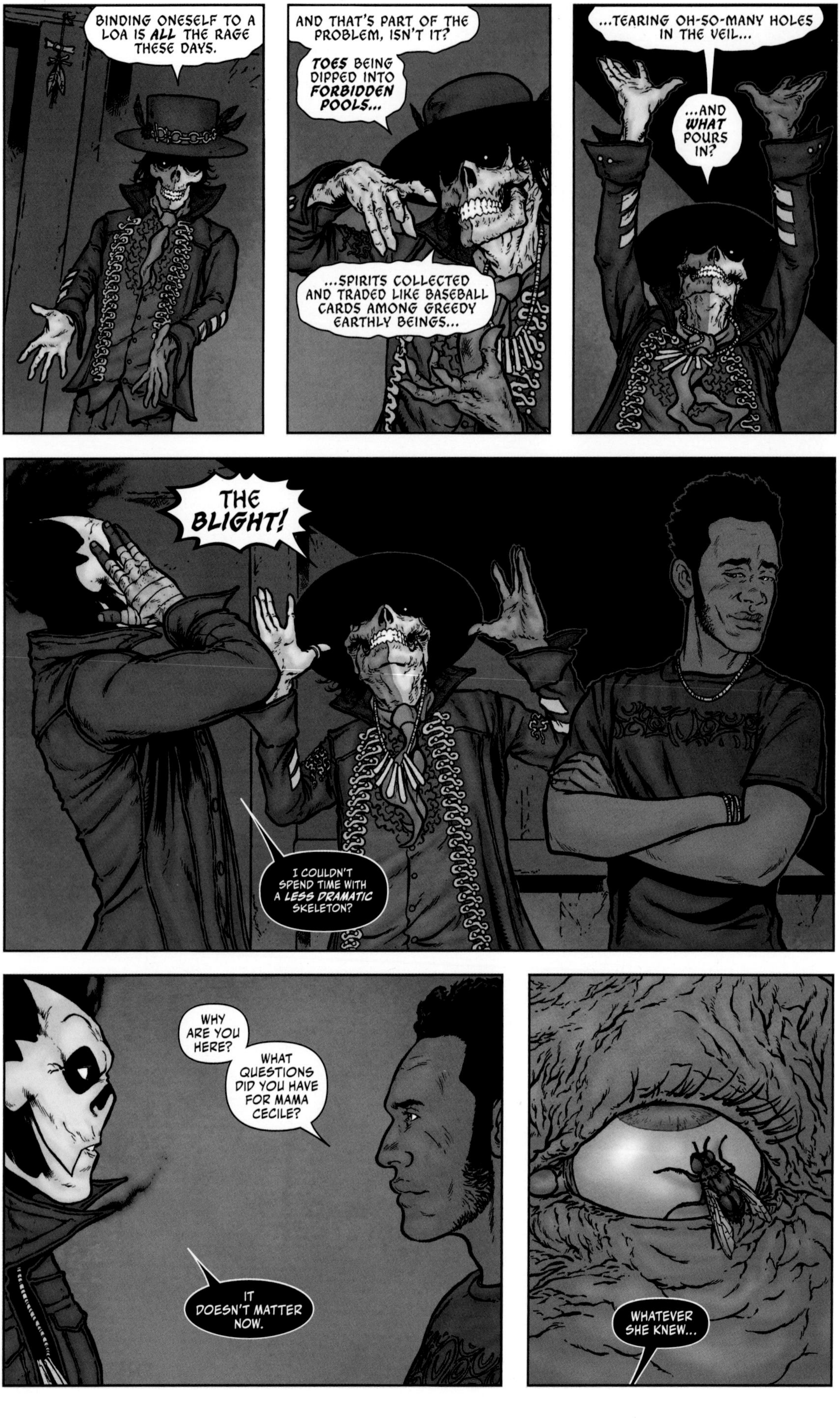
BINDING ONESELF TO A LOA IS ALL THE RAGE THESE DAYS.
AND THAT'S PART OF THE PROBLEM, ISN'T IT?
TOES BEING DIPPED INTO FORBIDDEN POOLS...
...SPIRITS COLLECTED AND TRADED LIKE BASEBALL CARDS AMONG GREEDY EARTHLY BEINGS...
...TEARING OH-SO-MANY HOLES IN THE VEIL...
...AND WHAT POURS IN?
THE BLIGHT!
I COULDN'T SPEND TIME WITH A LESS DRAMATIC SKELETON?
WHY ARE YOU HERE?
WHAT QUESTIONS DID YOU HAVE FOR MAMA CECILE?
IT DOESN'T MATTER NOW.
WHATEVER SHE KNEW...

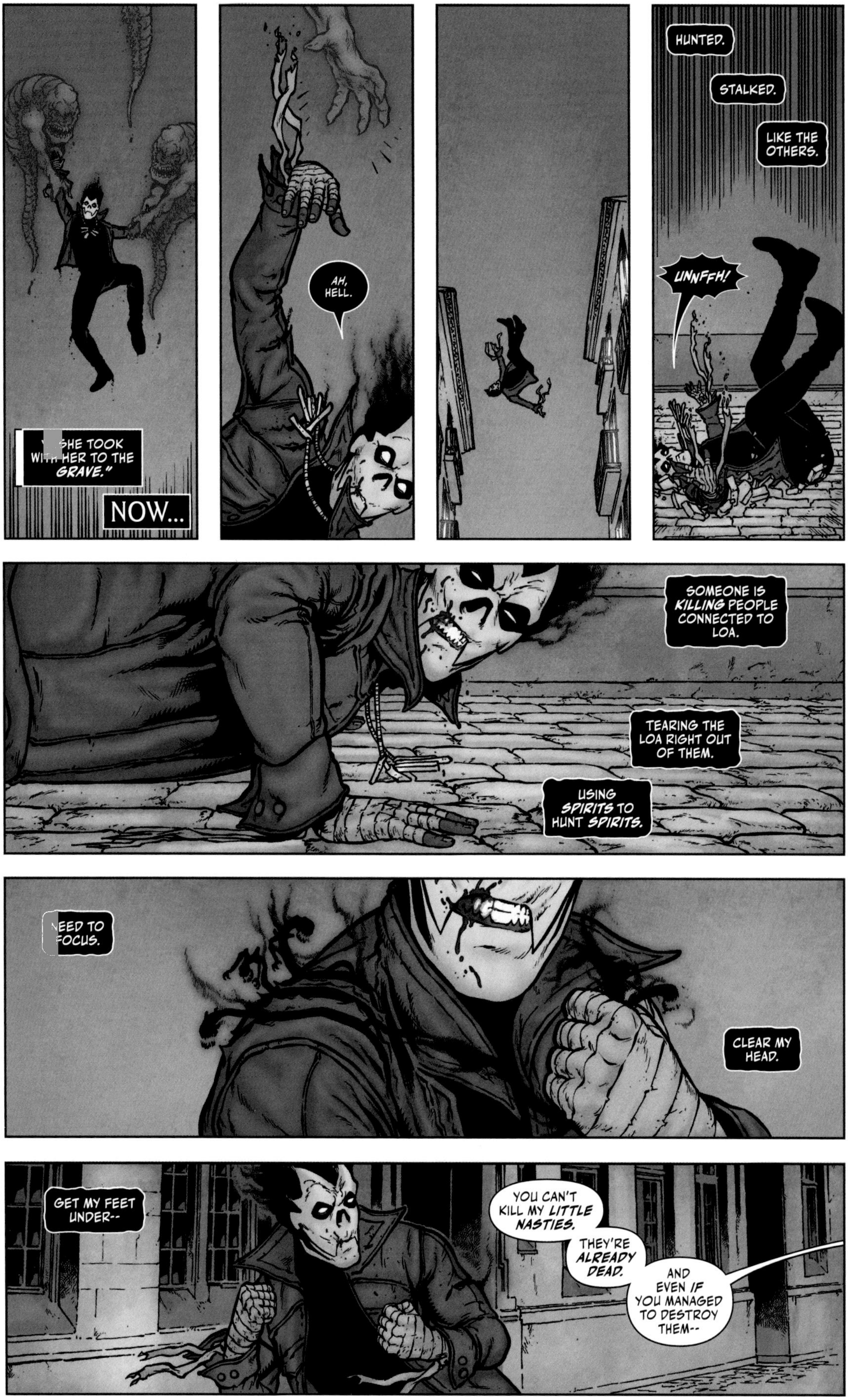
SHE TOOK WITH HER TO THE GRAVE."
NOW...
AH, HELL.
HUNTED.
STALKED.
LIKE THE OTHERS.
UNNFFH!
SOMEONE IS KILLING PEOPLE CONNECTED TO LOA.
TEARING THE LOA RIGHT OUT OF THEM.
USING SPIRITS TO HUNT SPIRITS.
NEED TO FOCUS.
CLEAR MY HEAD.
GET MY FEET UNDER--
YOU CAN'T KILL MY LITTLE NASTIES.
THEY'RE ALREADY DEAD.
AND EVEN IF YOU MANAGED TO DESTROY THEM--

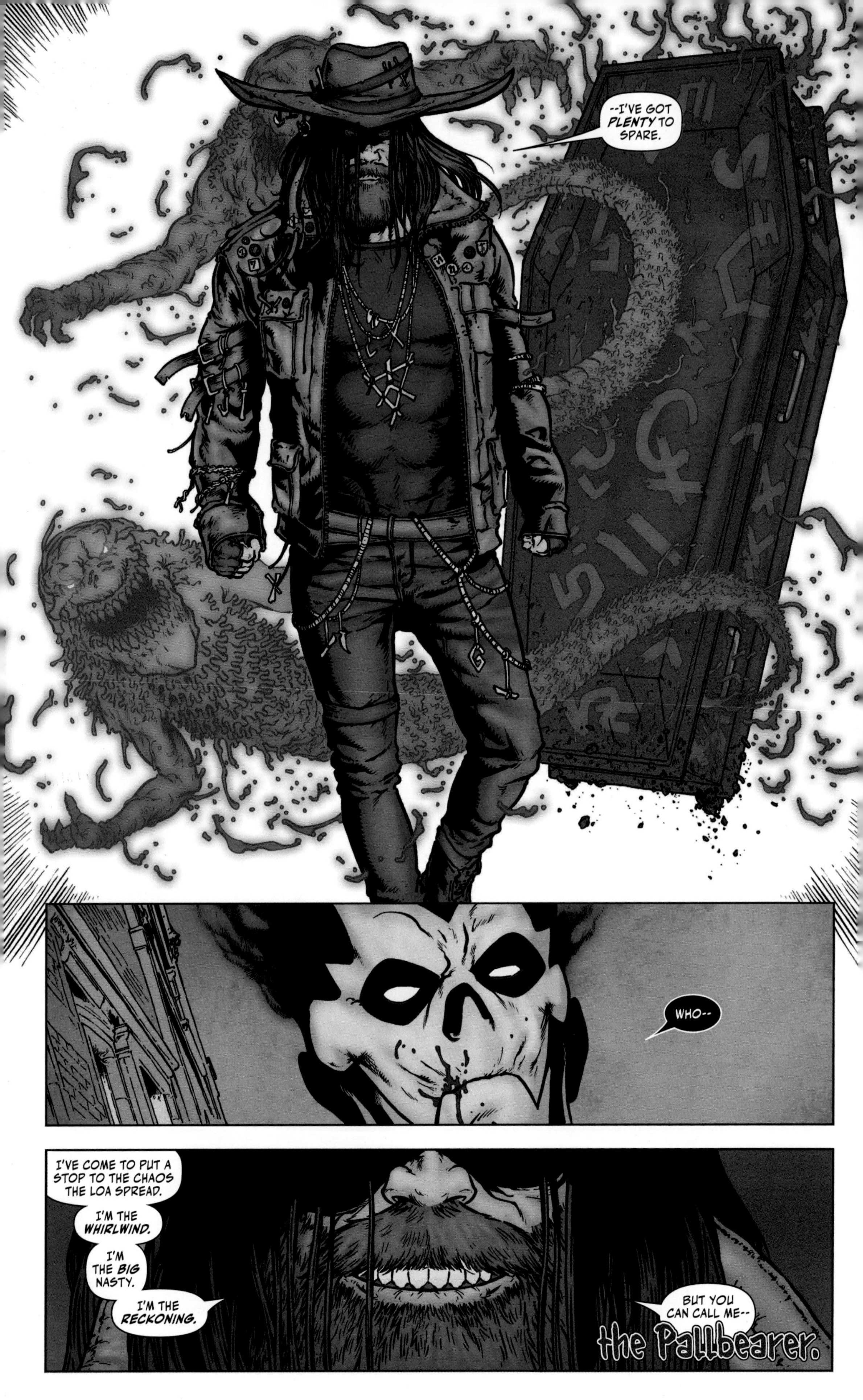
--I'VE GOT PLENTY TO SPARE.
WHO--
I'VE COME TO PUT A STOP TO THE CHAOS THE LOA SPREAD.
I'M THE WHIRLWIND.
I'M THE BIG NASTY.
I'M THE RECKONING.
BUT YOU CAN CALL ME--
the Pallbearer.

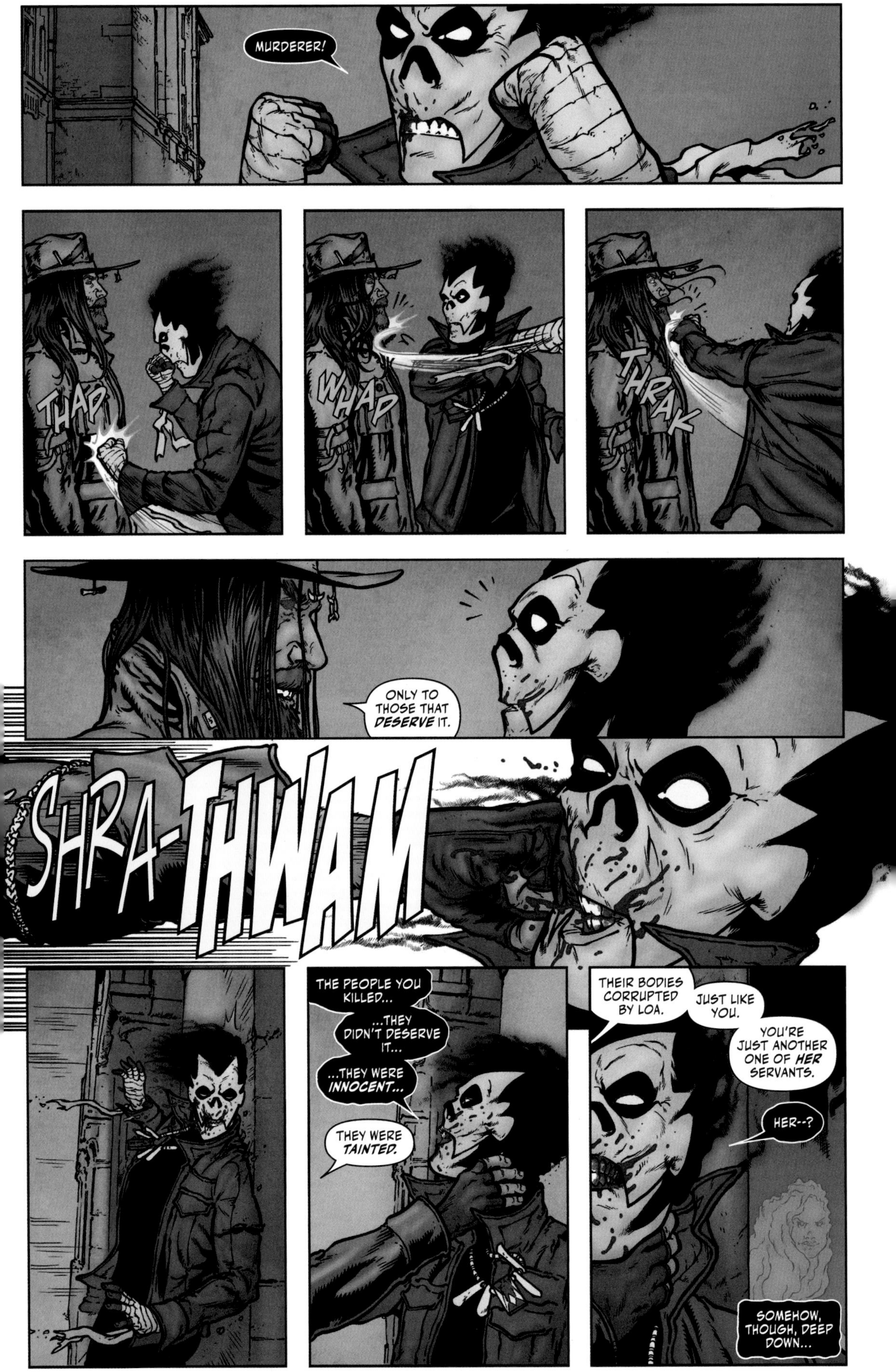

MURDERER!
THAP
WHAP
THRAK
ONLY TO THOSE THAT *DESERVE* IT.
SHRA-THWAM
THE PEOPLE YOU KILLED...
...THEY DIDN'T DESERVE IT...
...THEY WERE *INNOCENT...*
THEY WERE *TAINTED.*
THEIR BODIES CORRUPTED BY LOA.
JUST LIKE YOU.
YOU'RE JUST ANOTHER ONE OF *HER* SERVANTS.
HER--?
SOMEHOW, THOUGH, DEEP DOWN...

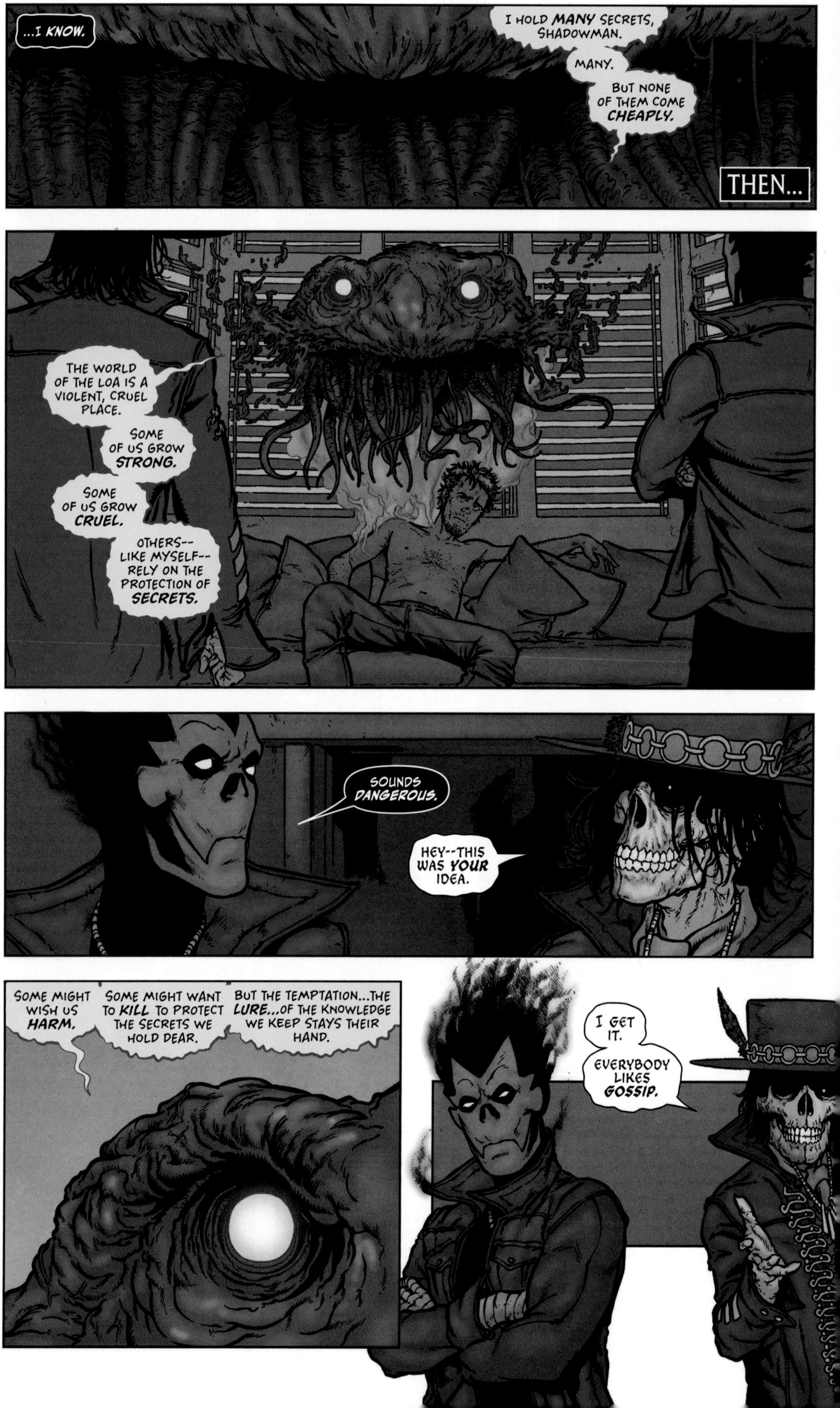

...I KNOW.
I HOLD MANY SECRETS, SHADOWMAN.
MANY.
BUT NONE OF THEM COME CHEAPLY.
THEN...
THE WORLD OF THE LOA IS A VIOLENT, CRUEL PLACE.
SOME OF US GROW STRONG.
SOME OF US GROW CRUEL.
OTHERS--LIKE MYSELF--RELY ON THE PROTECTION OF SECRETS.
SOUNDS DANGEROUS.
HEY--THIS WAS YOUR IDEA.
SOME MIGHT WISH US HARM.
SOME MIGHT WANT TO KILL TO PROTECT THE SECRETS WE HOLD DEAR.
BUT THE TEMPTATION...THE LURE...OF THE KNOWLEDGE WE KEEP STAYS THEIR HAND.
I GET IT.
EVERYBODY LIKES GOSSIP.

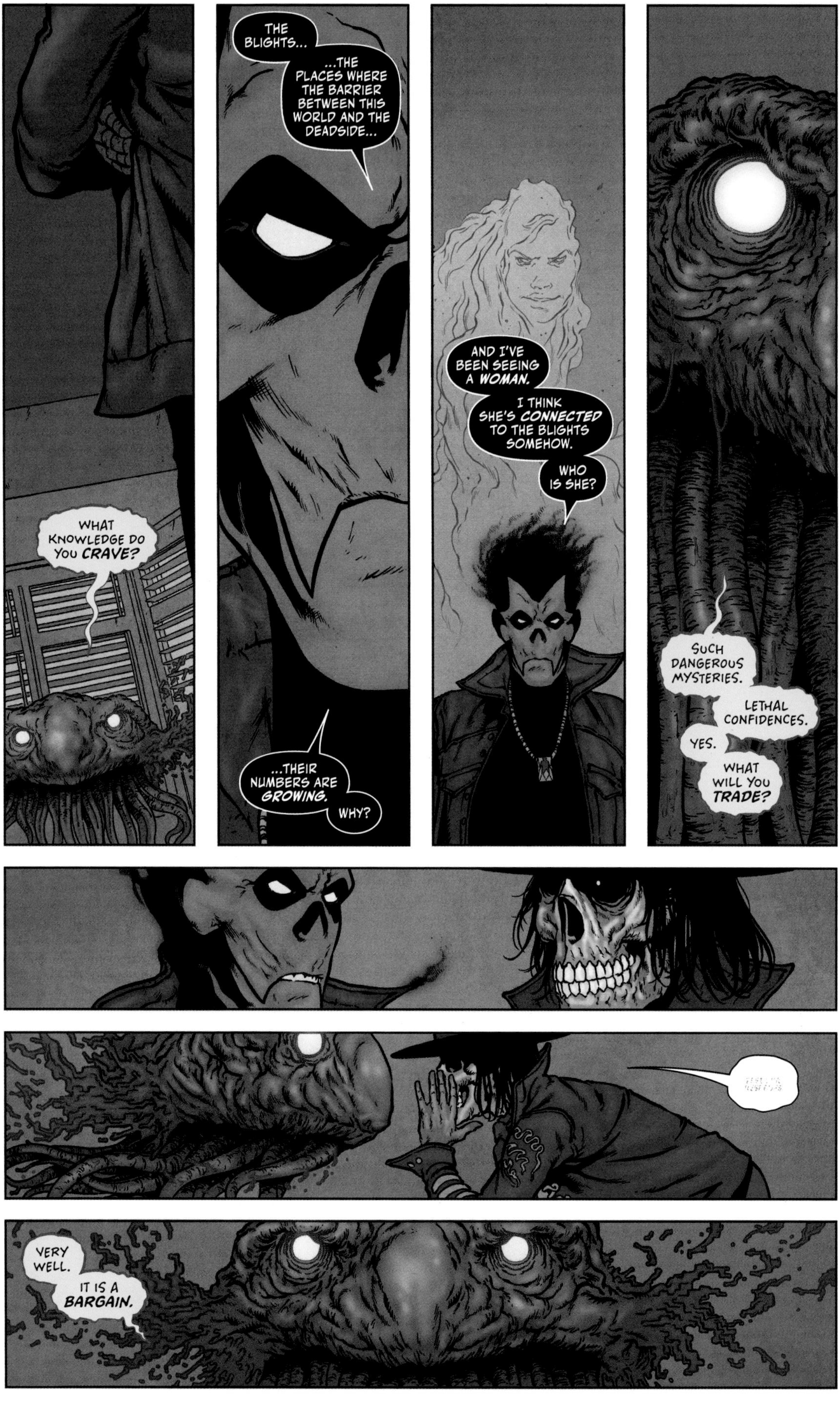
WHAT KNOWLEDGE DO YOU CRAVE?
THE BLIGHTS...
...THE PLACES WHERE THE BARRIER BETWEEN THIS WORLD AND THE DEADSIDE...
...THEIR NUMBERS ARE GROWING.
WHY?
AND I'VE BEEN SEEING A WOMAN.
I THINK SHE'S CONNECTED TO THE BLIGHTS SOMEHOW.
WHO IS SHE?
SUCH DANGEROUS MYSTERIES.
LETHAL CONFIDENCES.
YES.
WHAT WILL YOU TRADE?
VERY WELL.
IT IS A BARGAIN.

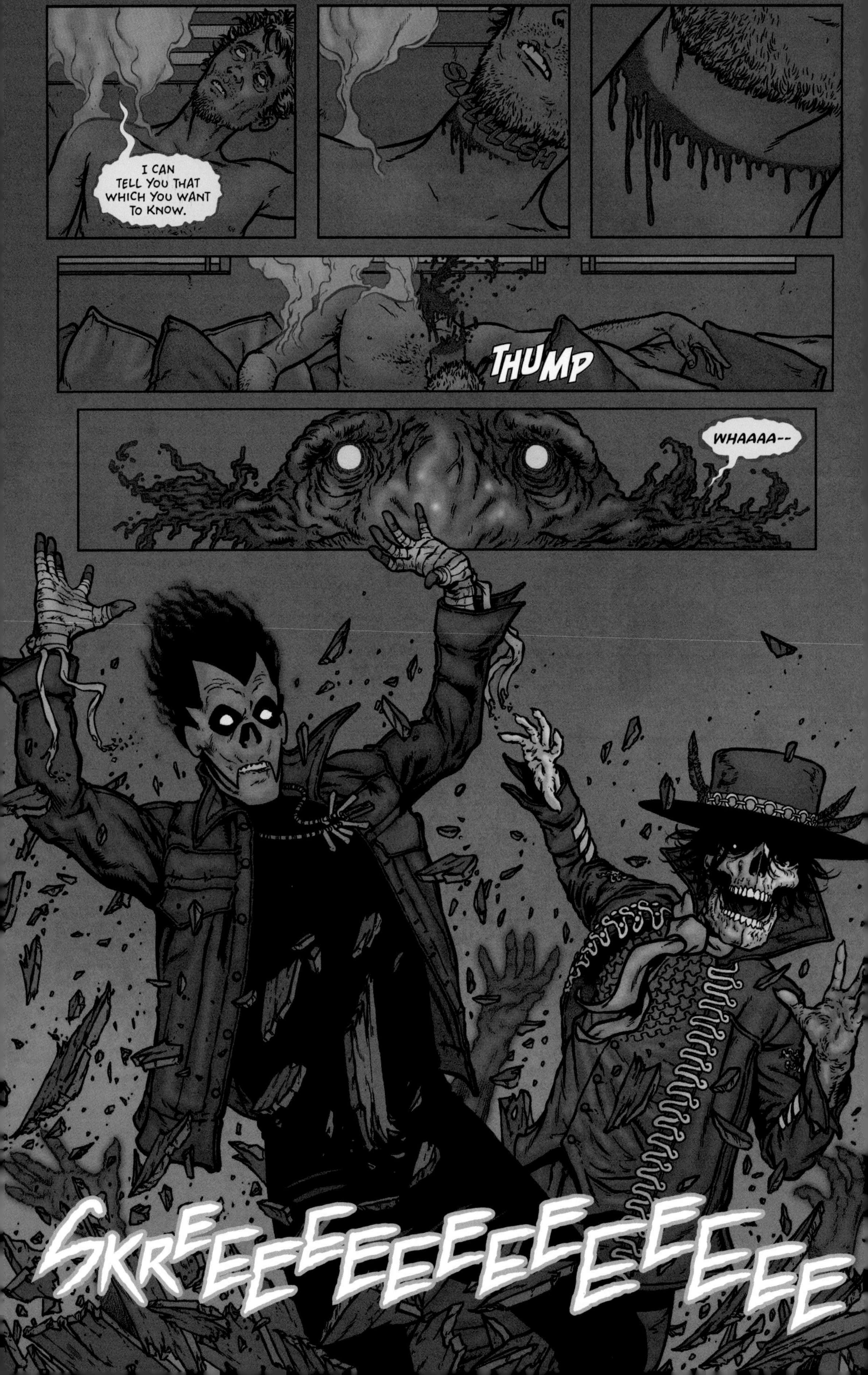
I CAN TELL YOU THAT WHICH YOU WANT TO KNOW.
SCHLLLLSH
THUMP
WHAAAA--
SKREEEEEEEEEEEEEEEEEE

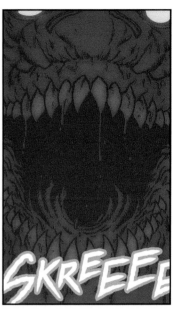

NO!
NO, PLEASE!

I CAN TRADE SECRETS!

SECRETS FOR MY LIFE!

SKREEEE

THESE SPIRITS...

...THEY'RE OLD...

...SO OLD...

...AND THEY HATE...

...HATE US SO MUCH...

THEY ARE LOA-KILLERS!

NNN--

RUN, JACK!

FLEE THIS PLACE!

RUN!

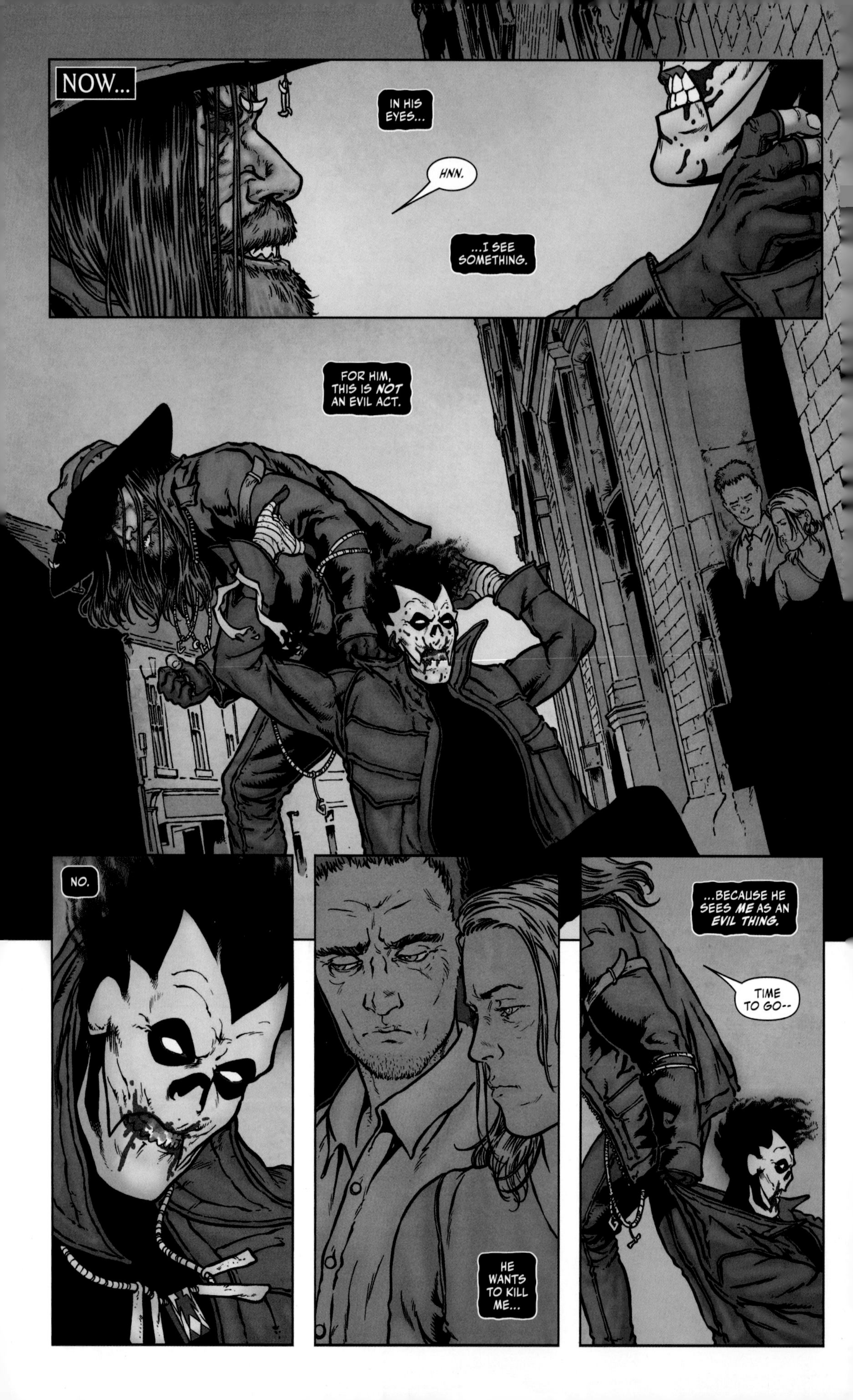
NOW...
IN HIS EYES...
HNN.
...I SEE SOMETHING.
FOR HIM, THIS IS NOT AN EVIL ACT.
NO.
HE WANTS TO KILL ME...
...BECAUSE HE SEES ME AS AN EVIL THING.
TIME TO GO--

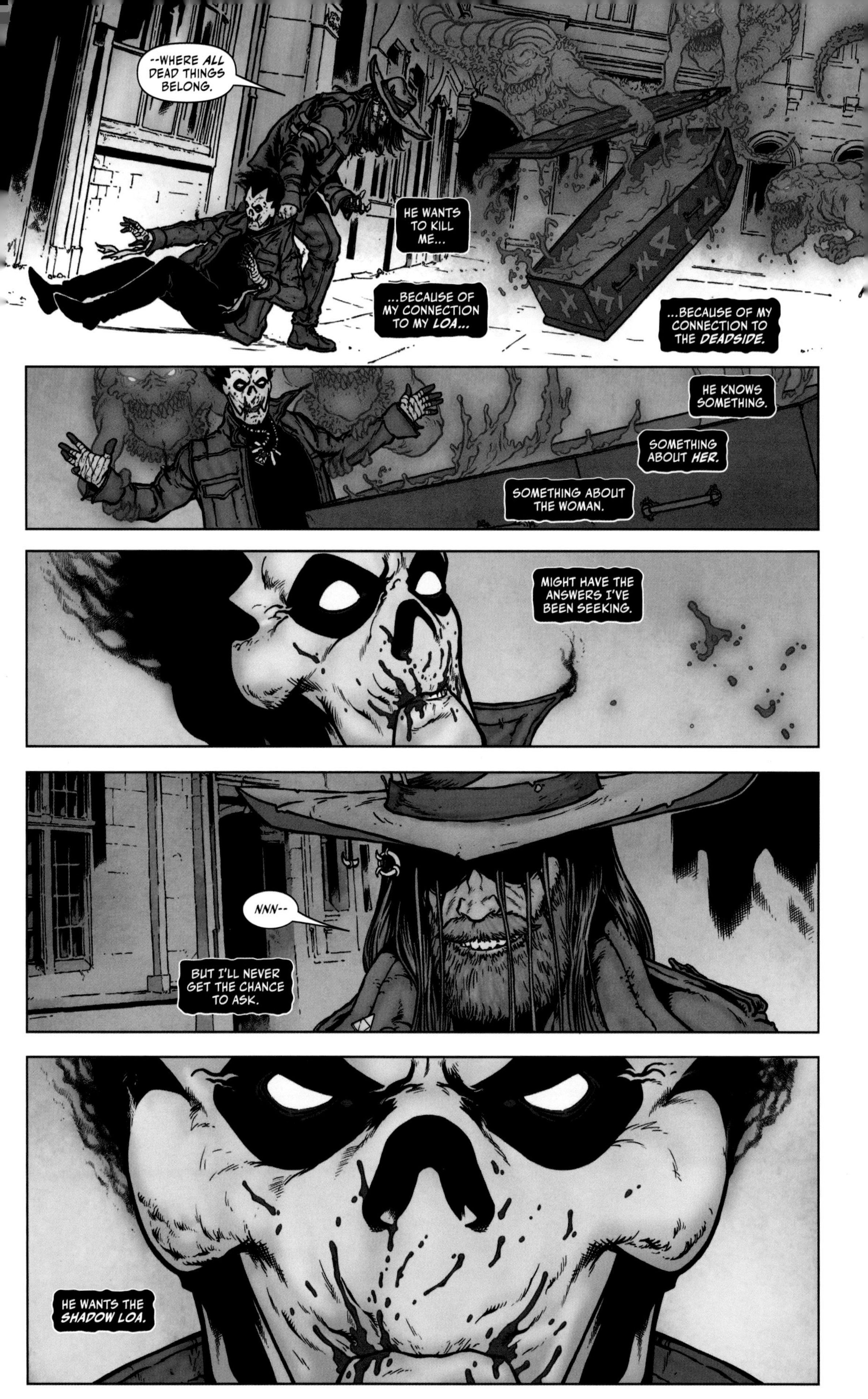
--WHERE ALL DEAD THINGS BELONG.
HE WANTS TO KILL ME...
...BECAUSE OF MY CONNECTION TO MY LOA...
...BECAUSE OF MY CONNECTION TO THE DEADSIDE.
HE KNOWS SOMETHING.
SOMETHING ABOUT HER.
SOMETHING ABOUT THE WOMAN.
MIGHT HAVE THE ANSWERS I'VE BEEN SEEKING.
NNN--
BUT I'LL NEVER GET THE CHANCE TO ASK.
HE WANTS THE SHADOW LOA.

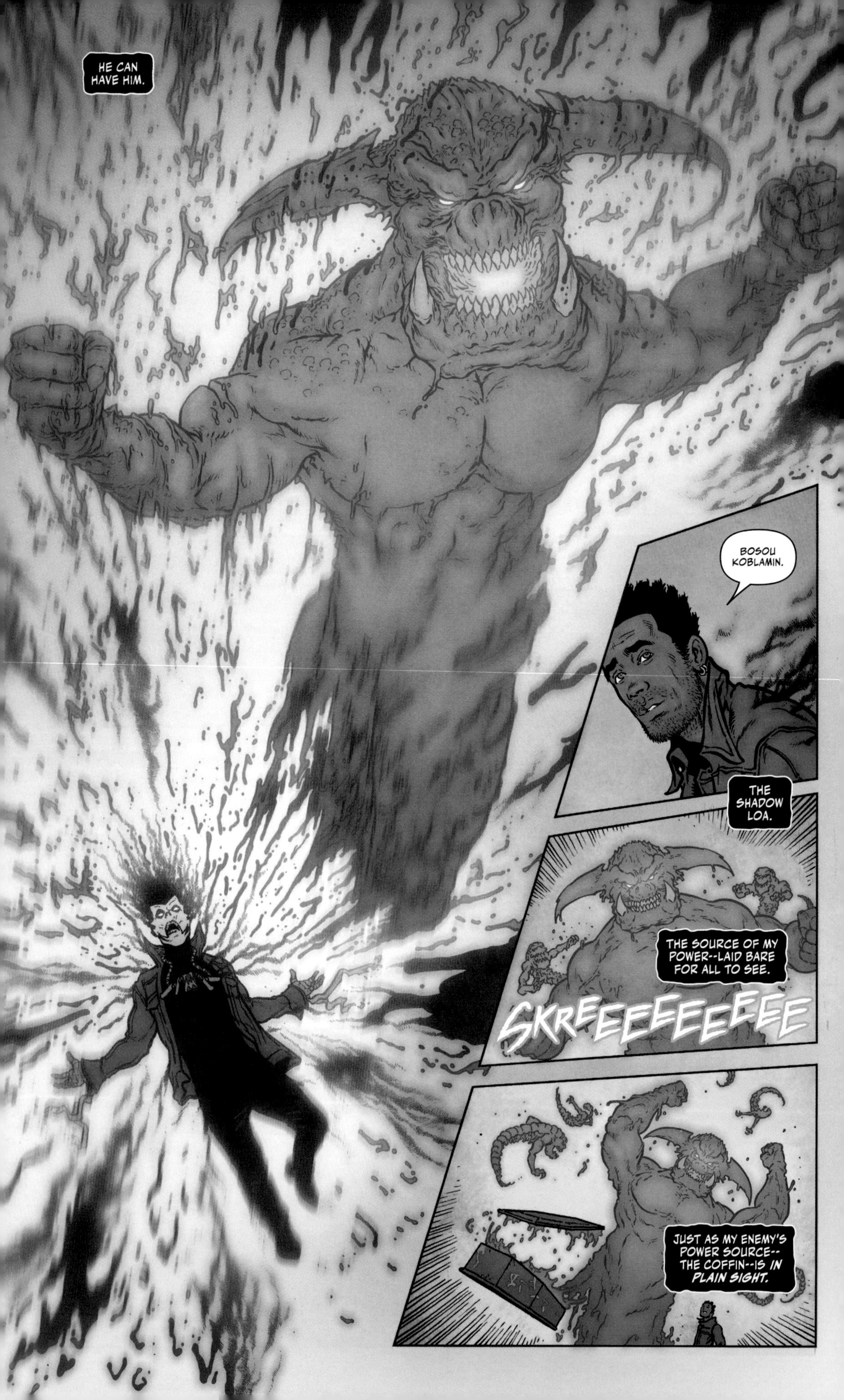
HE CAN HAVE HIM.
BOSOU KOBLAMIN.
THE SHADOW LOA.
THE SOURCE OF MY POWER--LAID BARE FOR ALL TO SEE.
SKREEEEEEEEEE
JUST AS MY ENEMY'S POWER SOURCE-- THE COFFIN--IS *IN PLAIN SIGHT.*

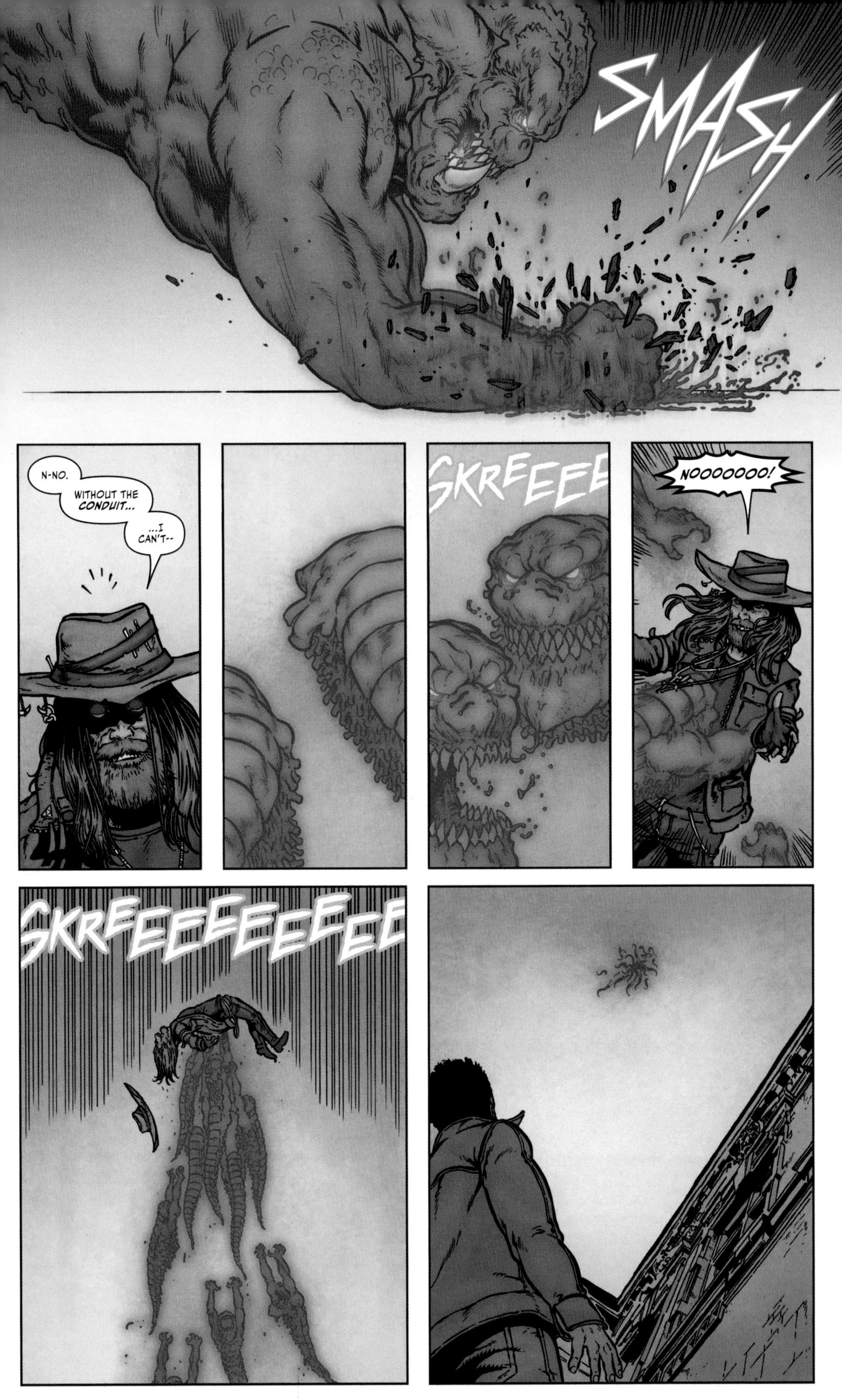
SMASH
N-NO.
WITHOUT THE CONDUIT...
...I CAN'T--
SKREEEE
NOOOOOOO!
SKREEEEEEEEEE

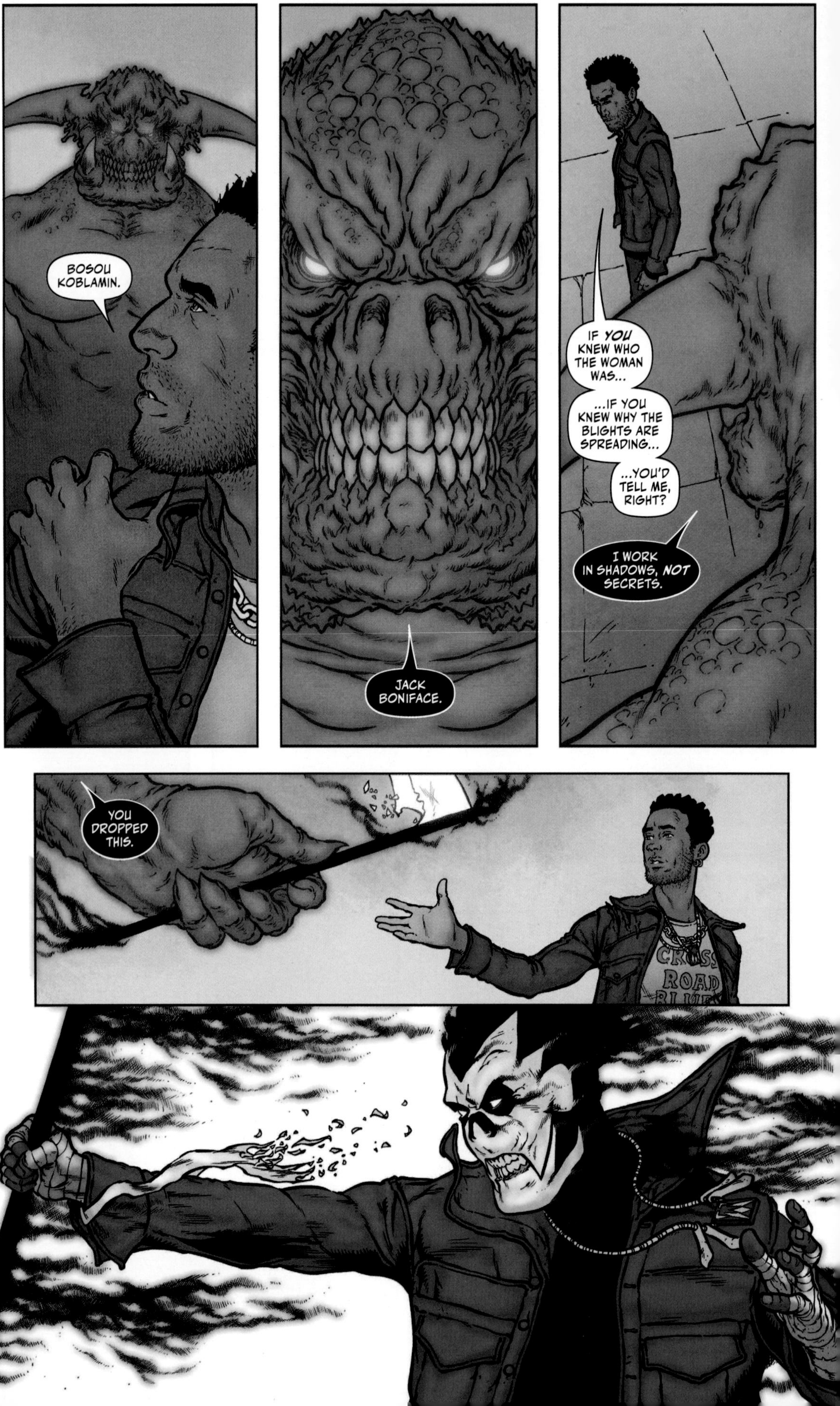
BOSOU KOBLAMIN.
JACK BONIFACE.
IF YOU KNEW WHO THE WOMAN WAS...
...IF YOU KNEW WHY THE BLIGHTS ARE SPREADING...
...YOU'D TELL ME, RIGHT?
I WORK IN SHADOWS, NOT SECRETS.
YOU DROPPED THIS.
CROSS ROAD

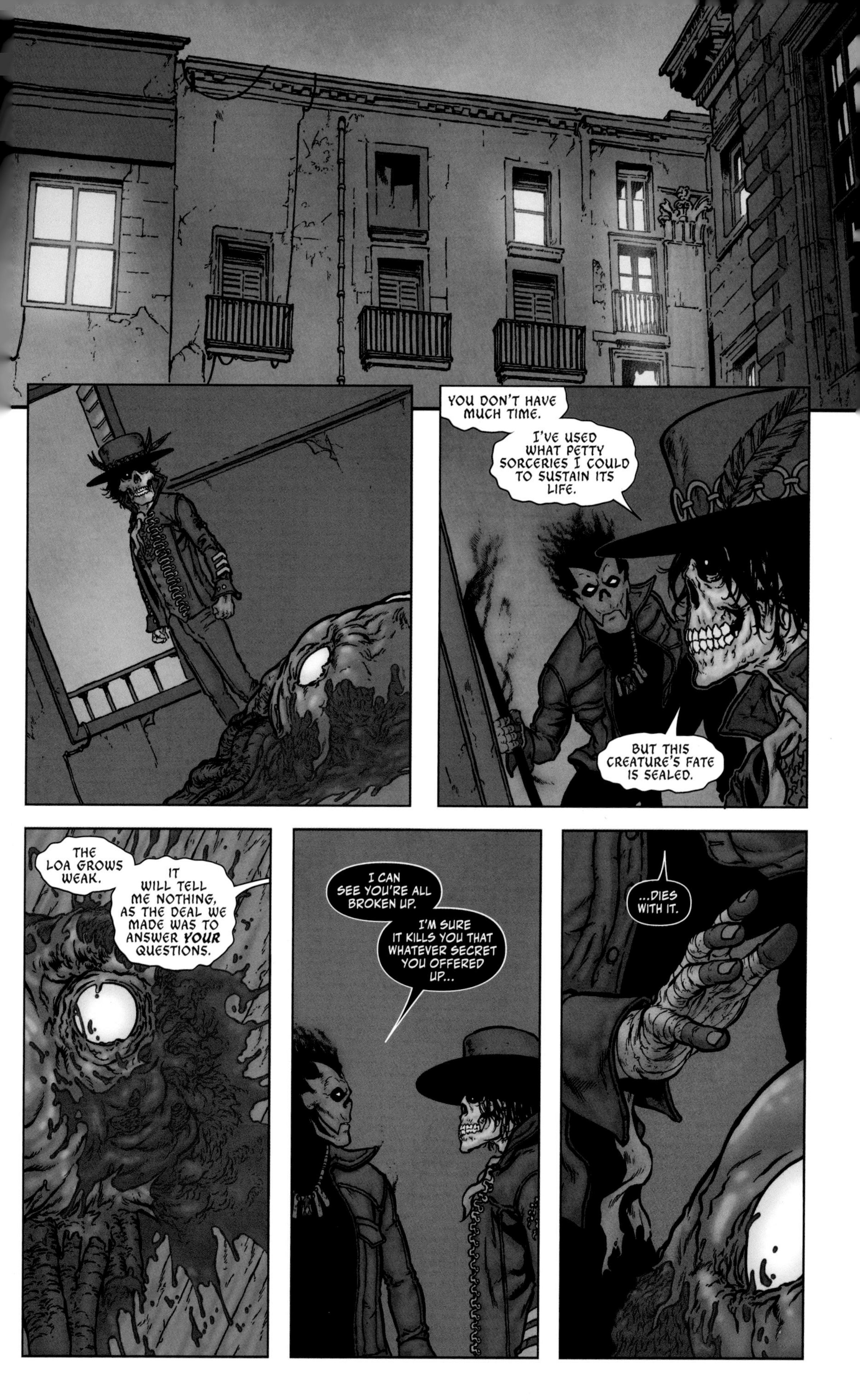
YOU DON'T HAVE MUCH TIME.
I'VE USED WHAT PETTY SORCERIES I COULD TO SUSTAIN ITS LIFE.
BUT THIS CREATURE'S FATE IS SEALED.
THE LOA GROWS WEAK.
IT WILL TELL ME NOTHING, AS THE DEAL WE MADE WAS TO ANSWER ***YOUR*** QUESTIONS.
I CAN SEE YOU'RE ALL BROKEN UP.
I'M SURE IT KILLS YOU THAT WHATEVER SECRET YOU OFFERED UP...
...DIES WITH IT.

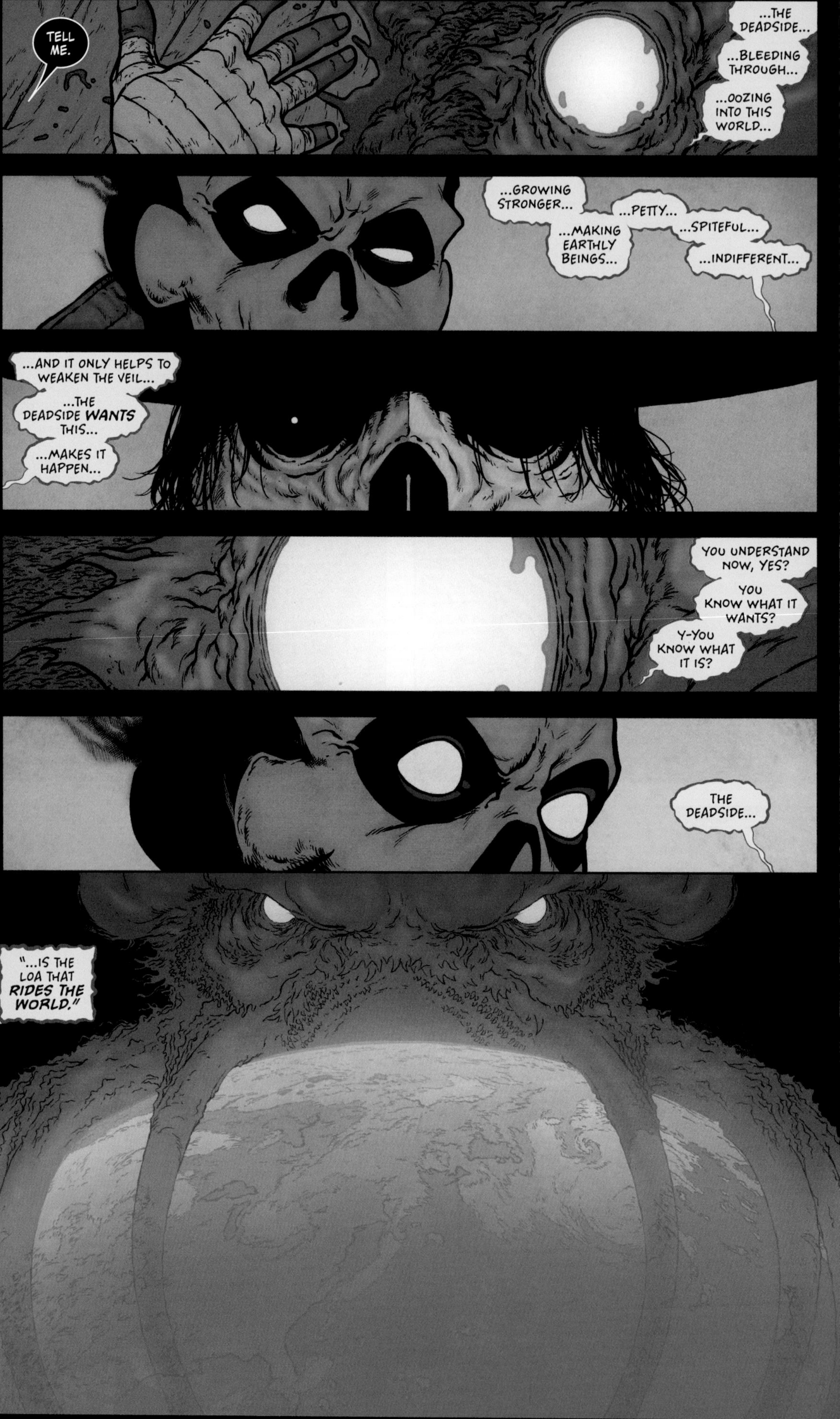

TELL ME.
...THE DEADSIDE...
...BLEEDING THROUGH...
...OOZING INTO THIS WORLD...
...GROWING STRONGER...
...MAKING EARTHLY BEINGS...
...PETTY...
...SPITEFUL...
...INDIFFERENT...
...AND IT ONLY HELPS TO WEAKEN THE VEIL...
...THE DEADSIDE **WANTS** THIS...
...MAKES IT HAPPEN...
YOU UNDERSTAND NOW, YES?
YOU KNOW WHAT IT WANTS?
Y-YOU KNOW WHAT IT IS?
THE DEADSIDE...
"...IS THE LOA THAT ***RIDES THE WORLD.***"

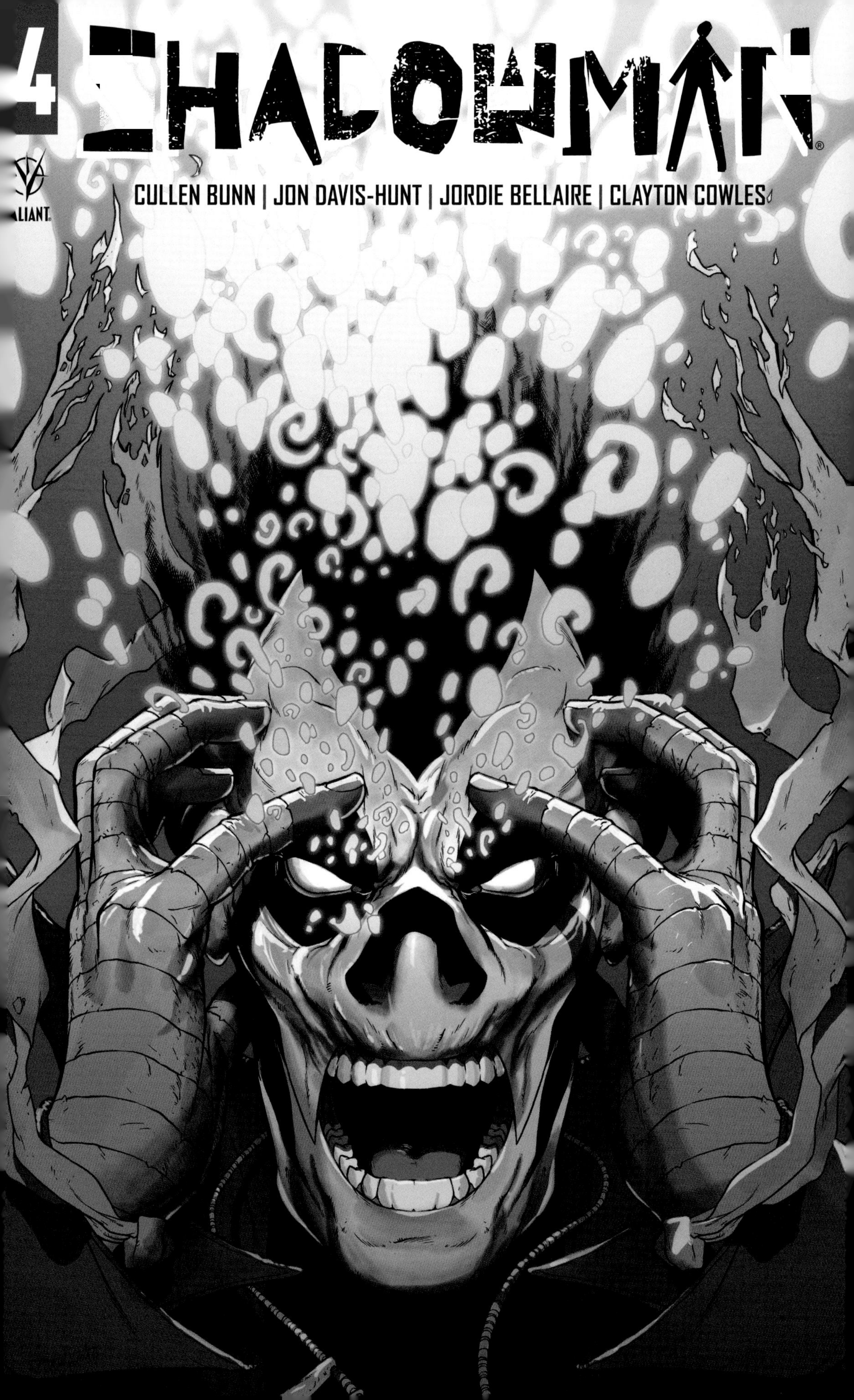
4
SHADOWMAN
VALIANT
CULLEN BUNN | JON DAVIS-HUNT | JORDIE BELLAIRE | CLAYTON COWLES

SHADOWMAN #4

WRITER: Cullen Bunn
ARTIST: Jon Davis-Hunt
COLORIST: Jordie Bellaire
LETTERER: Clayton Cowles
COVER ARTIST: Jon Davis-Hunt
EDITORIAL ASSISTANT: Audrey Meeker
ASSOCIATE EDITOR: David Menchel
SENIOR EDITORS: Heather Antos and Lysa Hawkins

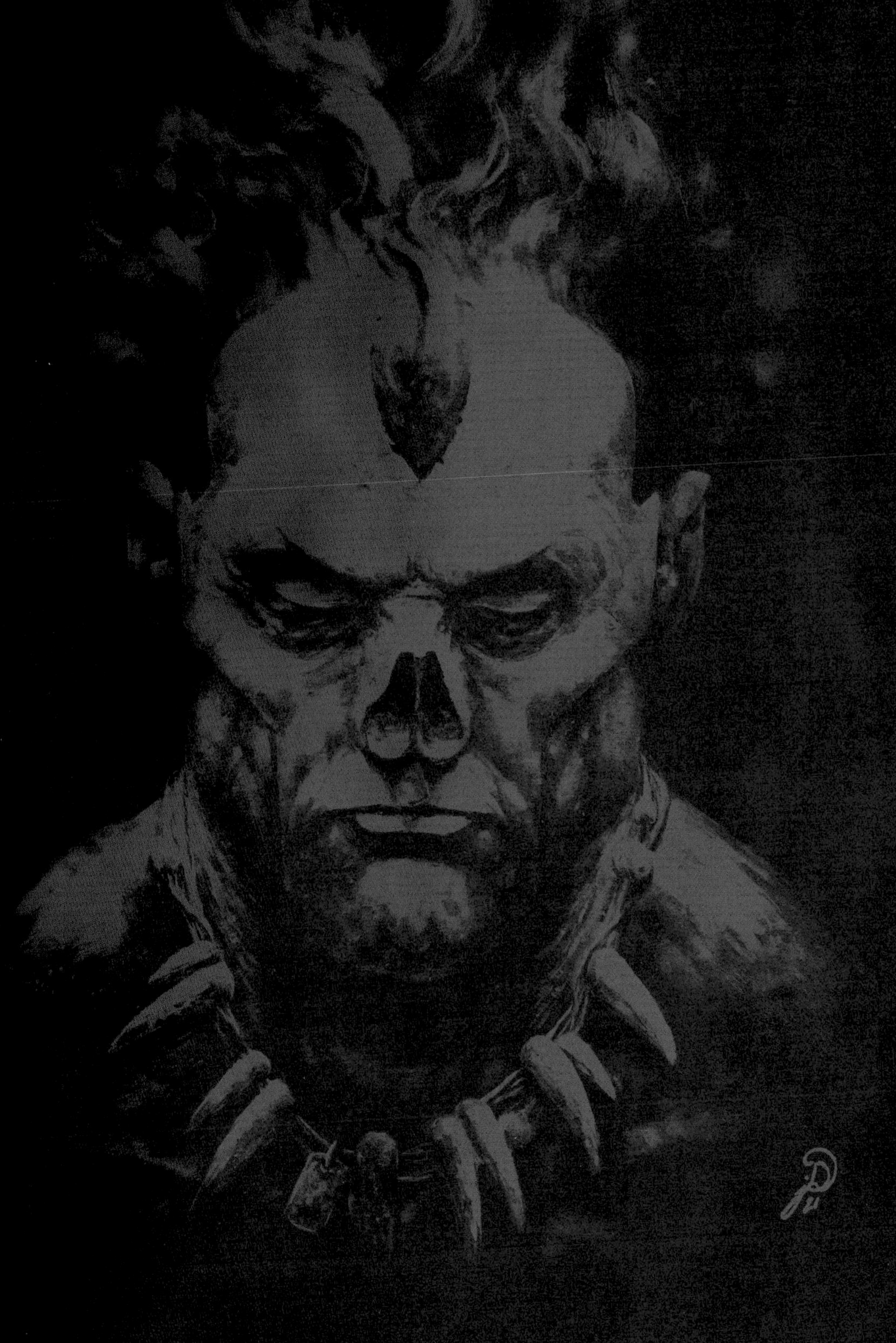

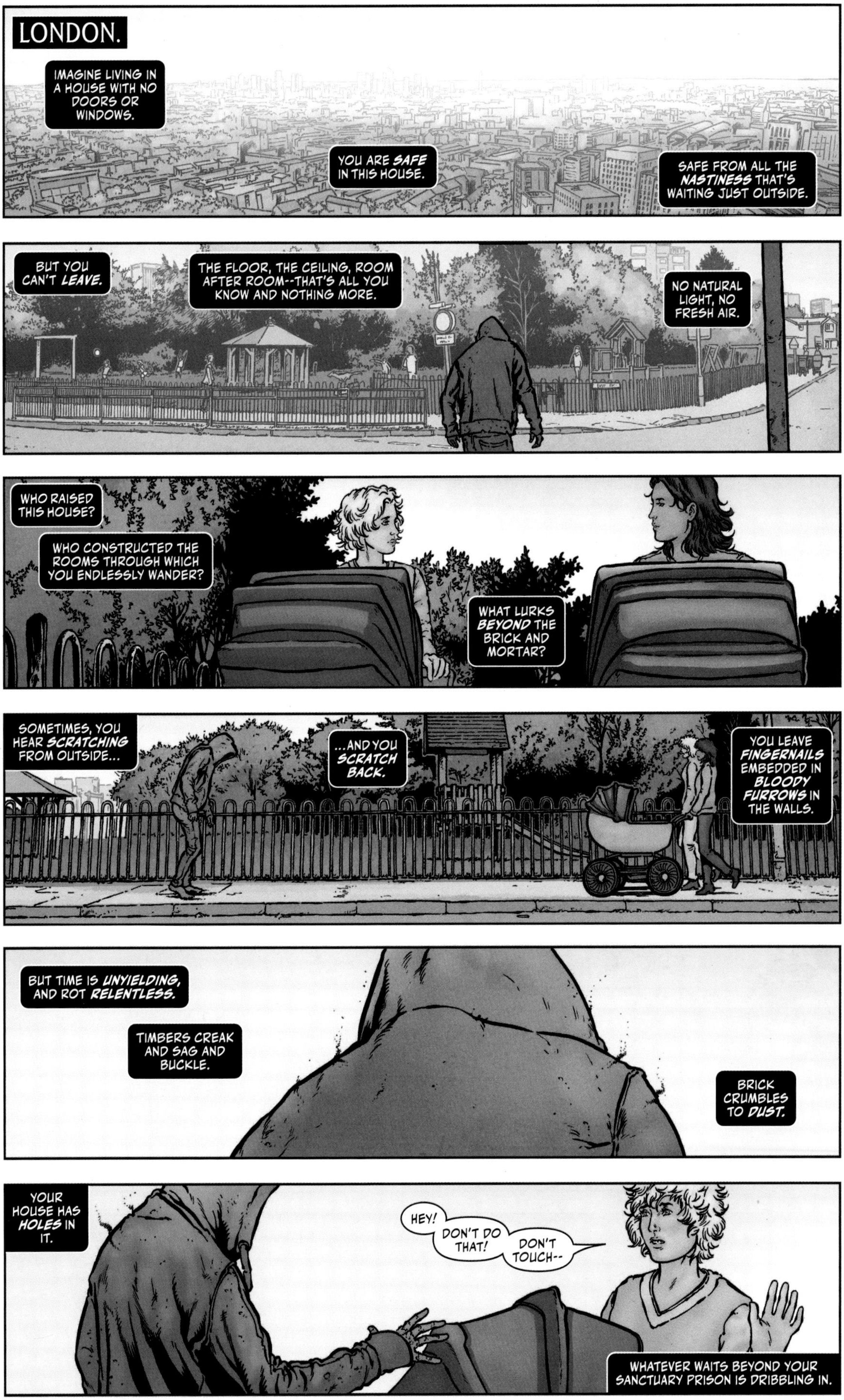

LONDON.
IMAGINE LIVING IN A HOUSE WITH NO DOORS OR WINDOWS.
YOU ARE SAFE IN THIS HOUSE.
SAFE FROM ALL THE NASTINESS THAT'S WAITING JUST OUTSIDE.
BUT YOU CAN'T LEAVE.
THE FLOOR, THE CEILING, ROOM AFTER ROOM--THAT'S ALL YOU KNOW AND NOTHING MORE.
NO NATURAL LIGHT, NO FRESH AIR.
WHO RAISED THIS HOUSE?
WHO CONSTRUCTED THE ROOMS THROUGH WHICH YOU ENDLESSLY WANDER?
WHAT LURKS BEYOND THE BRICK AND MORTAR?
SOMETIMES, YOU HEAR SCRATCHING FROM OUTSIDE...
...AND YOU SCRATCH BACK.
YOU LEAVE FINGERNAILS EMBEDDED IN BLOODY FURROWS IN THE WALLS.
BUT TIME IS UNYIELDING, AND ROT RELENTLESS.
TIMBERS CREAK AND SAG AND BUCKLE.
BRICK CRUMBLES TO DUST.
YOUR HOUSE HAS HOLES IN IT.
HEY!
DON'T DO THAT!
DON'T TOUCH--
WHATEVER WAITS BEYOND YOUR SANCTUARY PRISON IS DRIBBLING IN.

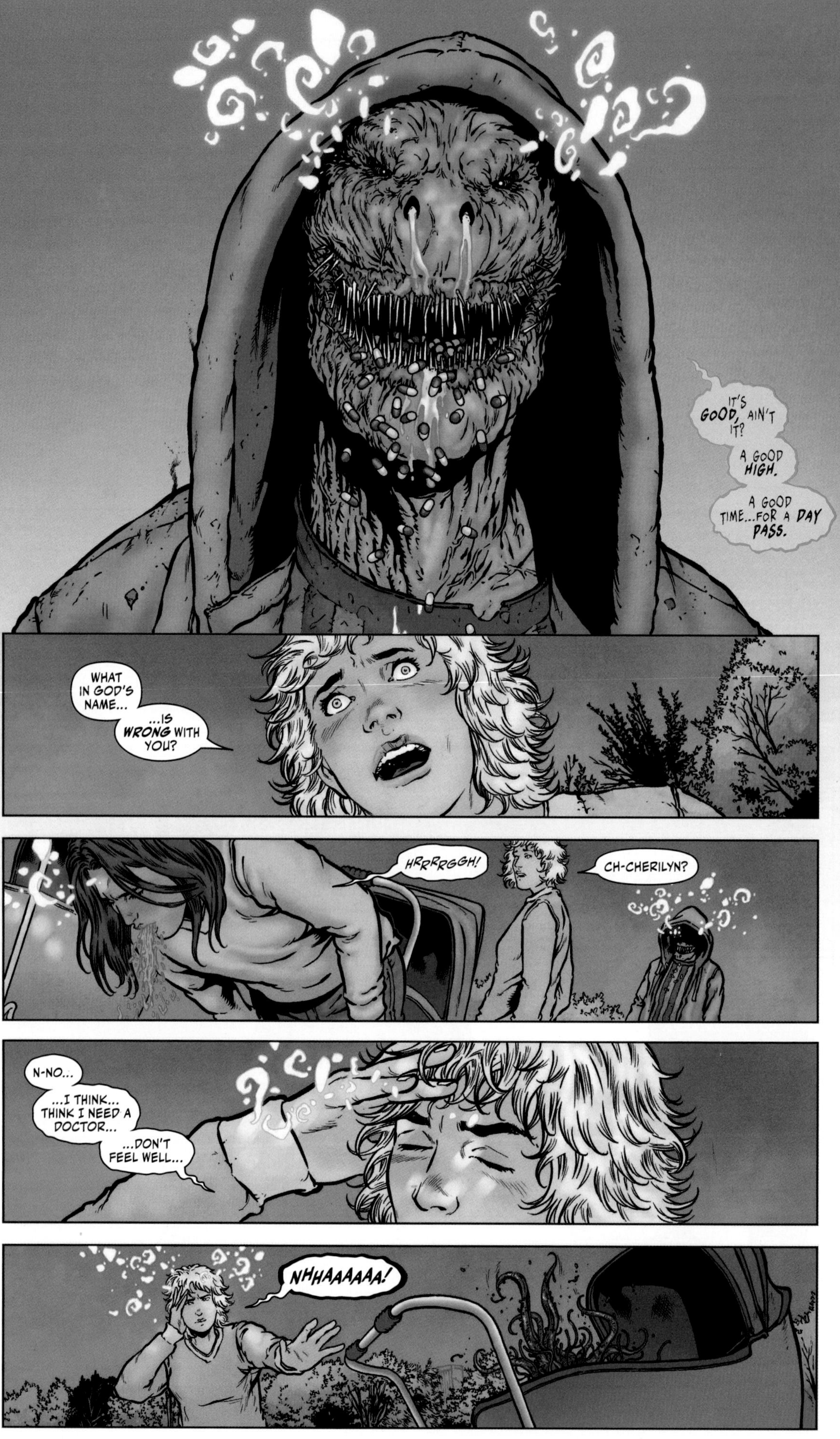
IT'S GOOD, AIN'T IT?
A GOOD HIGH.
A GOOD TIME...FOR A DAY PASS.
WHAT IN GOD'S NAME...
...IS WRONG WITH YOU?
HRRRRGGH!
CH-CHERILYN?
N-NO...
...I THINK... THINK I NEED A DOCTOR...
...DON'T FEEL WELL...
NHHAAAAAA!

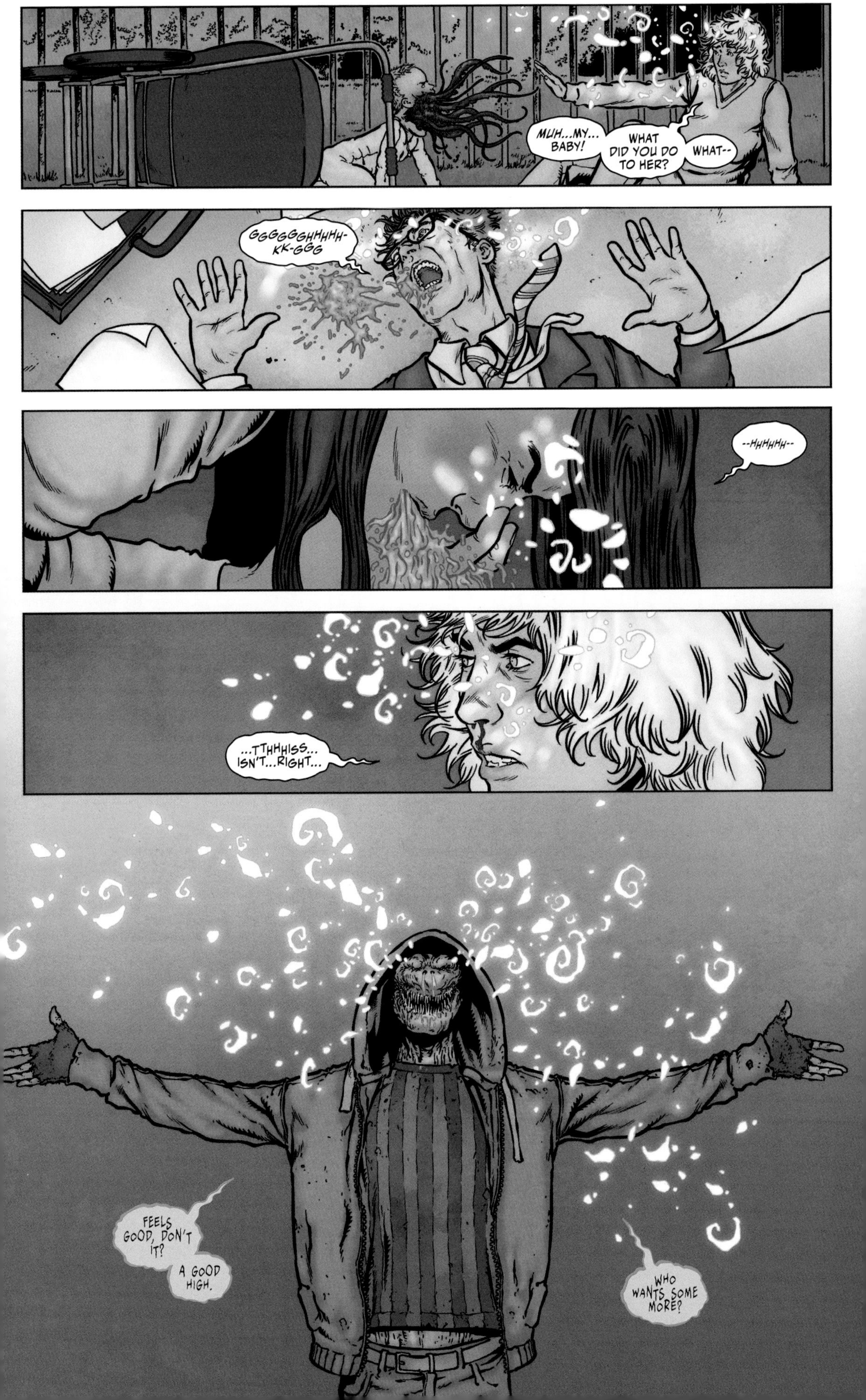
MUH...MY... BABY!
WHAT DID YOU DO TO HER?
WHAT--
GGGGGGHHHHH-KK-GGG
--HHHHHH--
...TTHHHISS... ISN'T...RIGHT...
FEELS GOOD, DON'T IT?
A GOOD HIGH.
WHO WANTS SOME MORE?

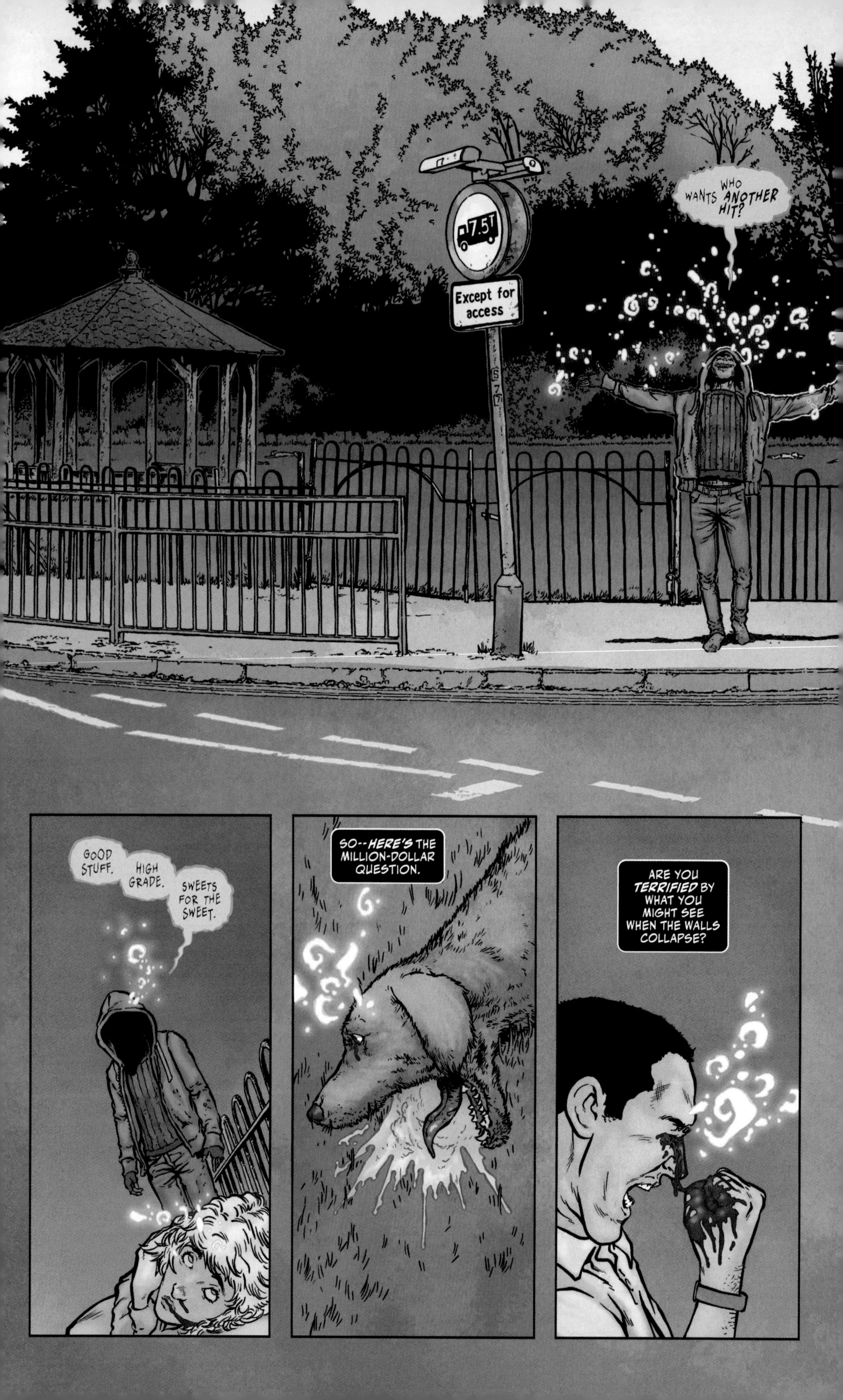
Except for access
WHO WANTS ANOTHER HIT?
GOOD STUFF.
HIGH GRADE.
SWEETS FOR THE SWEET.
SO--HERE'S THE MILLION-DOLLAR QUESTION.
ARE YOU TERRIFIED BY WHAT YOU MIGHT SEE WHEN THE WALLS COLLAPSE?

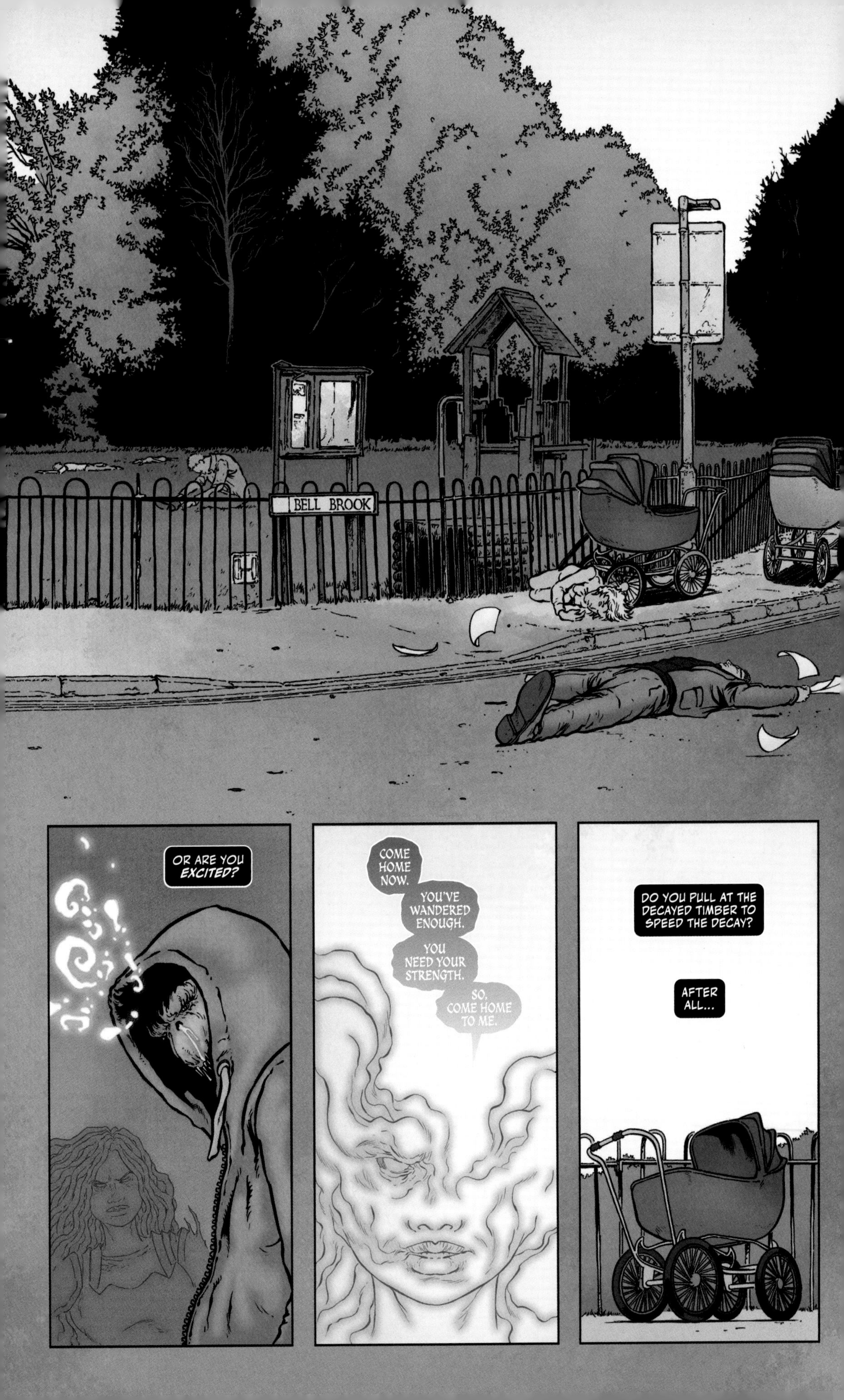
BELL BROOK
OR ARE YOU EXCITED?
COME HOME NOW.
YOU'VE WANDERED ENOUGH.
YOU NEED YOUR STRENGTH.
SO, COME HOME TO ME.
DO YOU PULL AT THE DECAYED TIMBER TO SPEED THE DECAY?
AFTER ALL...

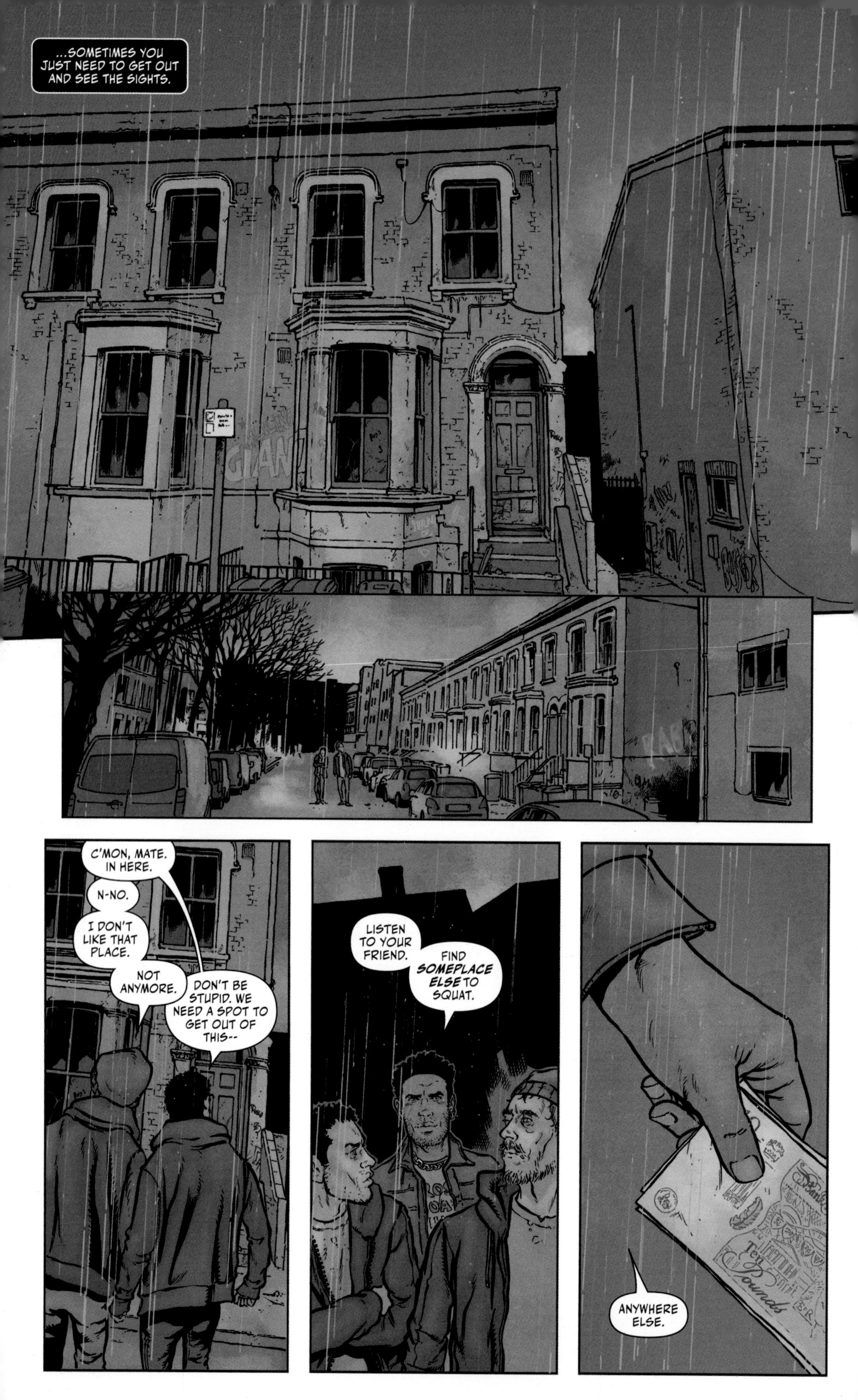

...SOMETIMES YOU JUST NEED TO GET OUT AND SEE THE SIGHTS.
C'MON, MATE. IN HERE.
N-NO.
I DON'T LIKE THAT PLACE.
NOT ANYMORE.
DON'T BE STUPID. WE NEED A SPOT TO GET OUT OF THIS--
LISTEN TO YOUR FRIEND.
FIND SOMEPLACE ELSE TO SQUAT.
ANYWHERE ELSE.

THEY'LL USE THAT MONEY FOR DRUGS.

DON'T BE *THAT* GUY.

WHATEVER'S KILLING PEOPLE...IT COMES FROM THIS PLACE.

TO BE FAIR, THERE ARE *MANY* DIFFERENT THINGS KILLING *MANY* DIFFERENT PEOPLE.

DEATH'S LIKE THAT.

IT *PLAYS THE FIELD.*

THERE'S A *BLIGHT* HERE, YES.

THE BARRIER BETWEEN THIS WORLD AND THE DEADSIDE IS CRUMBLING.

SOMETHING *CRAWLED OUT.*

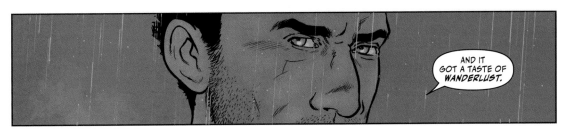

AND IT GOT A TASTE OF *WANDERLUST.*

PERHAPS YOU SHOULD PUT ON YOUR *GAME FACE.*

I WON'T BE LONG.

IT'S EASY TO SEE WHY THE VEIL IS COLLAPSING...

...BREAKING DOWN LIKE *DISEASED SKIN*...

...OPENING ITSELF UP TO *INFECTION.*

THE DEADSIDE BLEEDS THROUGH IN PLACES OF PAIN AND MISERY.

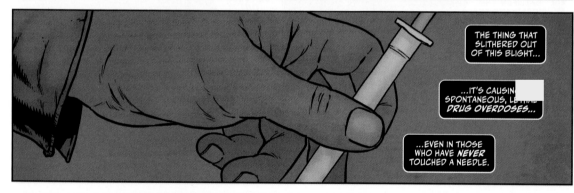

AND THERE'S *PLENTY* OF THAT TO GO AROUND.

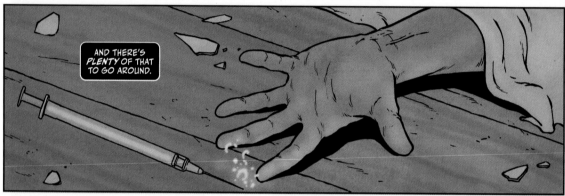

THE THING THAT SLITHERED OUT OF THIS BLIGHT...

...IT'S CAUSING SPONTANEOUS, LETHAL *DRUG OVERDOSES*...

...EVEN IN THOSE WHO HAVE *NEVER* TOUCHED A NEEDLE.

THE BUILDING'S A *DEATHTRAP.*

ALMOST ANYONE WHO STUMBLES IN SURE AS HELL ISN'T STUMBLING BACK OUT.

...THE MONSTER... THE DEMON...THE SPIRIT...HAS DECIDED TO GO OUT *EXPLORING.*

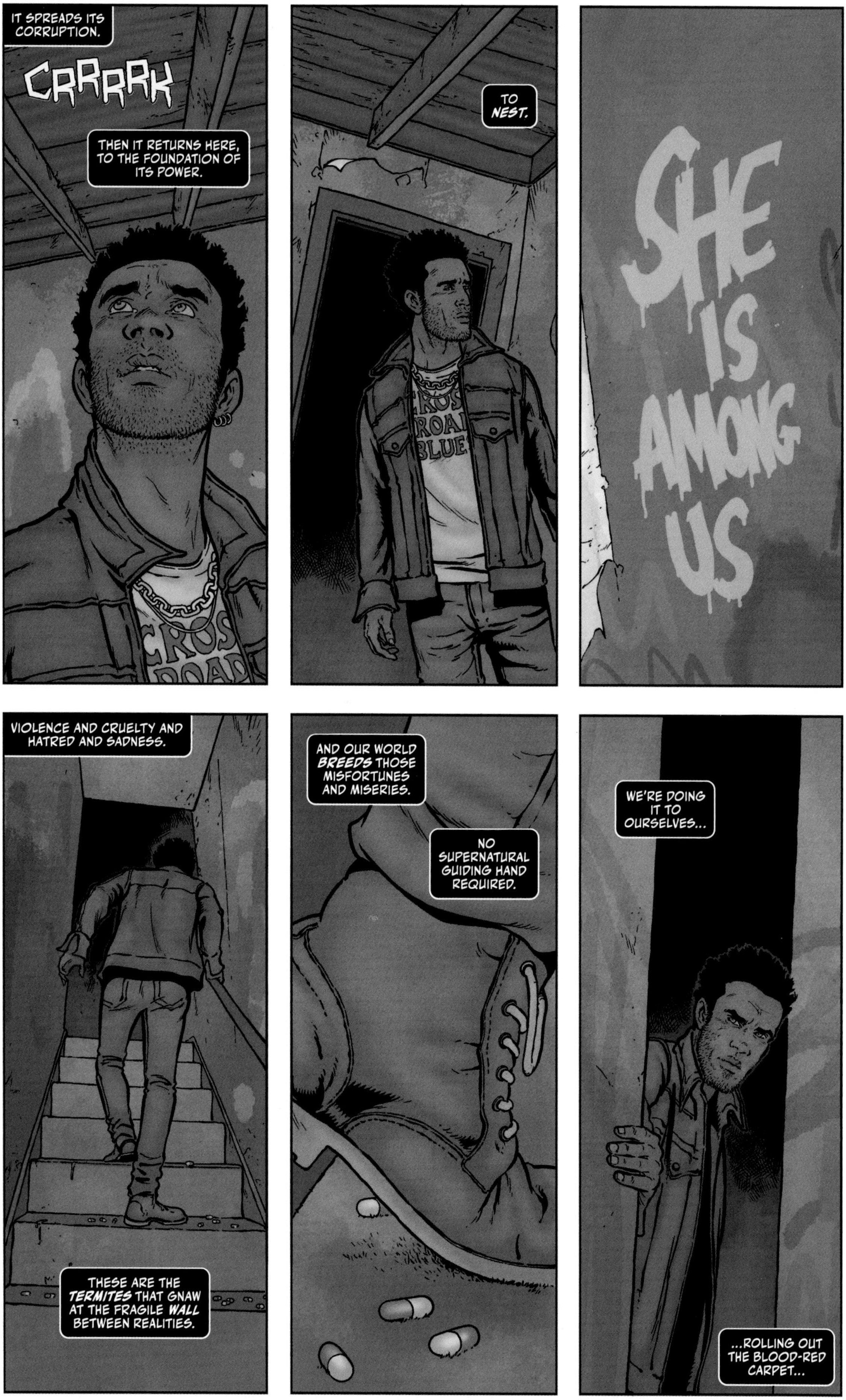
IT SPREADS ITS CORRUPTION.
CRRRRK
THEN IT RETURNS HERE, TO THE FOUNDATION OF ITS POWER.
TO *NEST.*
SHE IS AMONG US
VIOLENCE AND CRUELTY AND HATRED AND SADNESS.
THESE ARE THE *TERMITES* THAT GNAW AT THE FRAGILE *WALL* BETWEEN REALITIES.
AND OUR WORLD *BREEDS* THOSE MISFORTUNES AND MISERIES.
NO SUPERNATURAL GUIDING HAND REQUIRED.
WE'RE DOING IT TO OURSELVES...
...ROLLING OUT THE BLOOD-RED CARPET...

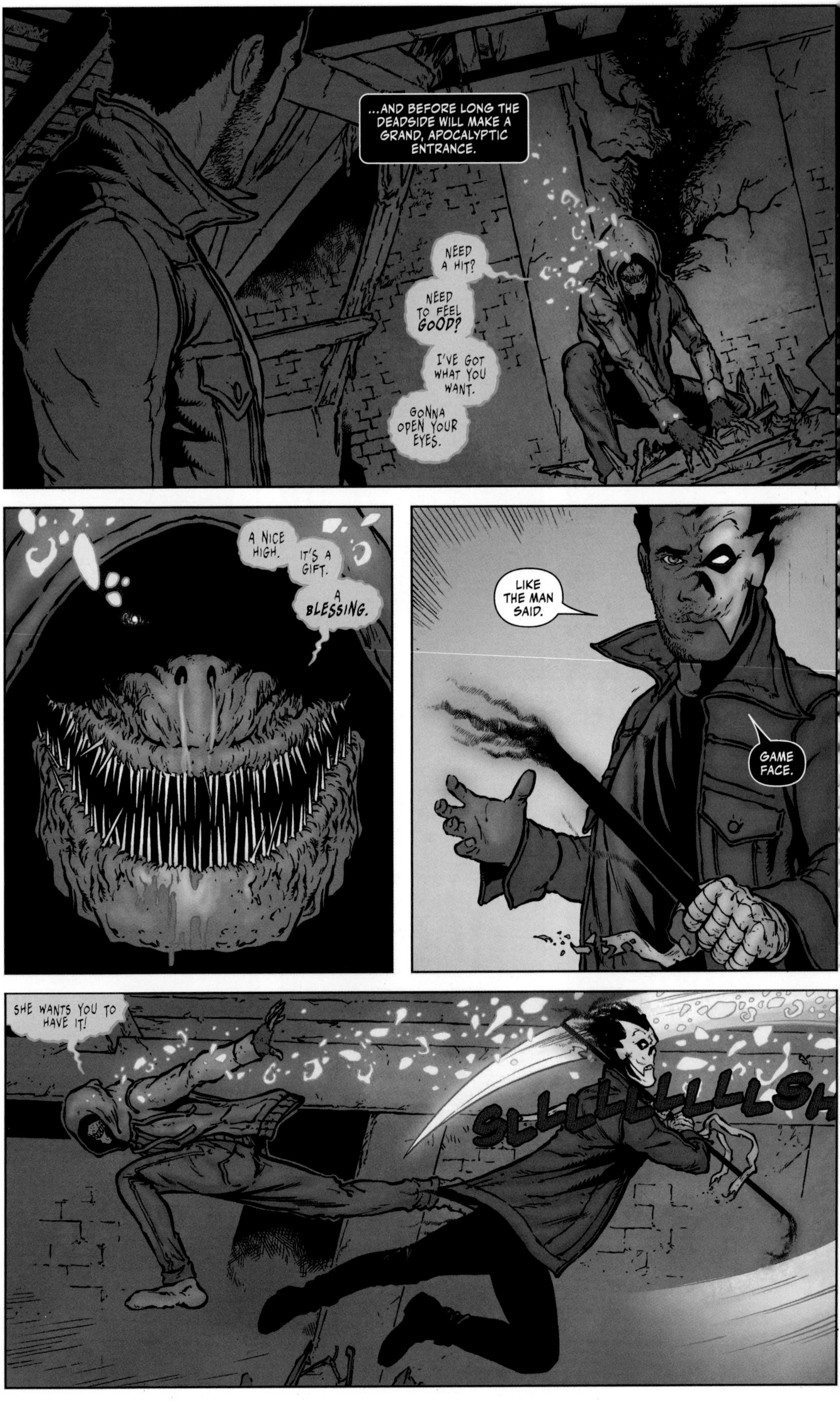
...AND BEFORE LONG THE DEADSIDE WILL MAKE A GRAND, APOCALYPTIC ENTRANCE.
NEED A HIT?
NEED TO FEEL GOOD?
I'VE GOT WHAT YOU WANT.
GONNA OPEN YOUR EYES.
A NICE HIGH.
IT'S A GIFT.
A BLESSING.
LIKE THE MAN SAID.
GAME FACE.
SHE WANTS YOU TO HAVE IT!
SLLLLLLLLLSH

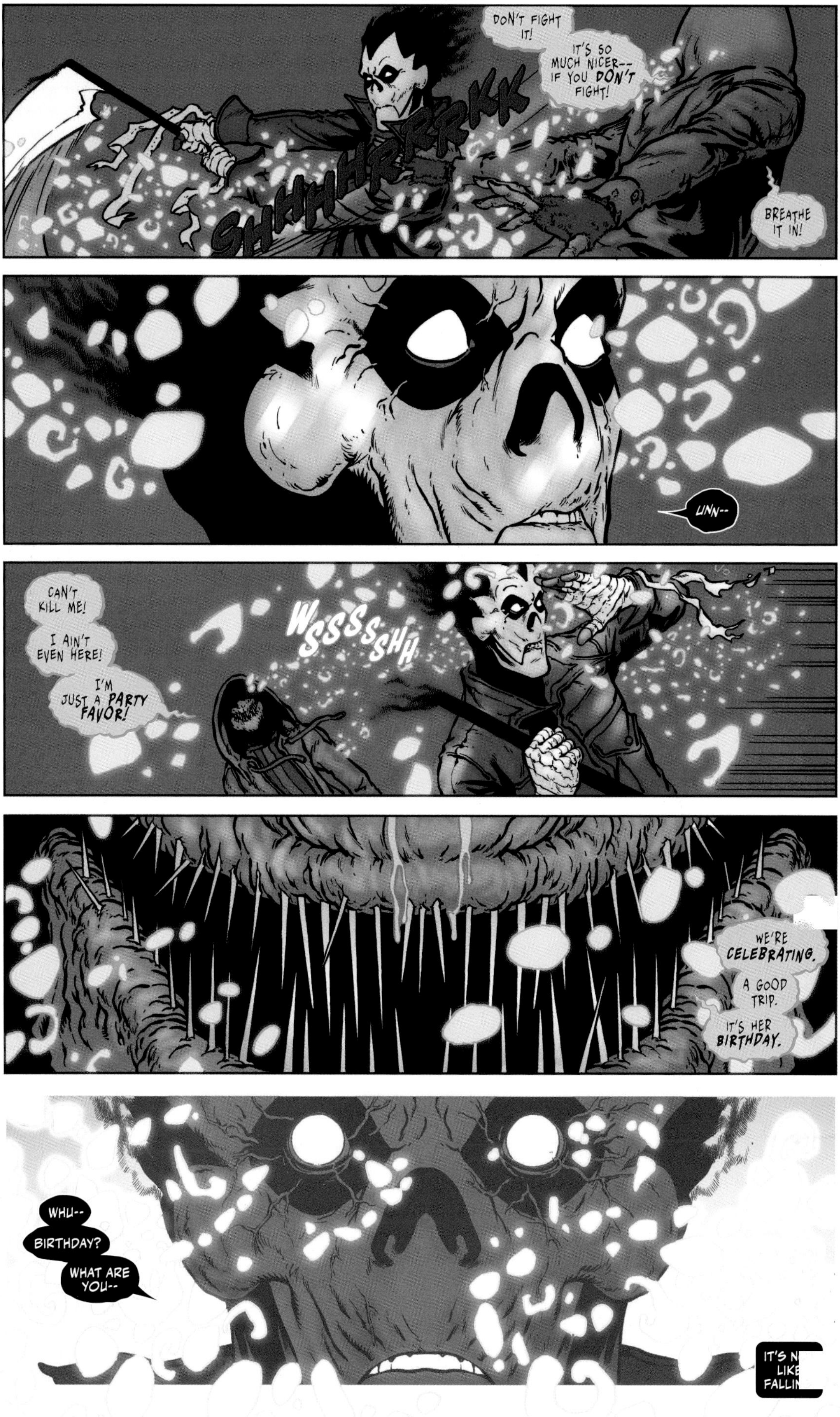
DON'T FIGHT IT!
IT'S SO MUCH NICER-- IF YOU DON'T FIGHT!
SHHHHRRRKK
BREATHE IT IN!
UNN--
CAN'T KILL ME!
I AIN'T EVEN HERE!
I'M JUST A PARTY FAVOR!
WSSSSHH
WE'RE CELEBRATING.
A GOOD TRIP.
IT'S HER BIRTHDAY.
WHU--
BIRTHDAY?
WHAT ARE YOU--

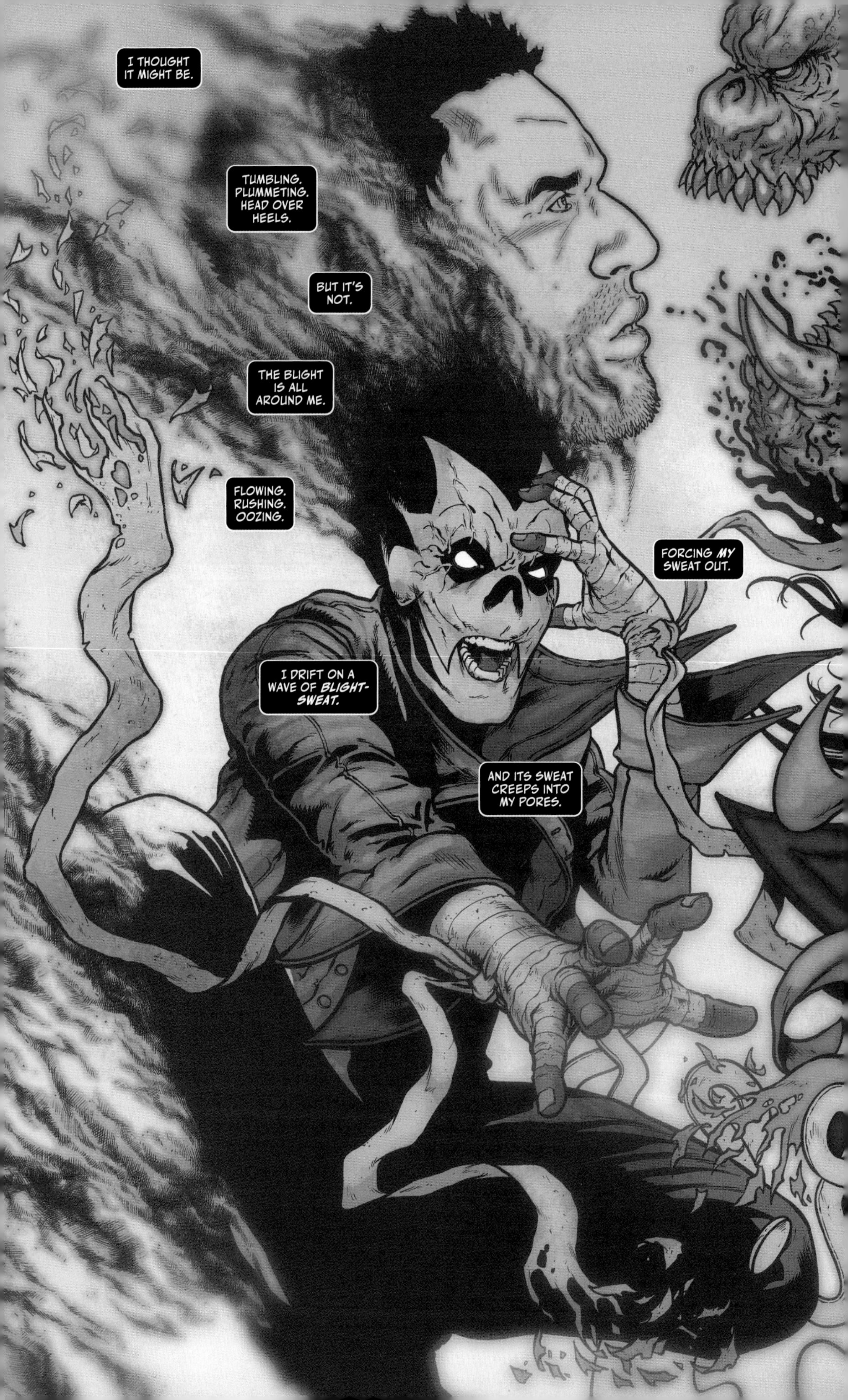
I THOUGHT IT MIGHT BE.
TUMBLING. PLUMMETING. HEAD OVER HEELS.
BUT IT'S NOT.
THE BLIGHT IS ALL AROUND ME.
FLOWING. RUSHING. OOZING.
FORCING *MY* SWEAT OUT.
I DRIFT ON A WAVE OF *BLIGHT-SWEAT.*
AND ITS SWEAT CREEPS INTO MY PORES.

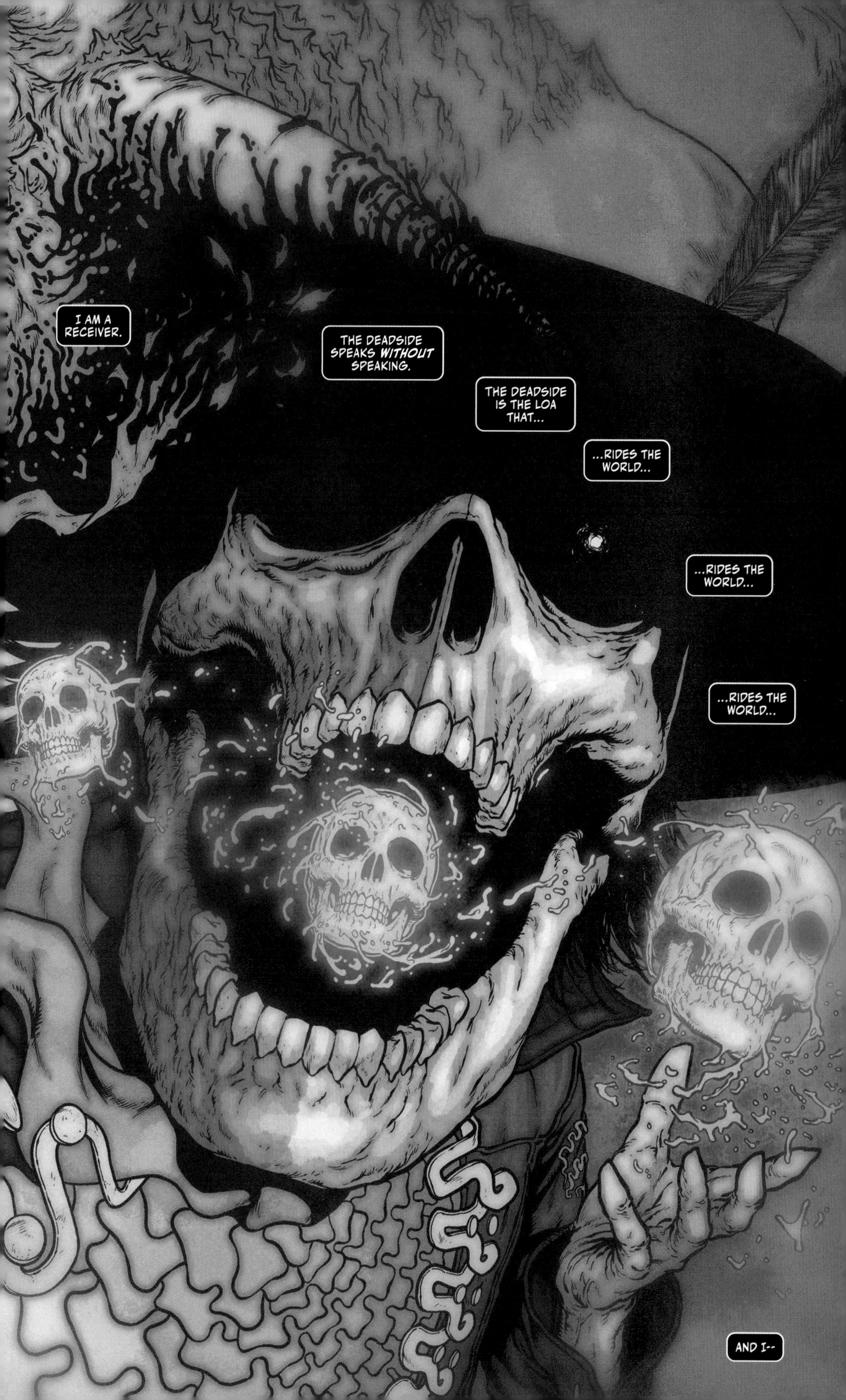
I AM A RECEIVER.
THE DEADSIDE SPEAKS *WITHOUT* SPEAKING.
THE DEADSIDE IS THE LOA THAT...
...RIDES THE WORLD...
...RIDES THE WORLD...
...RIDES THE WORLD...
AND I--

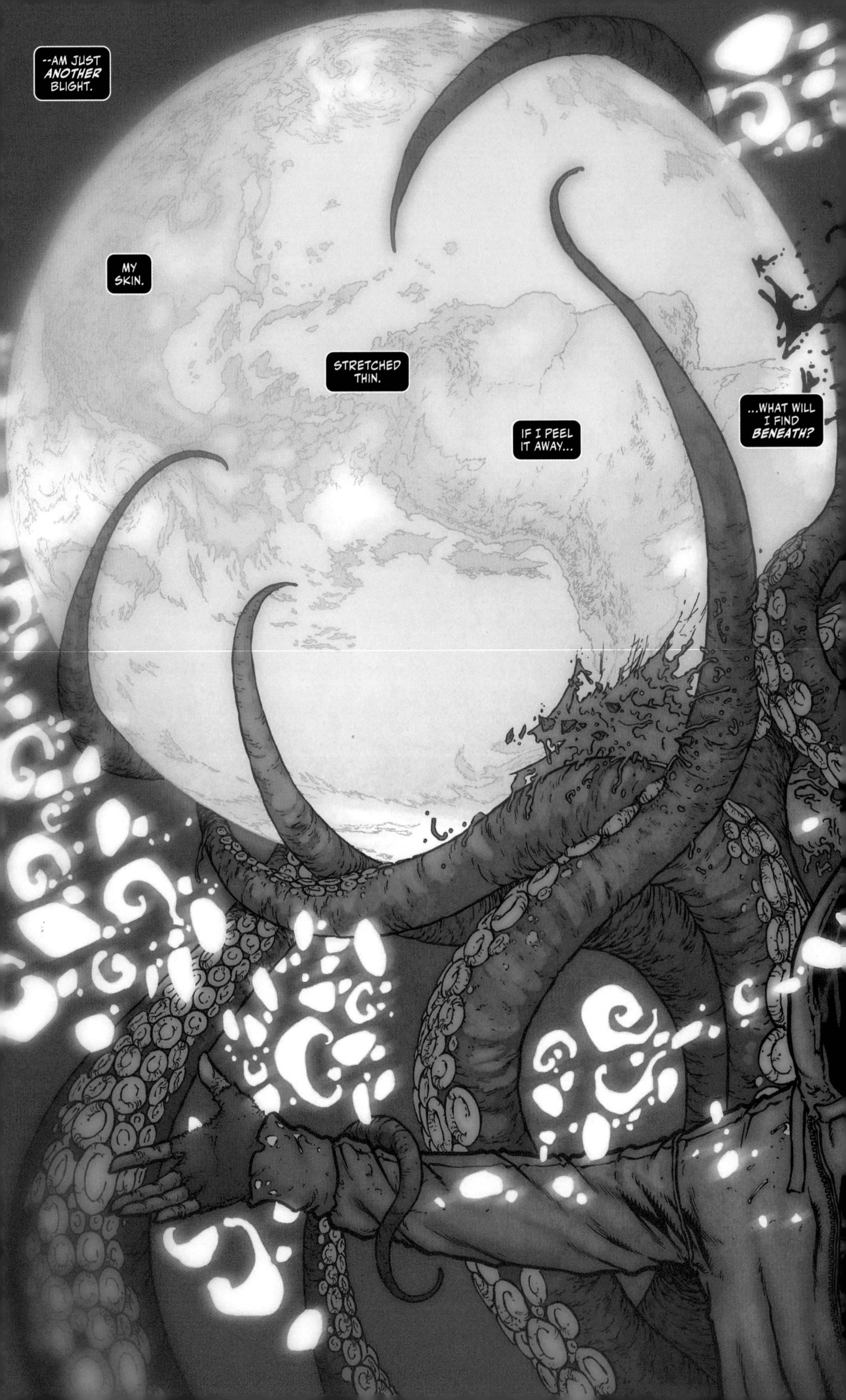
--AM JUST ANOTHER BLIGHT.
MY SKIN.
STRETCHED THIN.
IF I PEEL IT AWAY...
...WHAT WILL I FIND BENEATH?

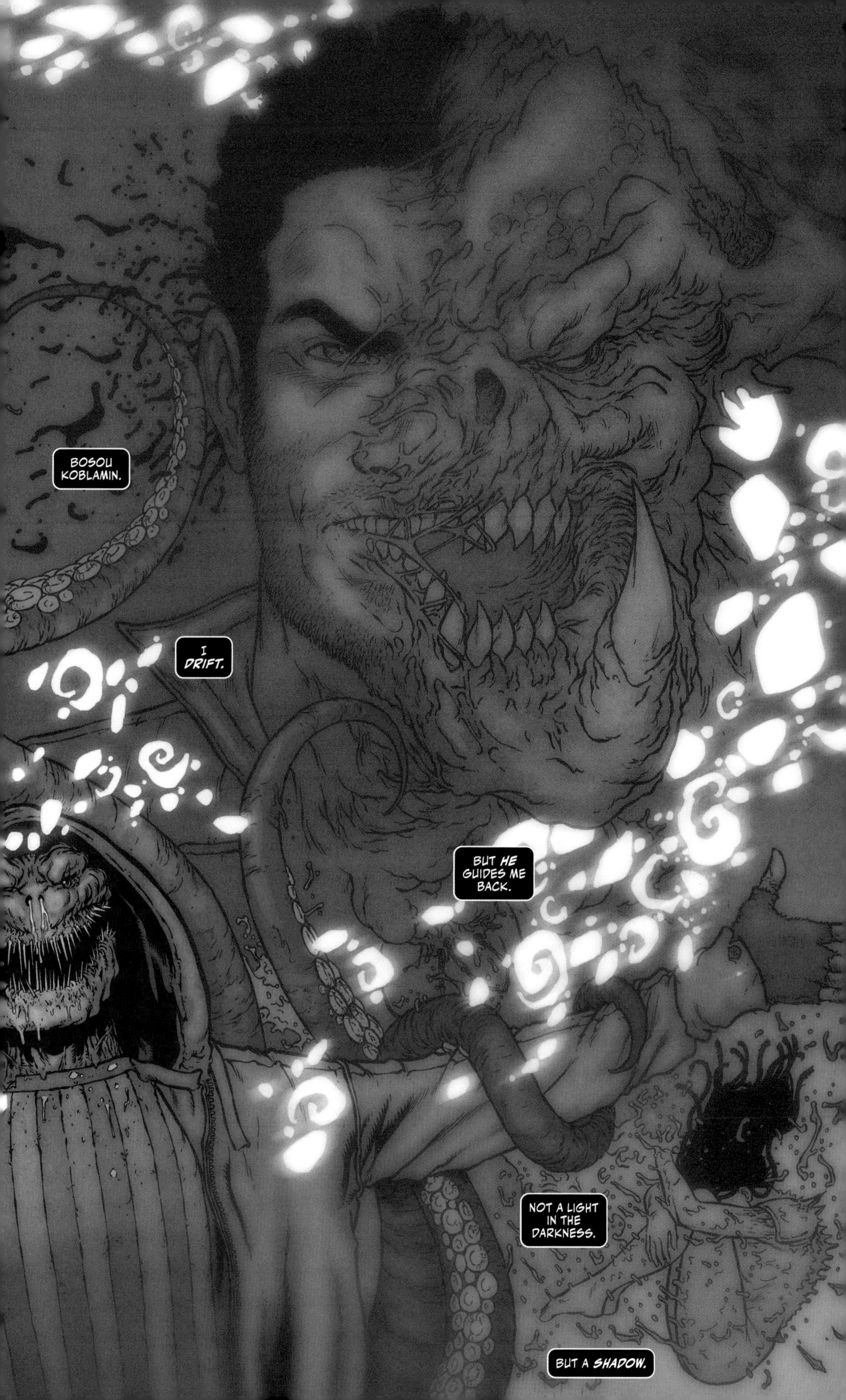
BOSOU KOBLAMIN.
I DRIFT.
BUT HE GUIDES ME BACK.
NOT A LIGHT IN THE DARKNESS.
BUT A SHADOW.

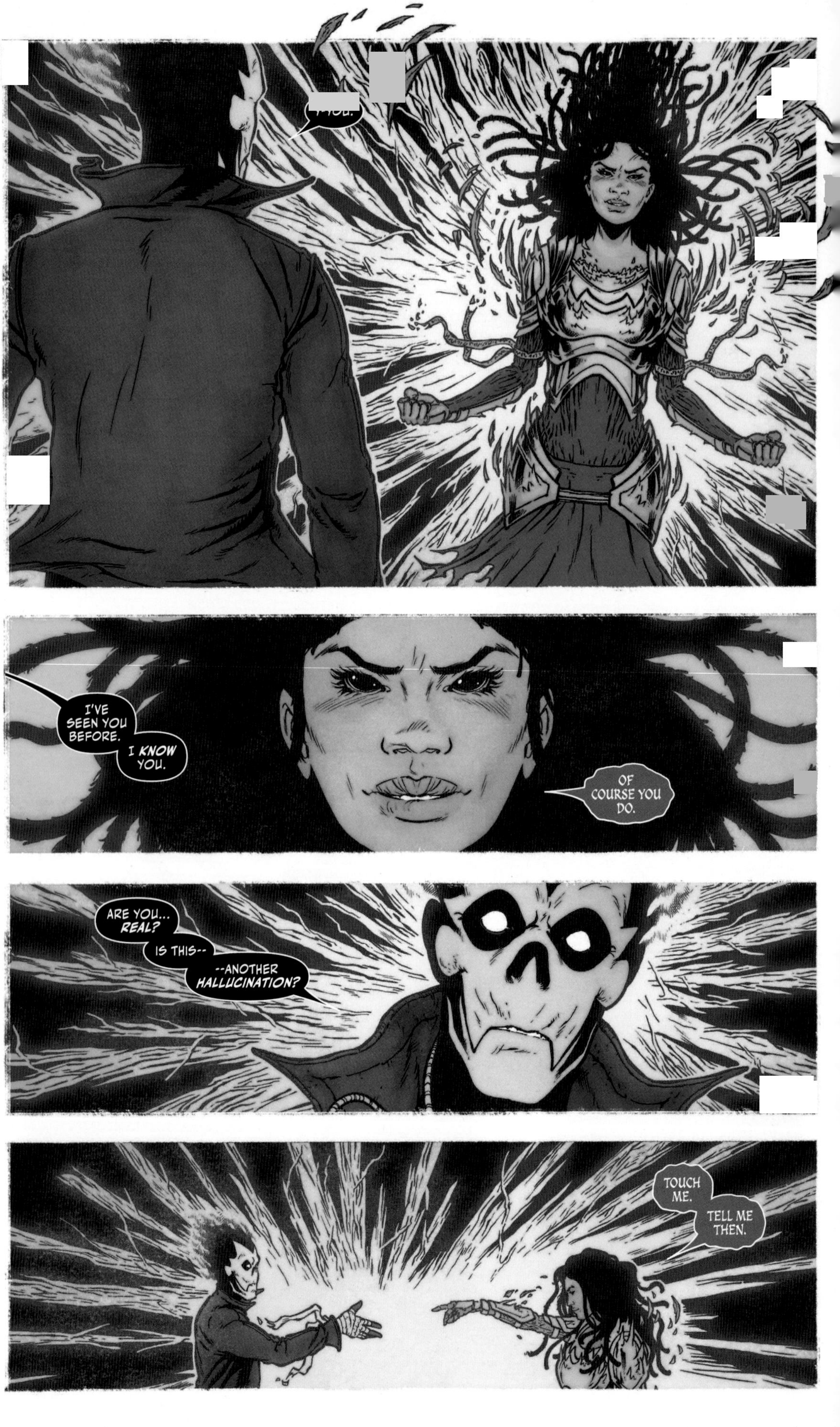
I'VE SEEN YOU BEFORE.
I KNOW YOU.
OF COURSE YOU DO.
ARE YOU... REAL?
IS THIS--
--ANOTHER HALLUCINATION?
TOUCH ME.
TELL ME THEN.

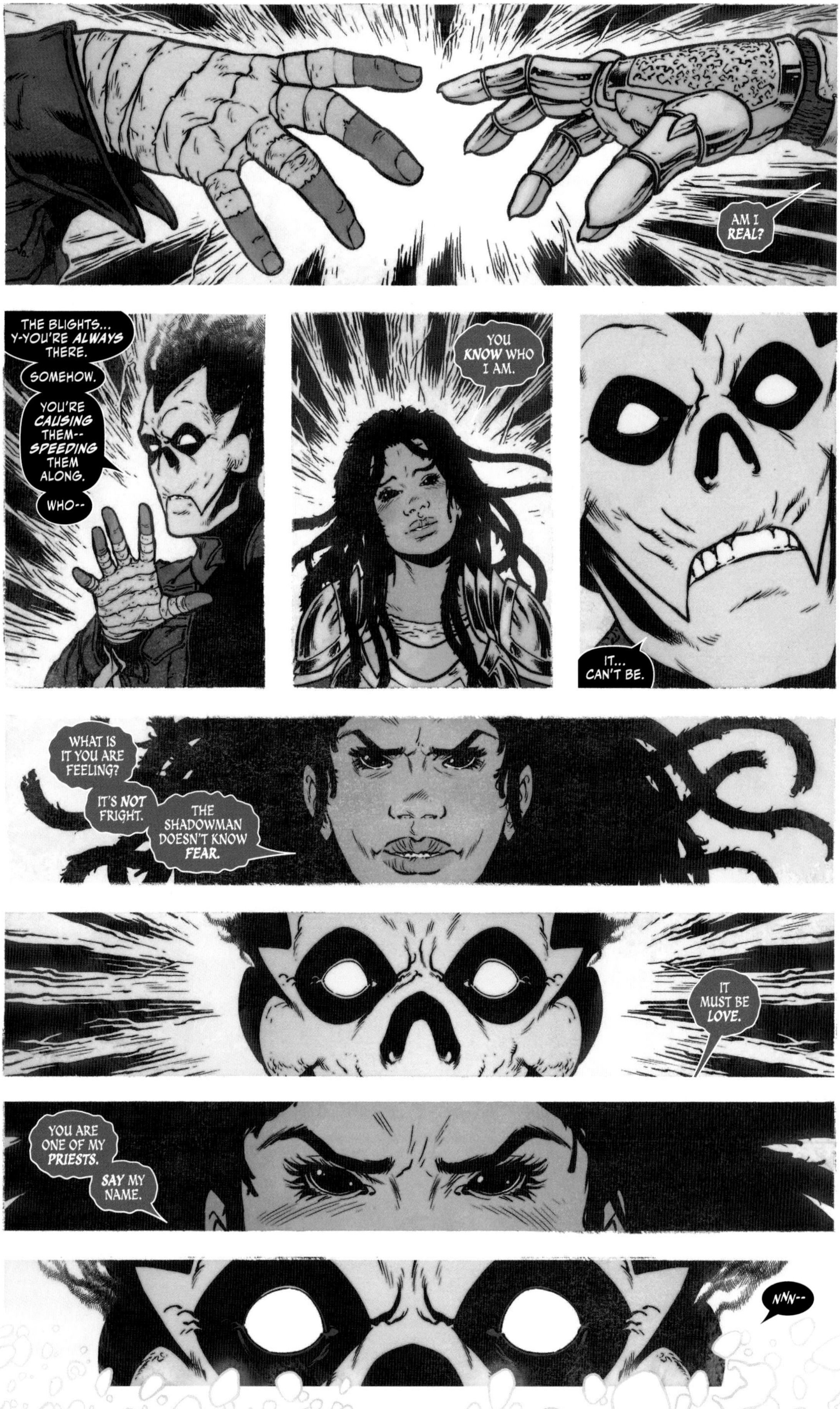
AM I REAL?
THE BLIGHTS... Y-YOU'RE ALWAYS THERE.
SOMEHOW.
YOU'RE CAUSING THEM-- SPEEDING THEM ALONG.
WHO--
YOU KNOW WHO I AM.
IT... CAN'T BE.
WHAT IS IT YOU ARE FEELING?
IT'S NOT FRIGHT.
THE SHADOWMAN DOESN'T KNOW FEAR.
IT MUST BE LOVE.
YOU ARE ONE OF MY PRIESTS.
SAY MY NAME.
NNN--

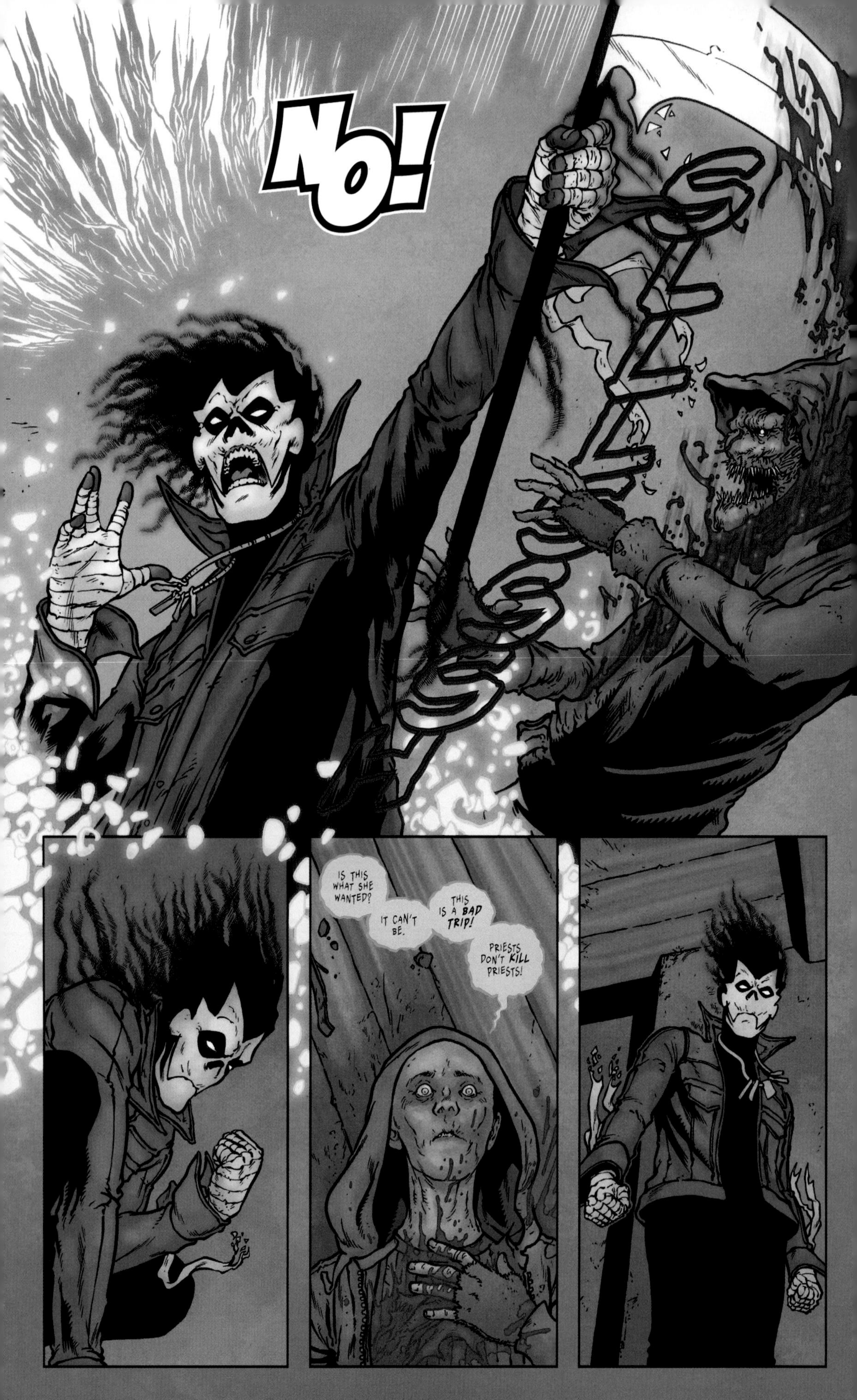
NO!
IS THIS WHAT SHE WANTED?
IT CAN'T BE.
THIS IS A BAD TRIP!
PRIESTS DON'T KILL PRIESTS!

SHE WANTED ME TO SEE.

SHE WANTED TO SHOW ME THAT CLOSING THESE BLIGHTS...

...ONE AT A TIME...

...IS ACCOMPLISHING *NOTHING.*

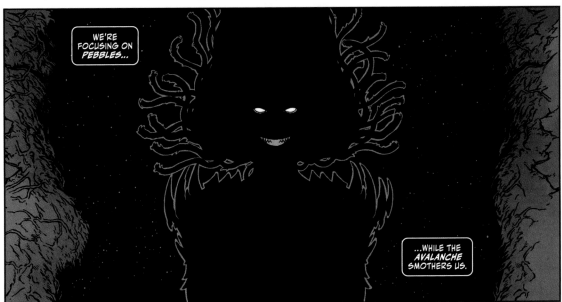

WE'RE FOCUSING ON *PEBBLES*...

...WHILE THE *AVALANCHE* SMOTHERS US.

BUT I DID LEARN SOMETHING.

SOMETHING I CAN *USE.*

"THE DEADSIDE IS THE LOA THAT RIDES THE WORLD."

WHEN WE STRUGGLE AGAINST IT...

...WHEN WE TRY TO REJECT IT...

WE *INVITE* STRIFE.

DID YOU KNOW?

I WAS STANDING RIGHT IN FRONT OF HER.

SHE WAS... *BEAUTIFUL.*

BUT SHE'S GOING TO DROWN THIS WORLD.

SHE?

THE DEADSIDE.

SHE'S TRYING TO TAKE *PHYSICAL FORM.*

I'VE LIED TO YOU *OFTEN* AND WITH *GREAT DELIGHT,* BUT I'M TELLING THE *TRUTH* NOW.

I DID NOT KNOW.

WE CAN'T STOP THE BLIGHTS.

THE WORLD IS *TOO FAR GONE* FOR THAT.

BUT THE SHADOW LOA SHOWED ME SOMETHING.

WHEN I *ACCEPTED* THE SHADOW LOA... MY POWERS GREW.

IF I CAN GUIDE THE PEOPLE OF THE WORLD...IF I CAN GIVE THEM A DEEPER UNDERSTANDING OF THE DEADSIDE...

...AND VICE VERSA...

...MAYBE ONE WORLD DOESN'T HAVE TO CONSUME THE OTHER.

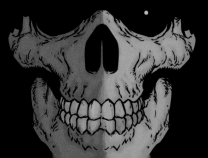

MAYBE... THIS WORLD AND THE DEADSIDE CAN *BECOME* ONE.

NEXT:

BOOK TWO

GALLERY

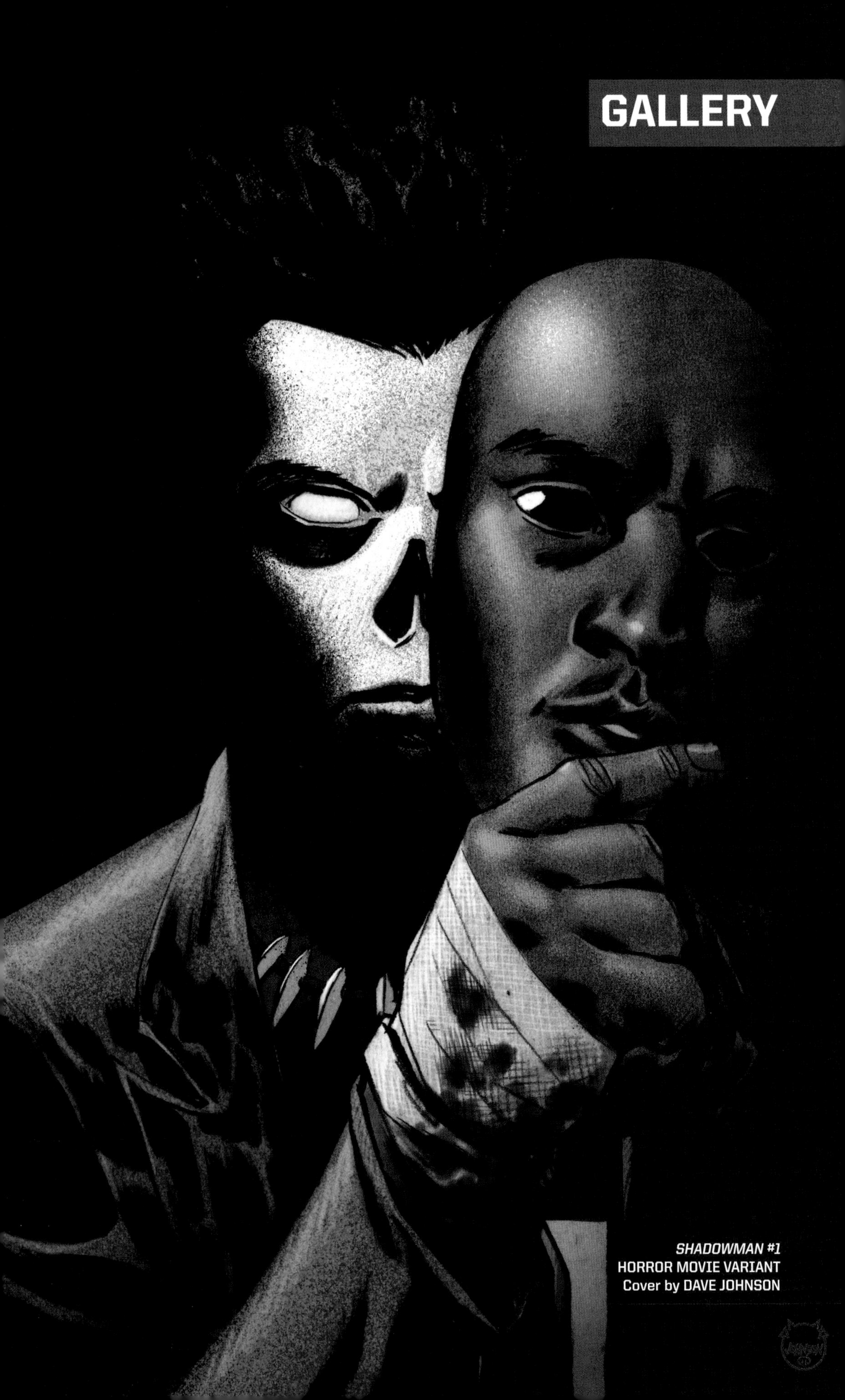

SHADOWMAN #1
HORROR MOVIE VARIANT
Cover by DAVE JOHNSON

LION DEMON:

The DEMON is a huge, hulking monstrosity. It is nearly ten feet tall, all muscle. Patches of hair grow all over it. Patches of ridged horns or tusks jut from its shoulders, knuckles, and elbows. Its head is massive, and something like a lion's head—if the skin of a lion's head had pulled back into writhing, barbed tentacles and the blood-dripping skull remained behind and started roaring in anger. Its teeth are huge and nasty.

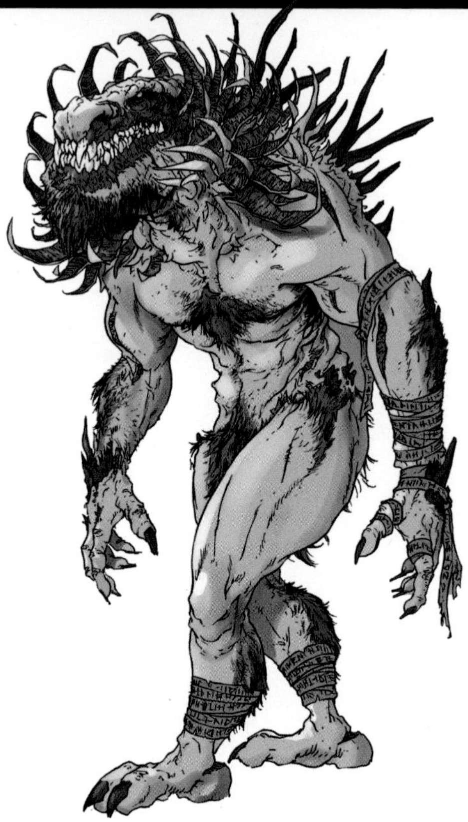

HELL BUGS:

Suddenly, the TWISTED, MANGLE BODY erupts, flesh tearing open in several places, and a CLOUD OF HELL-INSECTS comes out, moving in several undulating swarms from the body. The insects are small, but several of them fly into the foreground, giving us a good look at them. Each looks like a winged praying mantis. Clusters of long, wriggling tentacles (like the tentacles of a Portuguese Manowar) hang from the belly. The tentacles all end in fish hook-like barbs. They're really horrible looking little beasts.

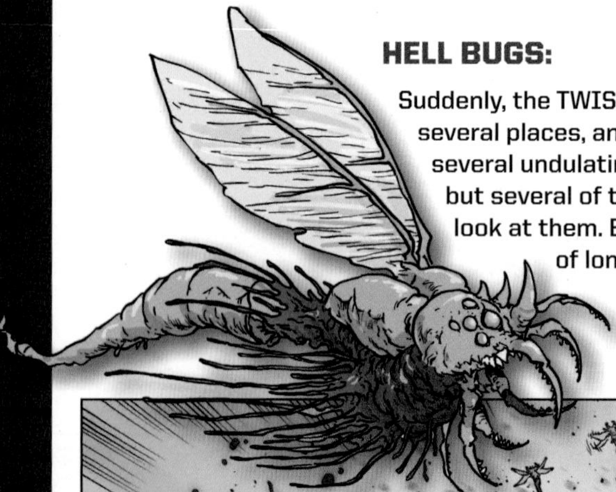

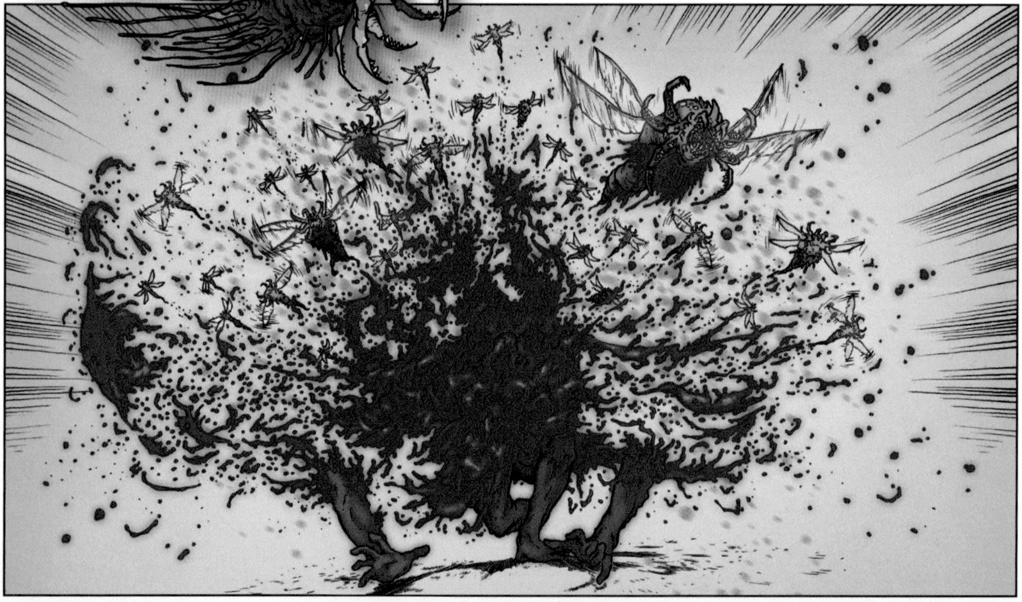

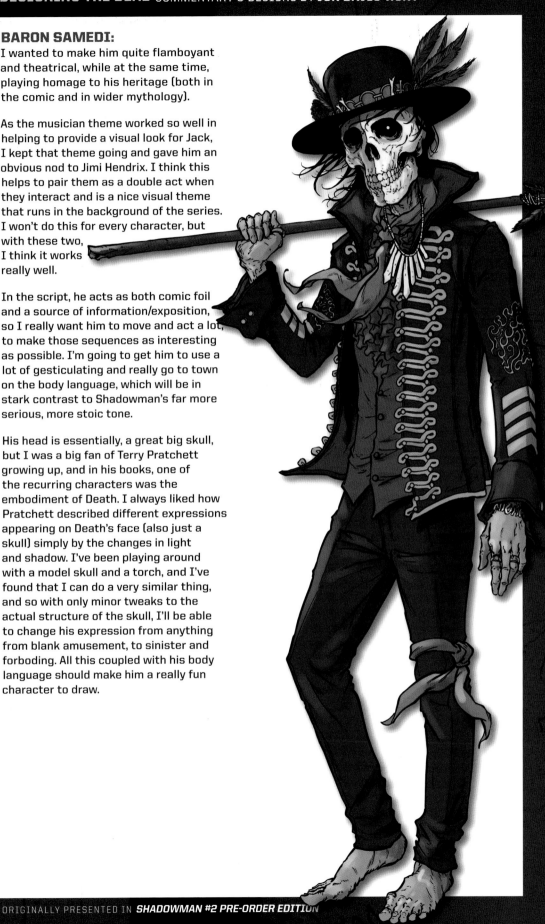

BARON SAMEDI:

I wanted to make him quite flamboyant and theatrical, while at the same time, playing homage to his heritage (both in the comic and in wider mythology).

As the musician theme worked so well in helping to provide a visual look for Jack, I kept that theme going and gave him an obvious nod to Jimi Hendrix. I think this helps to pair them as a double act when they interact and is a nice visual theme that runs in the background of the series. I won't do this for every character, but with these two, I think it works really well.

In the script, he acts as both comic foil and a source of information/exposition, so I really want him to move and act a lot, to make those sequences as interesting as possible. I'm going to get him to use a lot of gesticulating and really go to town on the body language, which will be in stark contrast to Shadowman's far more serious, more stoic tone.

His head is essentially, a great big skull, but I was a big fan of Terry Pratchett growing up, and in his books, one of the recurring characters was the embodiment of Death. I always liked how Pratchett described different expressions appearing on Death's face (also just a skull) simply by the changes in light and shadow. I've been playing around with a model skull and a torch, and I've found that I can do a very similar thing, and so with only minor tweaks to the actual structure of the skull, I'll be able to change his expression from anything from blank amusement, to sinister and forboding. All this coupled with his body language should make him a really fun character to draw.

There are places on this Earth -- St. Peter's Basillica, Amityville, and Aokigahara -- that are not entirely of this world. Locations where the membrane between our mundane world and the spiritual one is weaker; they are known as Thin Places. People have sought out these areas where pieces of the great beyond slip into this reality, in an attempt to access a semblance of power and introspection. The term originated in Ireland, in reference to these places where a heavenly and spiritual presence are believed to be closer to mankind.

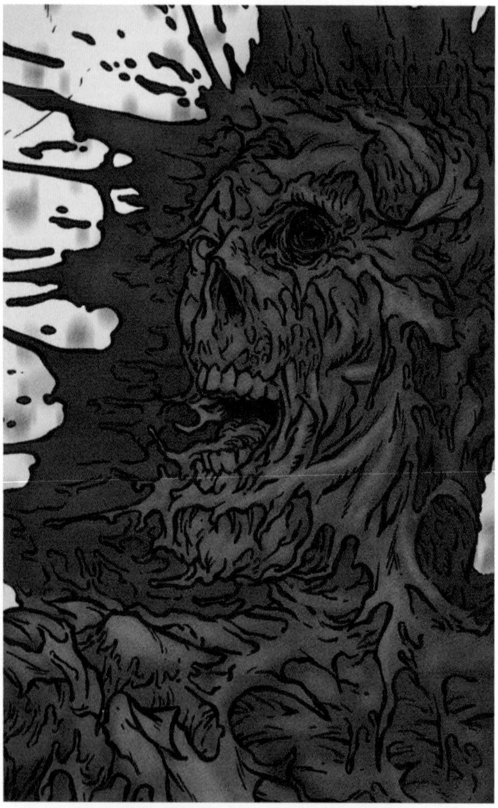

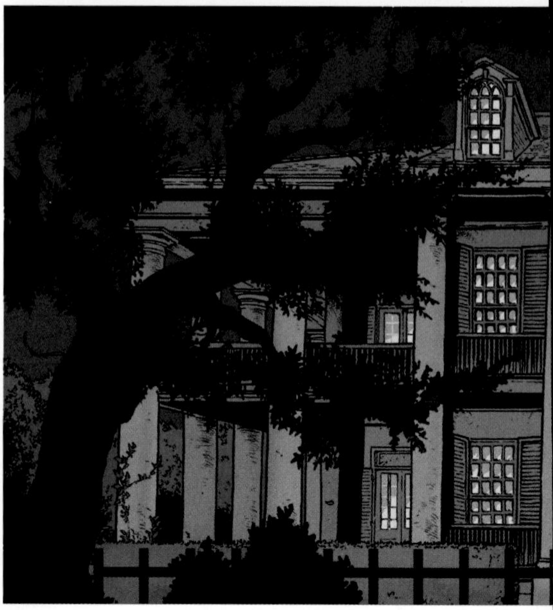

When discussing these anomalies, it is important to note that Thin Places do not only skew towards the heavens. The term is often used to describe these ethereal locations because the harrowing ones go by a more colloquial acknowledgment: hauntings. The more hauntings - also known as Blights - in one place, the thinner the veil has become, and the more at risk the world is of what may peak through...

THE BLIGHTS OF NEW ORLEANS:
New Orleans is a city populated by ghost stories and hauntings, suggesting that the boundary between our world and the next is thinner there than in most other places. Perhaps the most unsettling of New Orleans' ghastly repertoire is the tale of the LaLaurie Mansion.

Resting at 1140 Royale Street, the LaLaurie Mansion is home to nearly 200 mysteries. The focal point of

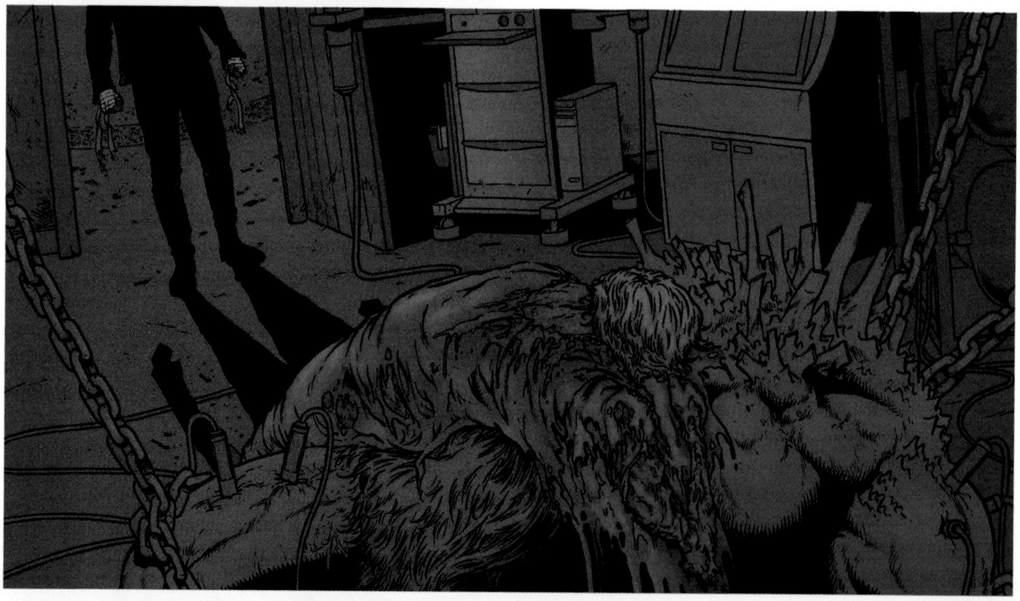

ARTWORK BY **JON DAVIS-HUNT** WITH **JORDIE BELLAIRE**

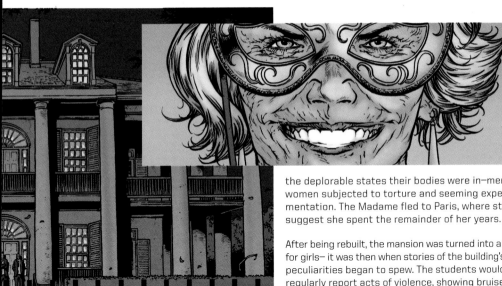

the supernatural occurrences? Delphine LaLaurie—also known as the Mad Madame. Born in the twilight of the 18th century to a wealthy French family, the Madame was married thrice, though her first two husbands both met untimely ends—the first passing of mysterious circumstances while on vacation with Delphine in Havana, the second transpiring under similar conditions at home in New Orleans. But it was her third husband - a physician named Leonard LaLaurie - that would give their haunted mansion its namesake.

The two fought constantly, according to accounts from their neighbors, leading Leonard to finally leave his tumultuous marriage and the mansion in 1834. Those who knew Delphine stated that her relationship with Leonard had broken her, pushing her into madness, though evidence painted a different picture - a year prior, rumors brewed that it was Delphine who pushed a young girl to her death off a second floor balcony. On an evening in 1834, shortly after the departure of Leonard, a fire broke out in the kitchen of the LaLaurie Mansion. Set by a slave woman who was chained to the stove, the fire was meant to protest the egregious conditions that Delphine had subjugated her slaves to. And while only a part of the mansion was destroyed in the blaze, investigators uncovered a secret room in the attic where atrocities had gone unpunished. Slaves were chained to the walls, starved and emaciated. Liberal accounts recall

the deplorable states their bodies were in—men and women subjected to torture and seeming experimentation. The Madame fled to Paris, where stories suggest she spent the remainder of her years.

After being rebuilt, the mansion was turned into a school for girls— it was then when stories of the building's peculiarities began to spew. The students would regularly report acts of violence, showing bruises on their arms, legs, and sometimes faces. Whenever the teachers would investigate, the girls only ever spoke of one attacker: a woman, matching Delphine LaLaurie's description. Only, no woman like that existed on the school's grounds. Students also reported hearing screaming, pleading and heavy breathing coming from the attic... the site of the Mad Madame's torture chamber. Since then, 1140 Royale Street was converted into an apartment complex where tenants heard footsteps of invisible strangers down their halls, reports of strange noises coming from the attic and, most startlingly, a tenant being discovered brutally murdered in his room. No suspect was ever found or charged. Most recently, workmen hired to refurbish the mansion have uncovered skeletons buried beneath the manor, some missing limbs and others with holes drilled into their skulls.

While this story is New Orleans' most infamous, and perhaps its most gruesome, it's no coincidence that the city is home to so many haunted accounts—it's because of the dissolving boundary between our world and the next.

As it stands, these hauntings are innocent enough until provoked. However, with more interest in the occult, and more people poking at what lurks in the shadows, the world beyond these Blights is stirring. It may not be long before someone -- or something -- finds its way through the shadows that cannot so easily be sent back... ▪

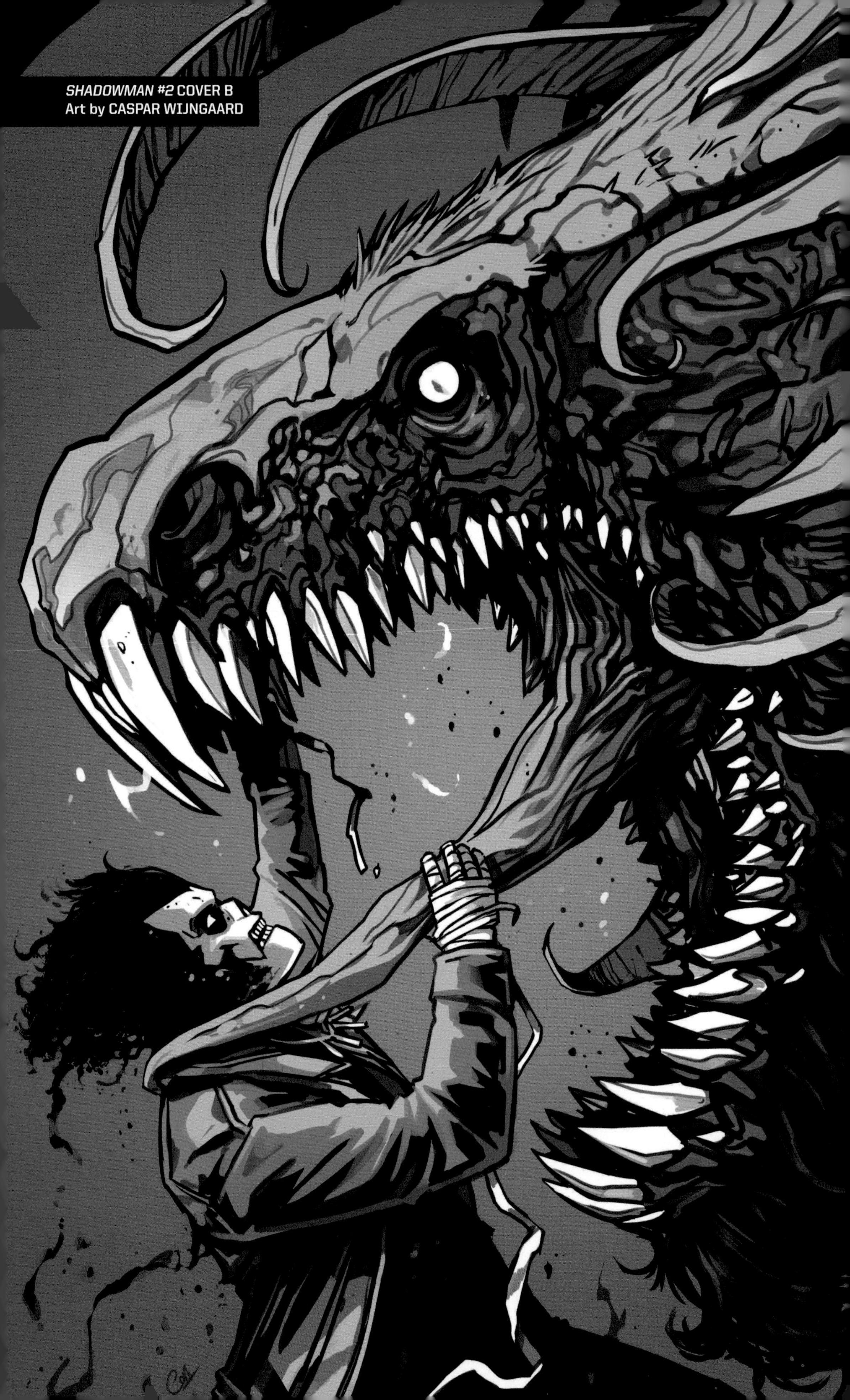

SHADOWMAN #2 COVER B
Art by CASPAR WIJNGAARD

SHADOWMAN #2 PRE-ORDER EDITION COVER
Art by ANNIE WU

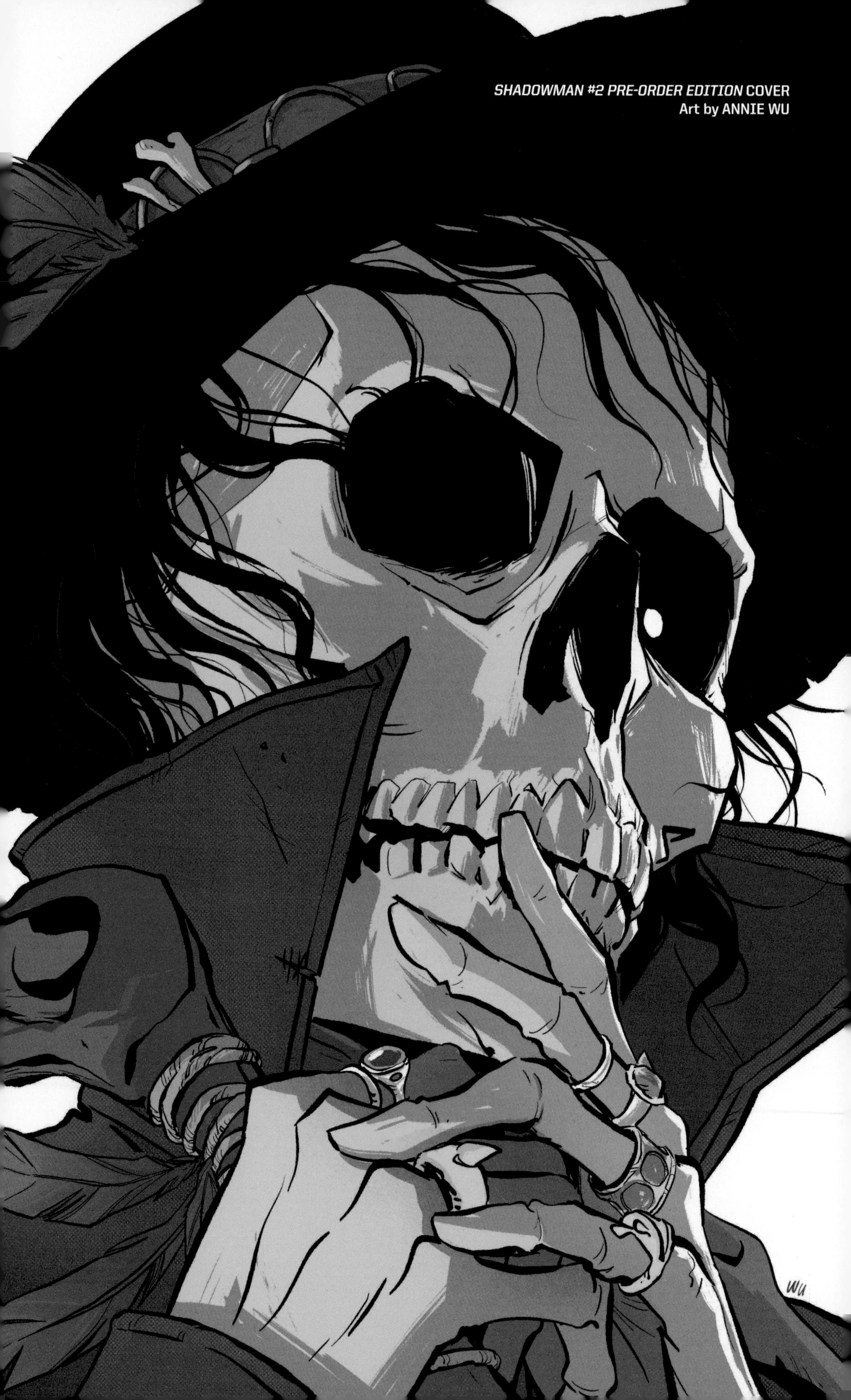
WU

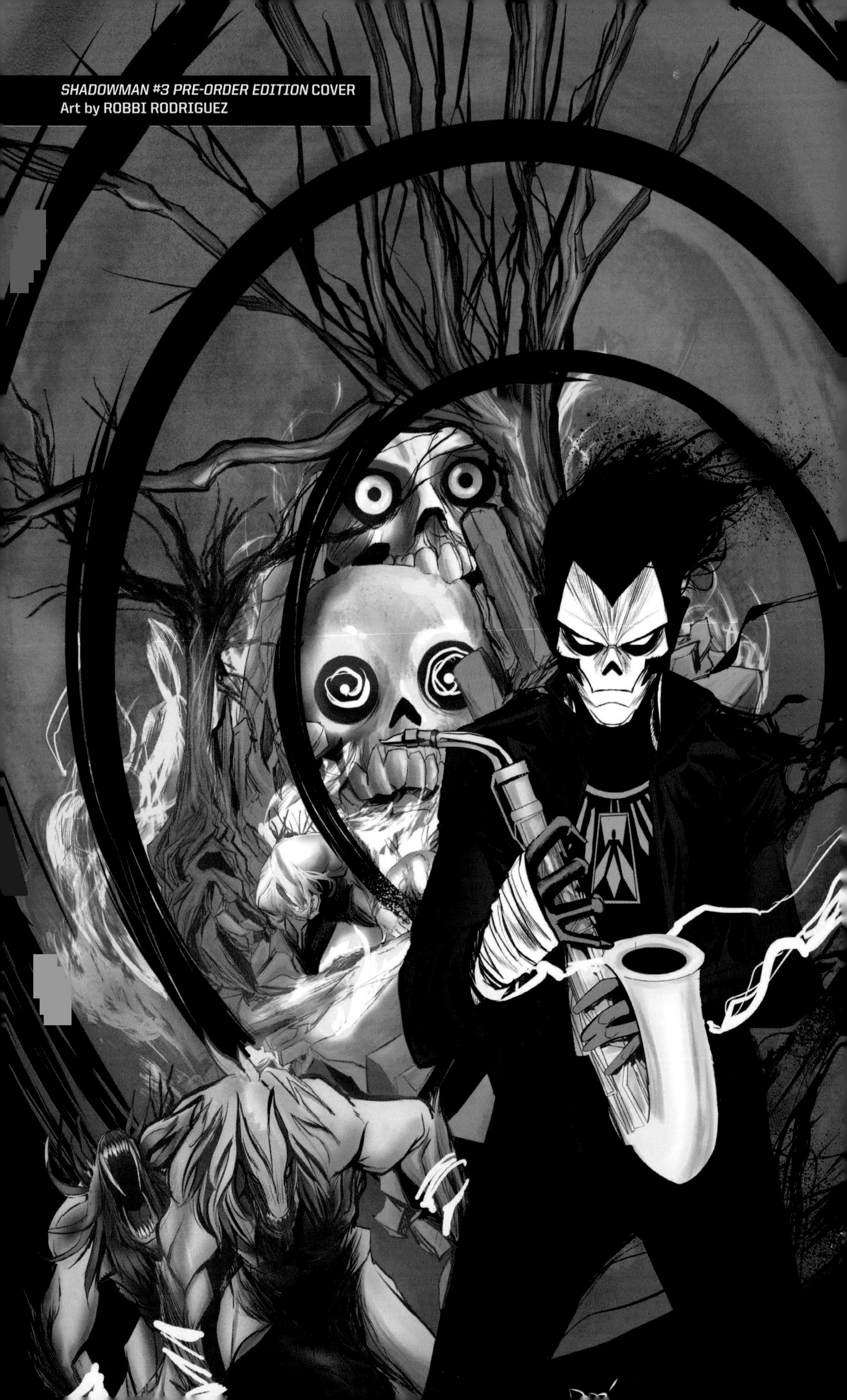

SHADOWMAN #3 PRE-ORDER EDITION COVER
Art by ROBBI RODRIGUEZ

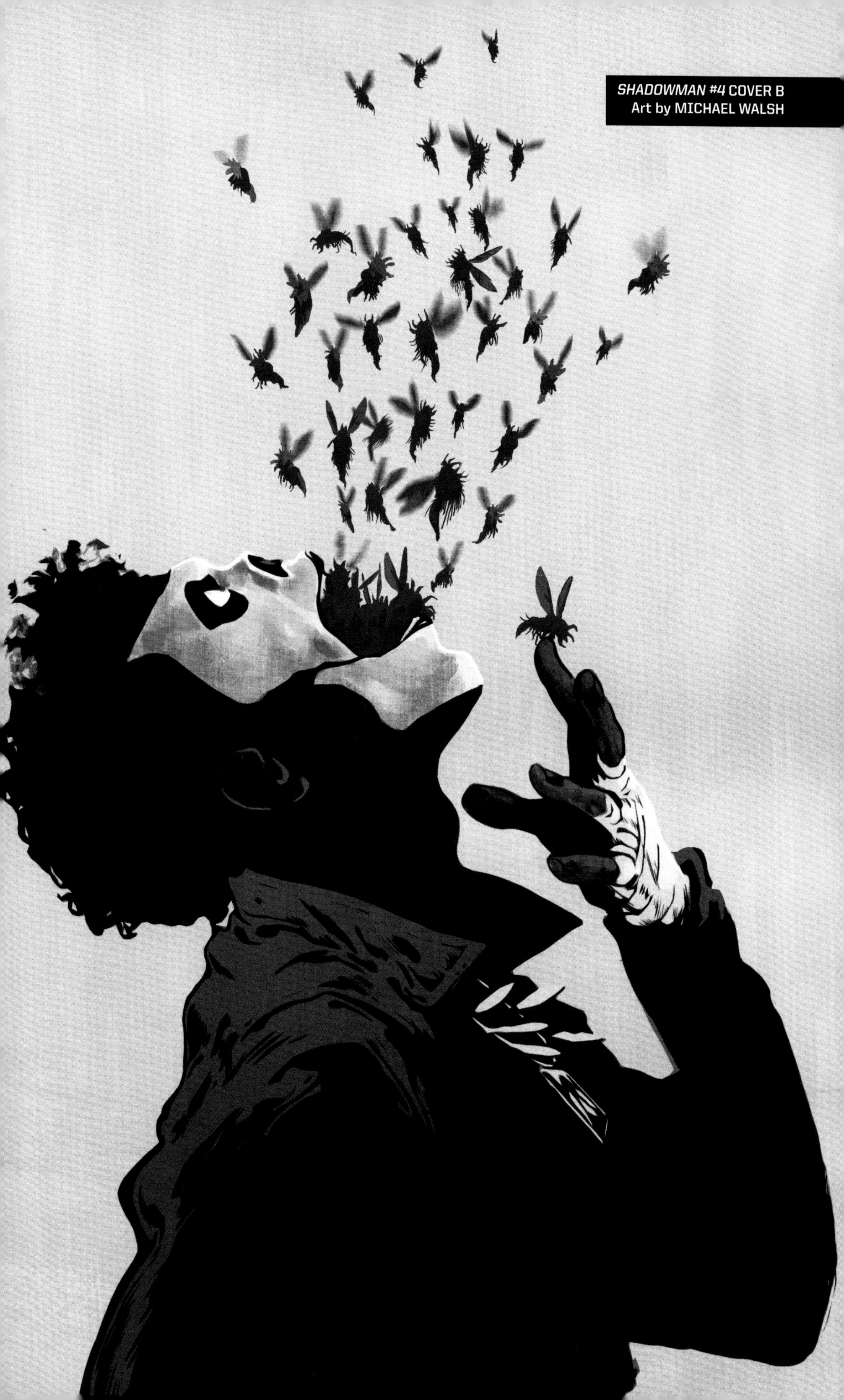

SHADOWMAN #4 COVER B
Art by MICHAEL WALSH

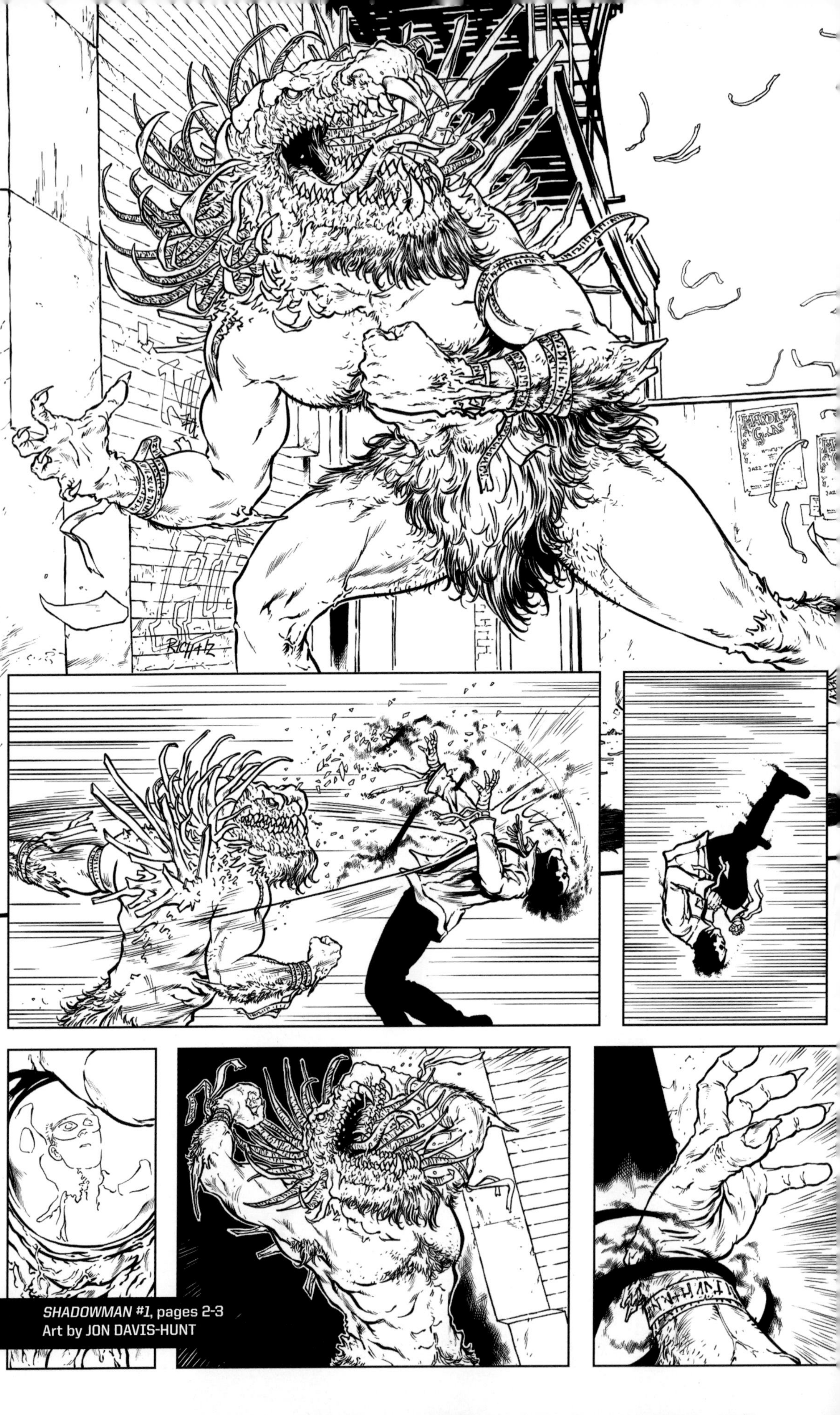
MARDI GRAS

SHADOWMAN #1, pages 2-3
Art by JON DAVIS-HUNT

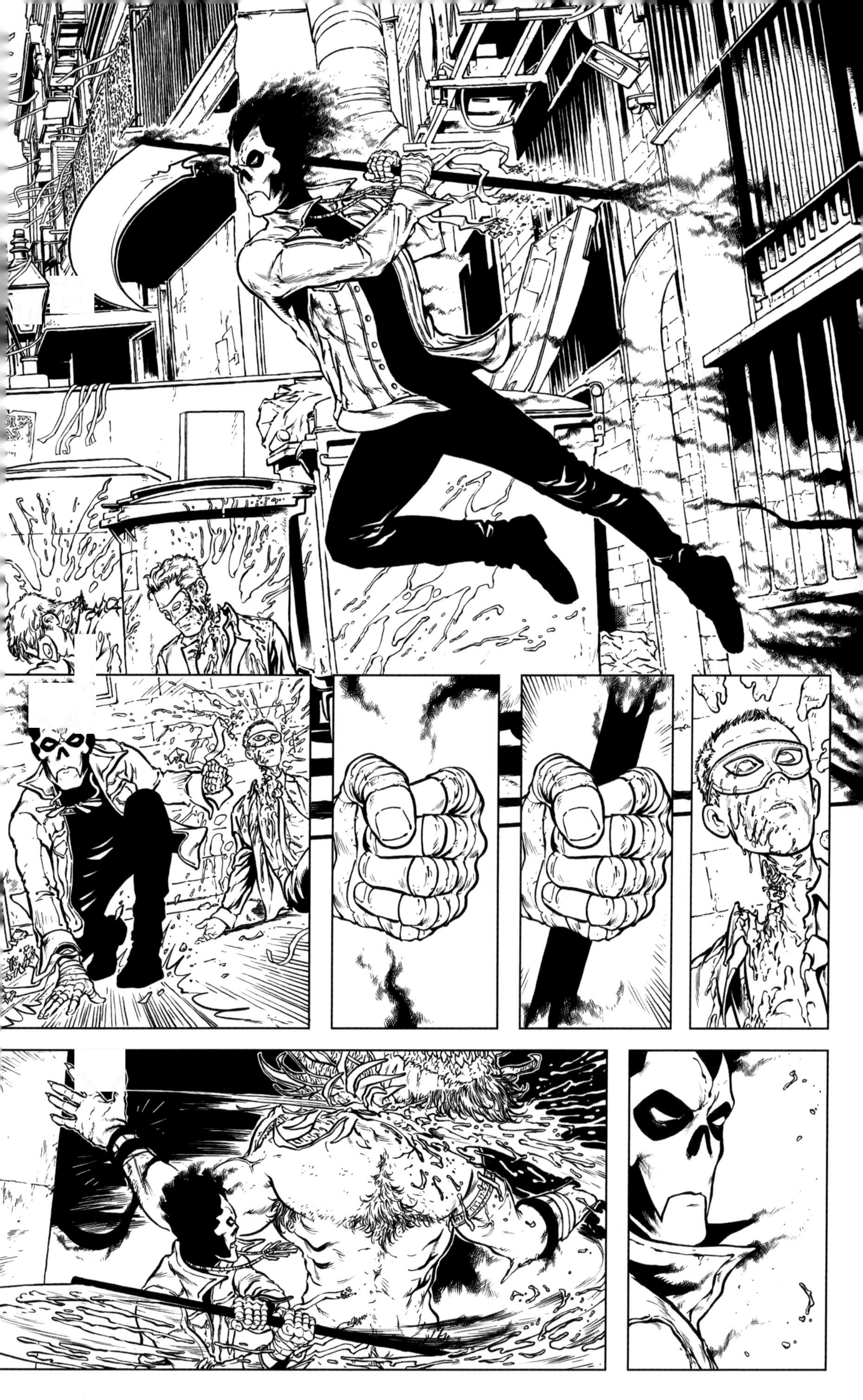

SHADOWMAN #2, pages 17, 18, and (facing) 19
Art by JON DAVIS-HUNT

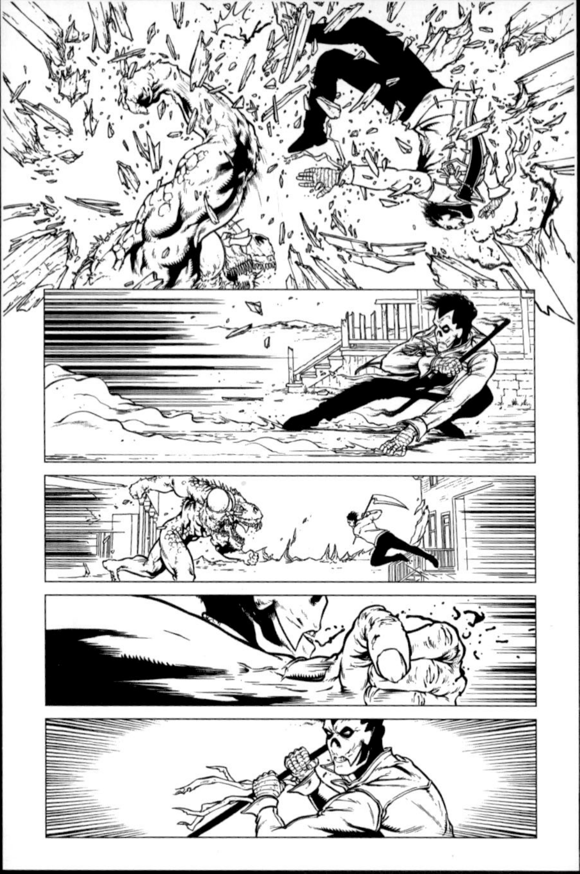

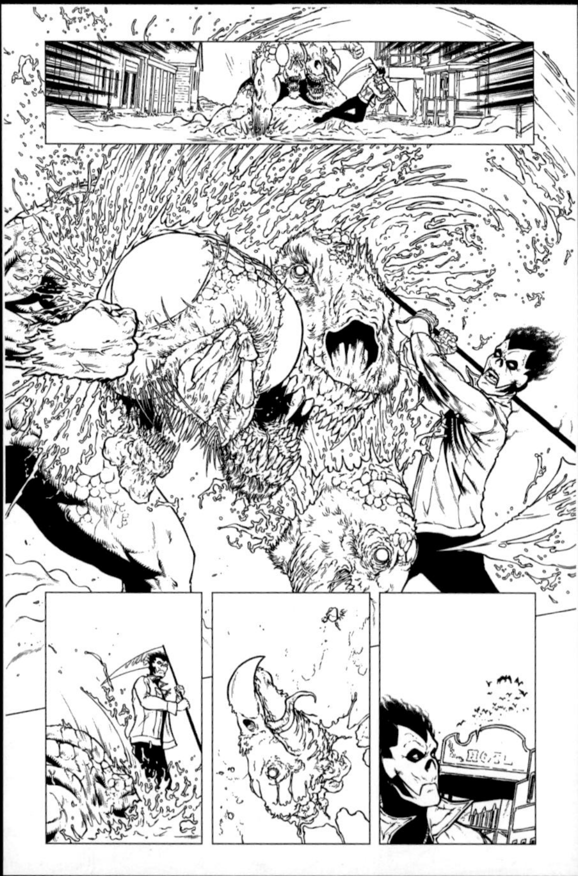

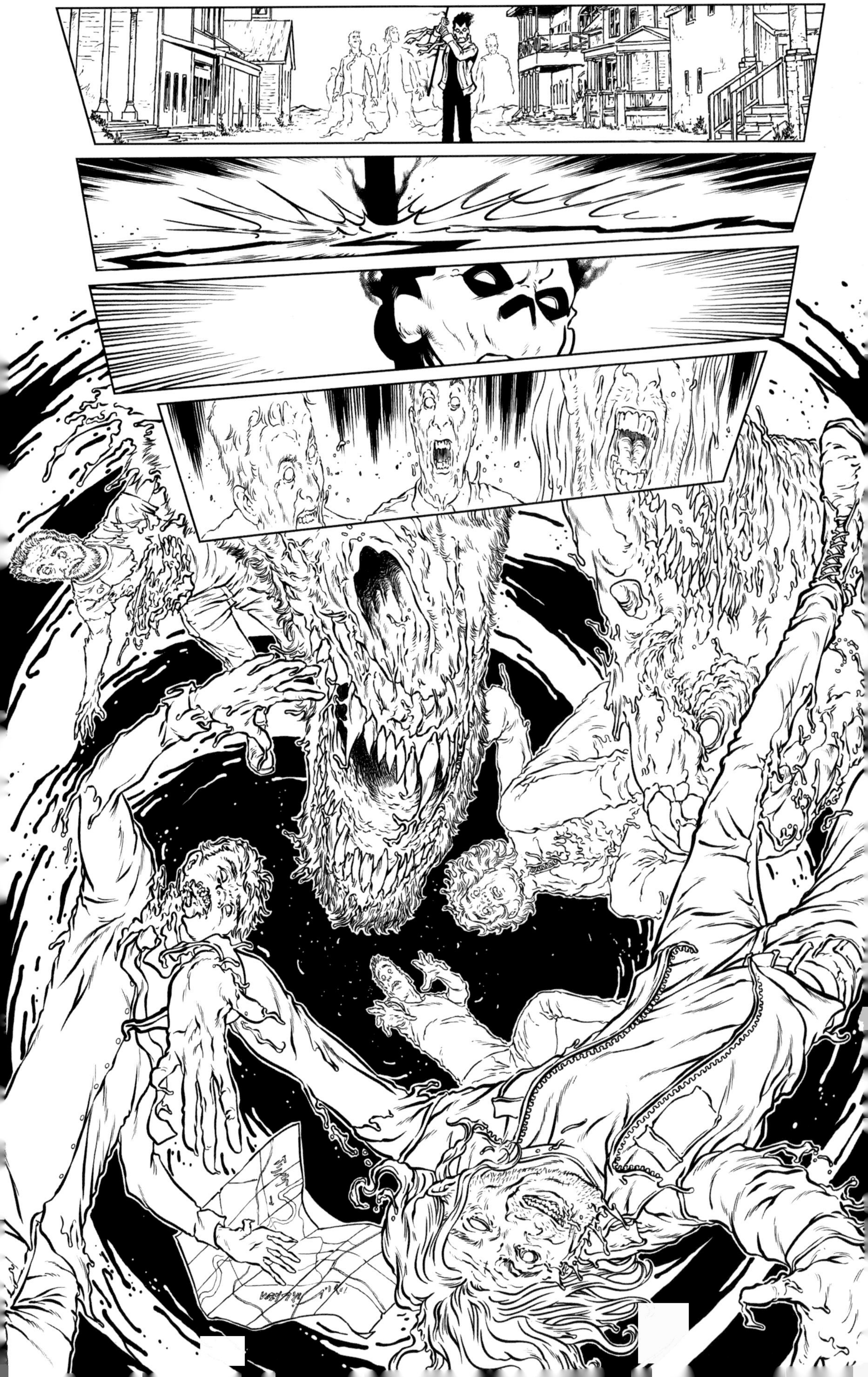

SHADOWMAN #3, pages 14, 15, and (facing) 16
Art by JON DAVIS-HUNT

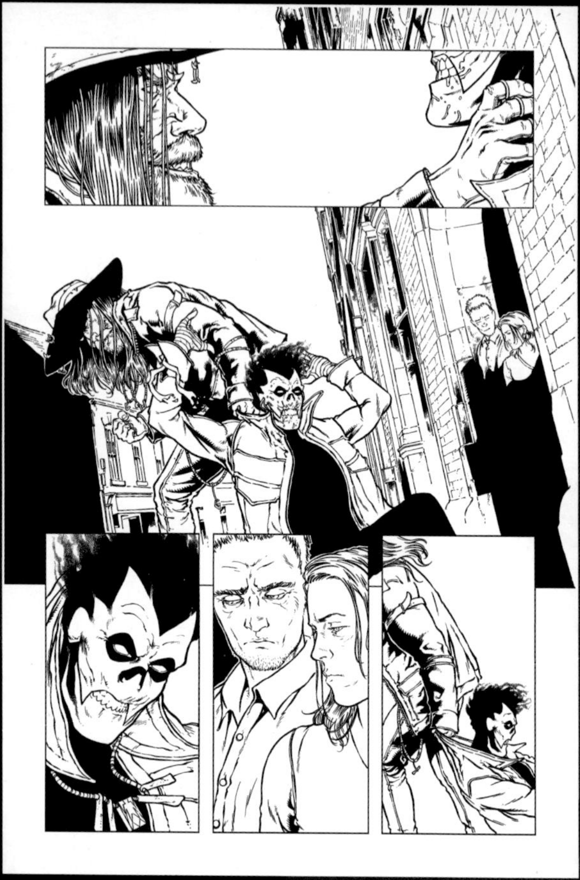

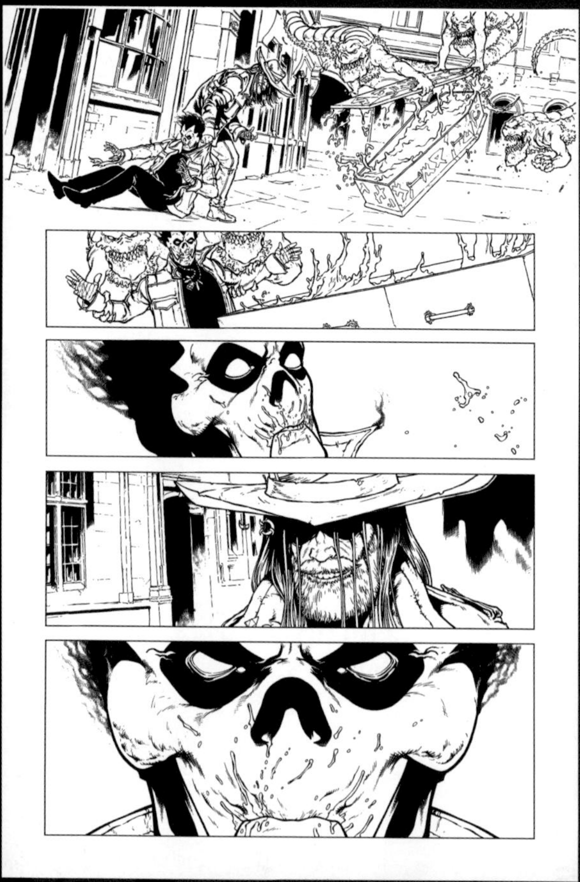

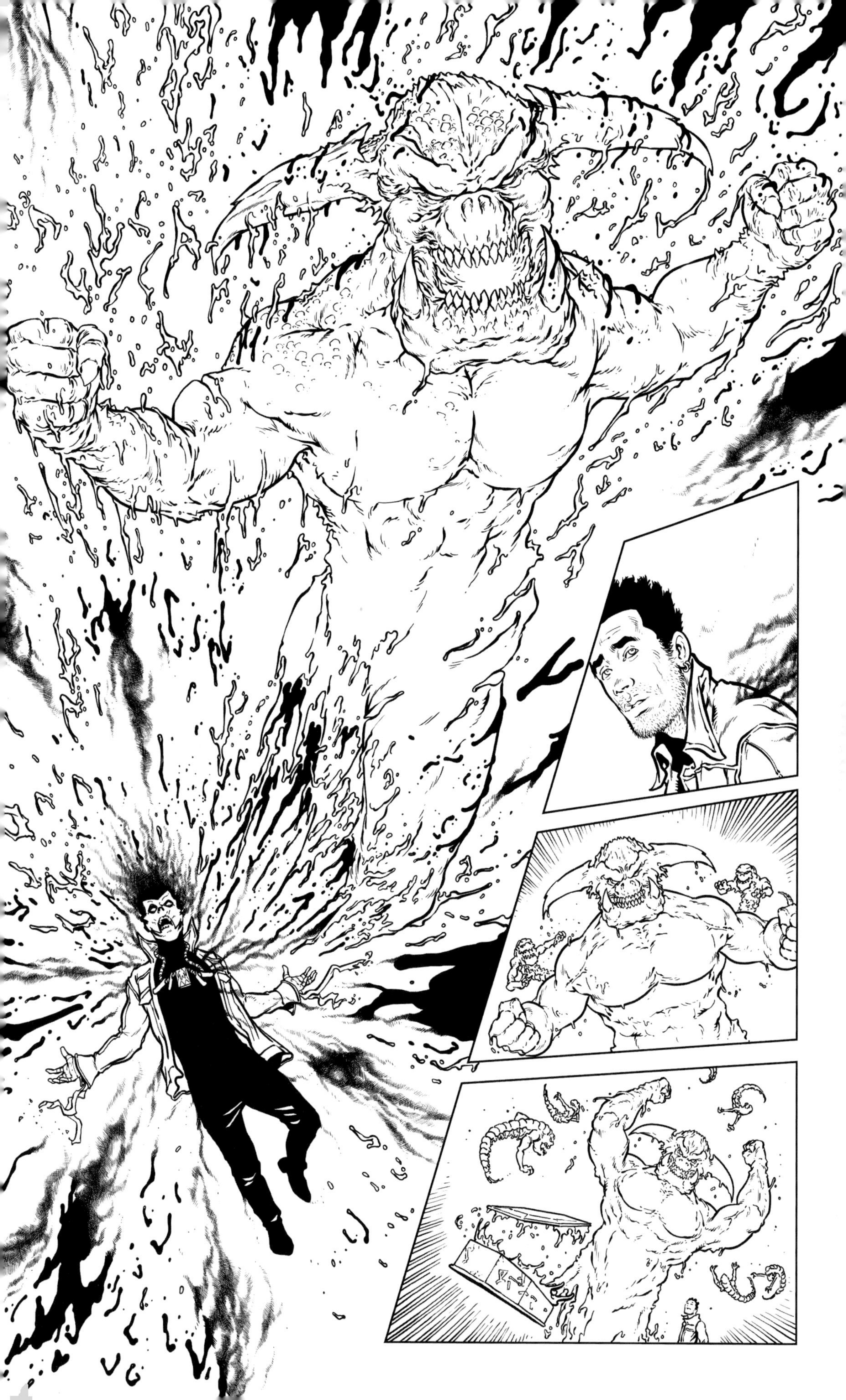

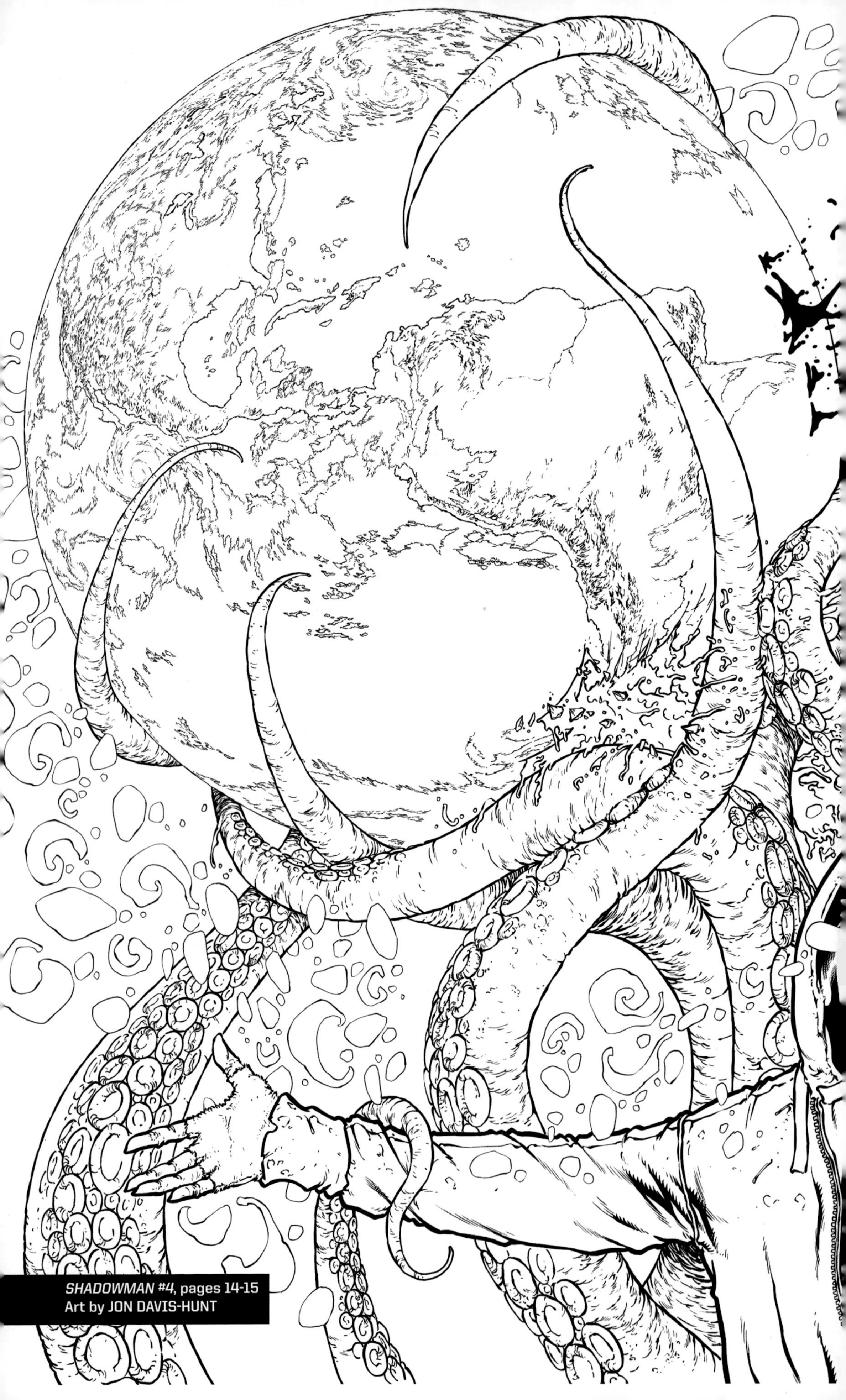

SHADOWMAN #4, pages 14-15
Art by JON DAVIS-HUNT

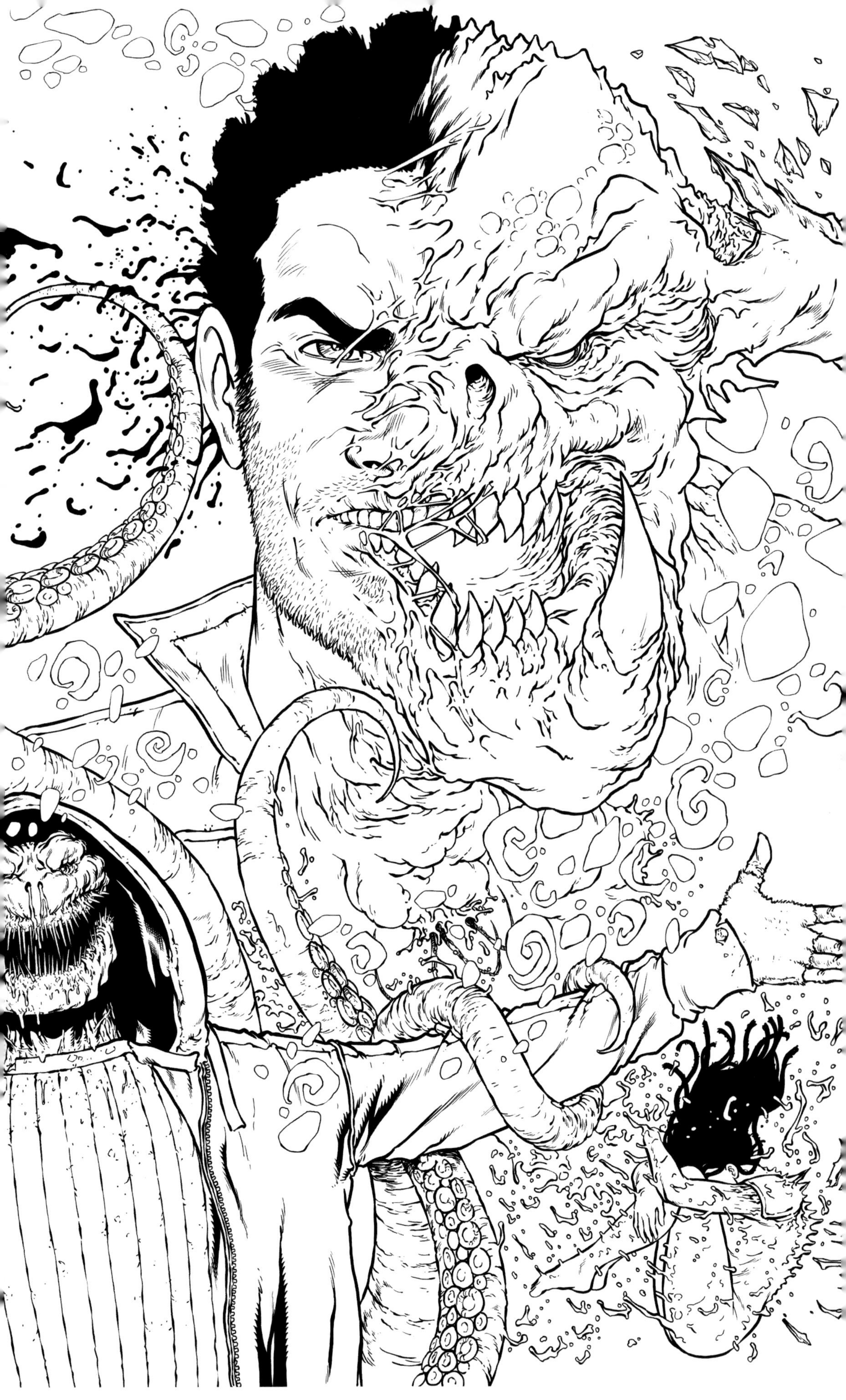

EXPLORE THE VALIANT U

ACTION & ADVENTURE

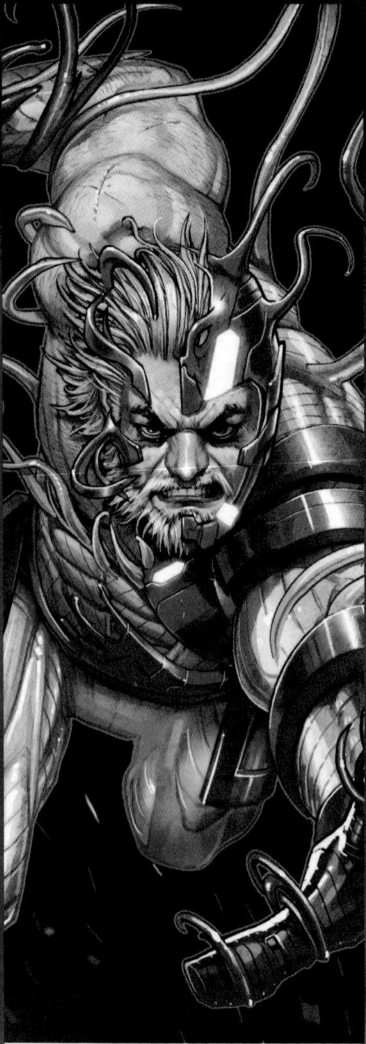

BLOODSHOT BOOK ONE
ISBN: 978-1-68215-255-3
NINJA-K VOL. 1: THE NINJA FILES
ISBN: 978-1-68215-259-1
WRATH OF THE ETERNAL WARRIOR VOL. 1: RISEN
ISBN: 978-1-68215-123-5
X-O MANOWAR (2019) BOOK ONE
ISBN: 978-1-68215-368-0

COMEDY

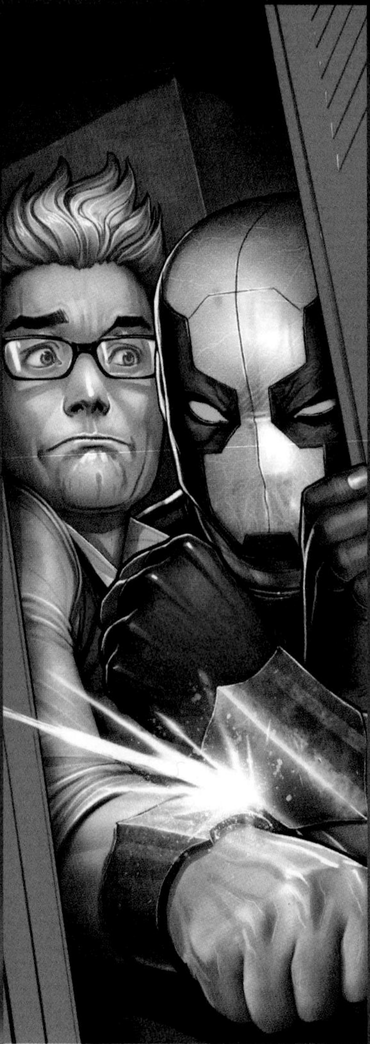

A&A: THE ADVENTURES OF ARCHER & ARMSTRONG VOL. 1: IN THE BAG
ISBN: 978-1-68215-149-5
THE DELINQUENTS
ISBN: 978-1-939346-51-3
QUANTUM AND WOODY! (2020): EARTH'S LAST CHOICE
ISBN: 978-1-68215-362-8

BLOCKBUSTER ADVENTURE

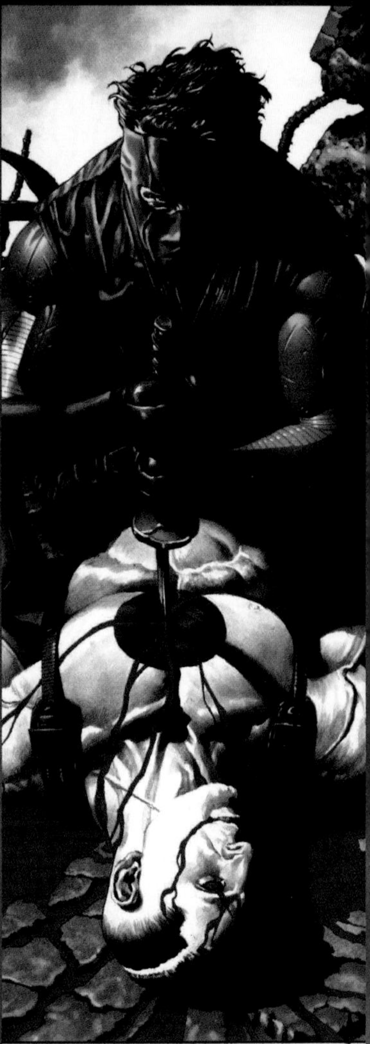

4001 A.D.
ISBN: 978-1-68215-143-3
ARMOR HUNTERS
ISBN: 978-1-939346-45-2
BOOK OF DEATH
ISBN: 978-1-939346-97-1
FALLEN WORLD
ISBN: 978-1-68215-331-4
HARBINGER WARS
ISBN: 978-1-939346-09-4
HARBINGER WARS 2
ISBN: 978-1-68215-289-8
INCURSION
ISBN: 978-1-68215-303-1
THE VALIANT
ISBN: 978-1-939346-60-5

IVERSE STARTING AT $9.99

HORROR & MYSTERY

SCIENCE FICTION & FANTASY

TEEN ADVENTURE

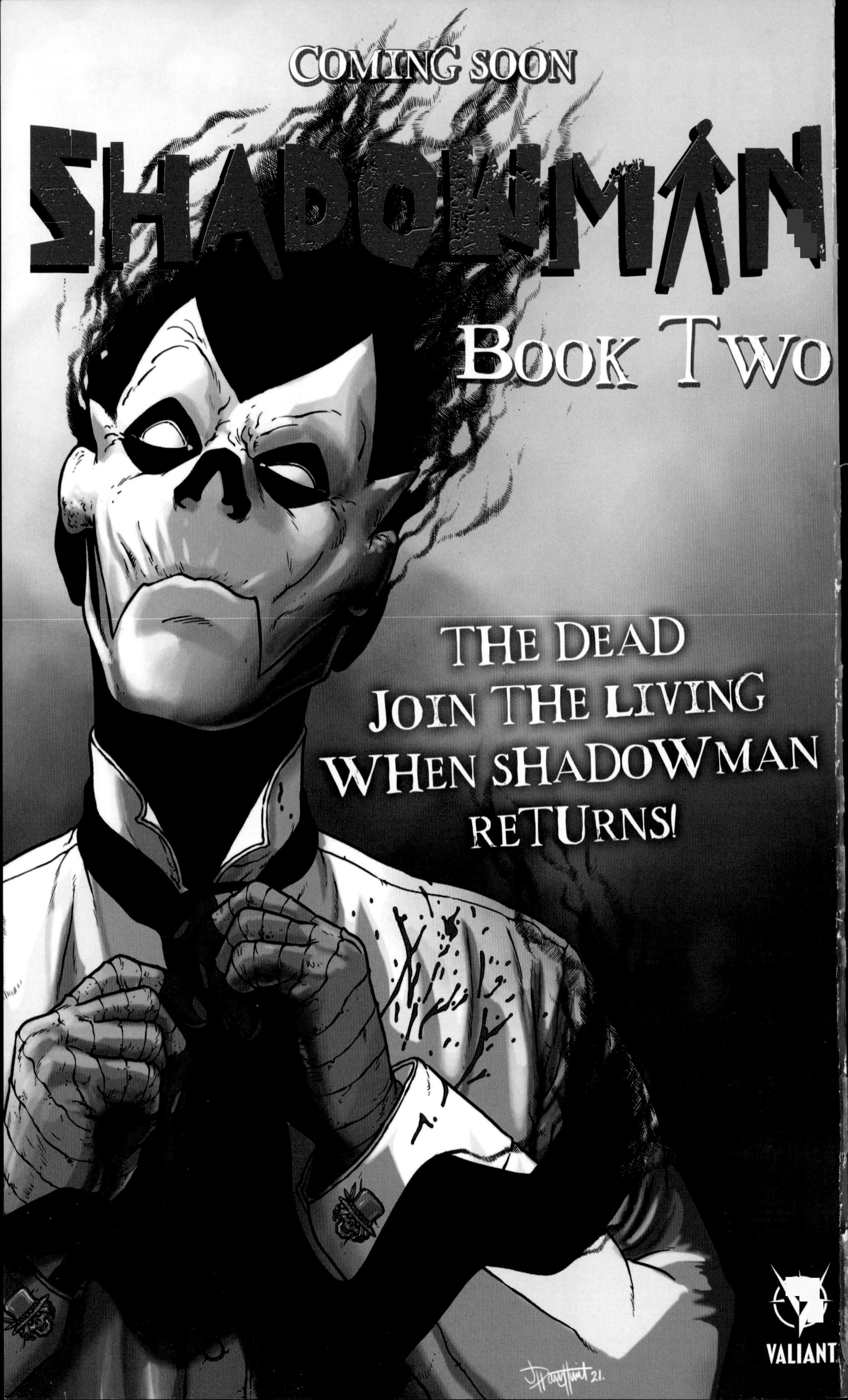
COMING SOON
SHADOWMAN
BOOK TWO
THE DEAD
JOIN THE LIVING
WHEN SHADOWMAN
RETURNS!
VALIANT